# The Mind of War
## John Boyd and American Security

# THE MIND OF WAR

## JOHN BOYD AND AMERICAN SECURITY

### GRANT T. HAMMOND

SMITHSONIAN BOOKS
WASHINGTON

To the men and women of the United States Armed Forces
and especially the mavericks among them

© 2001 by Smithsonian Institution

Editing by Lorraine Atherton
Production editing by Ruth Spiegel
Design by Janice Wheeler

Library of Congress Cataloging-in-Publication Data

Hammond, Grant Tedrick, 1945–
The mind of war : John Boyd and American security / Grant T. Hammond.
    p.    cm.
Includes bibliographical references and index.
ISBN 1-56098-941-6 (alk. paper)
    1. Boyd, John, 1927–1997.  2. Fighter pilots—United States—Biography.  3. United States.
Air Force—Biography.  4. Military art and science—United States—History—20th century.
5. Fighter plane combat. I. Title.
UG626.2.B69   H35 2001
358.4′3′092—dc21
[B]                                                                                          00-046311

A paperback reissue (ISBN 1-58834-178-X) of the original cloth edition

Manufactured in the United States of America
10 09                              5  4  3


⊖ The paper used in this book meets the requirements of American National Standard for
Information Sciences—Permanence of Paper for Printed Library Materials, ANSI Z39.48-1984.
Binding materials were selected for strength and durability.

For permission to reproduce illustrations appearing in this book, please correspond directly with
the author. Smithsonian Books does not retain reproduction rights for these illustrations individu-
ally or maintain a file of addresses for photo sources.

The views expressed in this book are those of the author and do not necessarily reflect those of
the Air University, the U.S. Air Force, the Department of Defense, or any portion of the U.S.
government.

# Contents

Preface **vii**
Acknowledgments **xi**

**1. The Man and His Mind**  1
**2. The Making of a Maverick**  18
**3. Air-to-Air Combat**  35
**4. Energy Maneuverability**  51
**5. Designing Fighters: The F-15**  67
**6. Designing Fighters: The F-16**  83
**7. The Military Reform Movement**  101
**8. Patterns of Conflict**  118
**9. From Patterns of Conflict to Maneuver Warfare**  136
**10. A Discourse on Winning and Losing**  155
**11. A Retired Fighter Pilot Who Reads a Lot**  175
**12. That Marvelous Pitch of Vision**  193

Epilogue to the Paperback Edition  **212**
Notes  **213**
Index  **227**

# Preface

This book began nearly a decade ago, in October 1991, when a colleague at the Air War College, Col. Ray Bishop, invited me to sit in on a session of a course he was teaching entitled "Strategy beyond Clausewitz." A guest speaker would be lecturing the class, a retired Air Force colonel named John Boyd, and Ray thought I would enjoy hearing what he had to say. A recent addition to the Air War College faculty as a civilian academic, I had become jaded rather quickly by the seemingly endless array of colonels and general officers that someone thought had something significant to say. I acknowledged the invitation and muttered something about trying to make it. Ray said, "No, Grant. He's not like the others. You really need to hear him. I promise you will find it rewarding." So I heard John Boyd's briefing, "A Discourse on Winning and Losing," for the first of many times.

Ray was right. It was clear that this was no ordinary former Air Force officer, nor an ordinary mind. A brusque, articulate, often profane, gravel-voiced man, Boyd moved catlike about the room during the briefing, his eyes sparkling. He stalked ideas and flushed them out of his audience. He led us to discover insights and connections before he had to tell us. He ranged widely over history, politics, technology, and economics. He could discuss by book, chapter, and section Sun Tzu's *Art of War* and Carl von Clausewitz's *On War* with equal aplomb and in fine detail. He appeared to be as knowledgeable about guerrilla warfare as air-to-air combat. I remember thinking that was an odd combination of interests and expertise. How could this be?

Boyd was entertaining, demanding, provocative, and stimulating. After the second day of hearing and talking with Boyd, I asked Ray Bishop if he had published anything or if anyone had written about him. Ray said no, not that he knew. I remember commenting that someone should do a book about this guy and his ideas. Ray said, "Why don't you?" I said I was far too busy with other projects and wasn't into biographies in any event. Within a few months, however, all that had changed. After reading through "The Green Book," the 327 pages of briefing slides that constitute "A Discourse on Winning and Losing," I was hooked. I had to learn more about these ideas and interpretations and how Boyd had come up with them.

So began a relationship that has been a transforming one. I don't agree with Boyd on all topics, and I found his sheer level of intensity difficult to take at times, but I valued our association and have profited greatly from it. What I have read and learned about how to read and learn, about a variety of subjects, some well beyond my ken, has changed me forever. I learned about the mechanics of flight and aircraft design, evolution, mathematics, bits of military history, theoretical physics, the workings of the brain, philosophy, industrial production, leadership, decision-making theory, time, Japanese management theories, and John Boyd's trinity of Gödel, Heisenberg, and the second law of thermodynamics. Reading the many works in Boyd's "Sources" for "A Discourse" (which he deemed valuable and essential to the evolution of his thought) was an education itself, equivalent to another graduate degree. For that I and many others owe John Boyd a debt we can never repay.

Writing a biography, the story of another person's life, is a difficult task because of the moral imperative one feels to get it right. This may be the most anyone, including longtime friends, will ever know of John Boyd and his ideas. To be accurate in the portrayal of each is a heavy responsibility, but writing a biography, personal and intellectual, of a living person is even more difficult, as it becomes part of a continuing dialogue and as such is never finished. To do so when one enjoys the learning process, is sympathetic to wide-ranging syntheses, and finds the impact of the process transforming makes it more difficult still. Hence, writing this book has been an effort to hold an inquisition with myself. That is not an easy task, but I have attempted it anyway and hope the results will weather the scrutiny of others and that the product is seen as useful. Boyd and his ideas are important, however flawed my chronicle of them may turn out to be. Sadly, it was the occasion of his death that made the final investigations possible and forced me to close the dialogue.

John Boyd was a larger-than-life character who touched many people and made waves in the military system over several years, both in uniform and out. He and his exploits have taken on a legendary quality. Stories about him have been embroidered over the years. Some were told by him, some by others, but all have become jumbled and may stray from the truth. Most were told by fighter pilots, who like Southerners enjoy the telling of the story as much as the story itself. (Like the Irish, who represent another oral tradition, fighter pilots also view writers as failed conversationalists.) Thus what is recorded here is the lore and the legend of John Boyd, corroborated where possible, taken from printed sources and interviews. Some anecdotes and interpretations are impossible to verify. The participants are either lost or dead, the stories from Boyd alone or reiterated by so many others so often that they have become the record, true or not. This book deals mainly with Boyd's ideas and their effect on others. It is less a validated record of Boyd than it is an intellectual biography. In that the stories are a part of the image that was Boyd, they are a part of this chronicle, but I cannot vouch for the veracity of all of them in their finer details. That some myths may thus be perpetuated may be regrettable, but it is also the stuff of which legends are made.

Boyd is known to a relatively small coterie of people. His name is hardly a household word. He attained success in his career on a number of issues, in a number of fields. He was a major contributor on air-to-air tactics, an aircraft designer, a military strategist, a bureaucratic in-fighter, a defense reformer, and a fighter pilot of great renown. He did not seek to capitalize on his considerable talents, his access to important people, or the value of his ideas. Others have chronicled portions of his life, his ideas, and impact. Jim Burton's *Pentagon Wars* and Jim Stevenson's *Pentagon Paradox* are the most salient and revealing efforts. Robert Coram's book, *Boyd: The Fighter Pilot Who Changed the Art of War*, written some time after this book was originally published, is a far more detailed biography of Boyd the man, but less focused on his ideas in the "Discourse on Winning and Losing." It is an exercise in synthesis, to understand the man, his ideas, and their importance. It is an attempt to combine the bits and pieces of the fighter pilot and intellectual, the aircraft designer and strategist, the maneuver warfare tactician and scientist. It seeks to combine the breadth of his insights, explain them, and reveal their significance to a broader public.

The book is in part a biography of John Boyd. It is also a book on how to win and lose in the competition of life. It is about planning and strategic thinking, as appropriate to the business shelf in a bookstore as one on military history. It assesses how we conceive of time and the process of evolution. It could just as easily occupy a place in the education section for its commentary on trade-off thinking and the importance of synthesis as well as analysis. It is in part a history of the U.S. Air Force and to some degree a commentary on recent scientific thought. It has as much to do with national security and weapons procurement as with air-to-air combat, with congressional politics and media relations as with creative thinking. It combines the tactics of maneuver warfare with some finer points of aircraft design, budget-building processes with guerrilla warfare, OODA loops with lightweight fighters. It is eclectic, and in that at least, it is an accurate reflection of John Boyd's life and thought.

It is still a thin substitute for transmitting the ideas on winning and losing as Boyd himself would have. However accurate or insightful, perceptive, and summative this chronicle of Boyd may be, it is a pale reflection of a larger-than-life figure to whom so many owe so much. He was, as James Fallows has written, "a priceless original," whose "ideas about weapons, leadership, and the very purpose of national security changed the modern military." I can convey some idea about that effort and the transformation Boyd accomplished, his successes and failures, but I can only begin to hint at the combination of wit, tenacity, genius, honesty, concentration, laughter, commitment, teaching skill, competitiveness, integrity, zest for learning, charm, and concern for other people that was John Boyd. Those of you who never knew him have been deprived of a precious gift. Those of us who did have been enriched, empowered, and ennobled by the experience. He was a demanding teacher, a model of integrity, and a man of action who made many contributions to the world. How and why he did so is the subject of this book.

# Acknowledgments

It has become de rigueur in the writing of books to thank those many people who have assisted in a variety of ways in the research, writing, and production of the finished product. The other usual aspect of this custom is to absolve all others from any mistakes of omission or commission and to accept responsibility for them oneself. I hasten to comply with both conventions. The efforts of those thanked below were necessary, if not sufficient, for this project to be completed. I thank them all for their time, gracious assistance, encouragement, and insights.

First and foremost, I owe an enormous debt to John Boyd for his many hours of interviews, correspondence, telephone calls, and visits. He displayed nearly endless patience in guiding me through mathematical and scientific concepts with which I was unfamiliar. He was generous in his introductions to the people and ideas that now populate my universe. He waited for me to ask the right question so the answer could fall into place for me without his having to tell me. For all that and more, I am grateful. He was a consummate teacher. To learn from John Boyd has been for me, as for many others, a high point of my life.

Getting to know some of Boyd's network of friends and colleagues from the past, themselves a diverse array of talent and dedication, has been another benefit of my work on this project. Much of what I know of Boyd and his work is due to their insights and generosity in sharing them with me. Some of those interviewed were close friends and associates; others were adversaries. Still others were admirers who had profited in some way from Boyd's wide-ranging expertise. Many were contemporaries who could shed light on the culture of the

Air Force, the state of doctrine or training in the Marine Corps and Army, or the political climate regarding weapons procurement at the Pentagon. In addition, I owe much to a host of former students and colleagues at the Air War College (too numerous to mention without giving offense to someone inadvertently left out), whose insights into fighter tactics, aircraft design, service culture, strategy, and doctrine were most helpful. The final product is better because of their efforts in assisting me to learn about the Air Force, its customs, culture, and idiosyncrasies.

Some of those interviewed spoke under the protection of nonattribution and wish to remain anonymous. Their contributions are nonetheless important for their anonymity, but I have honored their request. Others made no such stipulation. Among the scores of people whom I have interviewed or who have contributed to the project and are deserving of special mention are Tom Amlie, Jim Booth, Gen. Charles G. Boyd, Arthur Bredehoft, Mike Burns, Jim Burton, Bob Busch, Ron Catton, Tom Christie, Andrew Cockburn, Chuck Cooper, Bob Dilger, Gen. Mike Dugan, the late Jeff Ethell, Jim Fallows, John Fialka, Ernie Fitzgerald, Newt Gingrich, Gen. Al Gray, Eric Hehs, Harry Hillaker, I. B. Holley, Ray Leopold, Bill Lind, Gen. Mike Loh, Gen. Merrill McPeak, Dan Moore, Jim Morrison, Gen. Carl Mundy, Charlie Murphy, Chuck Myers, Roland Parks, Jeff Record, Rich Riccioni, Chet Richards, John Schmitt, Maj. Gen. Lance Smith, Chuck Spinney, Vern Spradling, Pierre Sprey, Jim Stevenson, Ole Stromgren, Win Wheeler, G. I. Wilson, and Mike Wyly. Many others (too numerous to mention) contributed a variety of insights and clarifications as well. Colleagues at the Air War College—Jae Engelbrecht, Ted Hailes, Tom Hughes, Dave Sorenson, Dick Szafranski, and Jim Toner—over the years also gave graciously of their time in discussing or reading parts of the manuscript.

I am most particularly indebted to two of Boyd's friends and colleagues, Gen. Paul K. Van Riper, USMC (ret.), and Barry Watts, of the Northrop-Grumman Analysis Center, and to Hugh Ahmann, retired Air Force oral historian, and Col. Mike Slinkard for their careful reading of the entire manuscript, keen insights, and corrections of factual errors. Their contributions greatly improved both my understanding and the book. To all, thank you for your time and contributions. The final product, however imperfect, is better for your efforts.

Then too, I must thank Dick Steeves, former executive director of the Air University Foundation, which supported the research for this book, and Mark Gatlin at the Smithsonian Institution Press, for his interest in and support of the project, as well as the staff there, particularly Ruth Spiegel and Lorraine Atherton, for their invaluable assistance. Without their efforts, this project could not have been completed. Wrestling with such a complex book that defied easy labeling was a frustrating experience for all of us, but one I hope is worth the effort. In addition, the help and assistance of the library staff at Air University Library, particularly Sue Goodman, Terry Hawkins, and Steve Chun, and those at the U.S. Marine Corps Archives and Research Center, Janet Kennelly and Kerri Strong, were superb. These librarians and archivists are the unsung heroes of much research and writing and deserving of more praise and compensation than most receive. Thank you all.

My thanks too to the Boyd family. Mary Boyd, John's long-suffering wife, saw her husband devote more time and attention to the Air Force, books, and the telephone than to his family. With me alone, John spent more than three hours a week on the telephone for over five years. Those calls were interspersed with half a dozen weeklong visits at Maxwell Air Force Base or in Delray Beach, Florida, as well as sessions at summer reunions of those involved in the military reform movement in West Virginia. John's children, particularly Mary Ellen Holton, also gave graciously of their time and shared recollections, photographs, and clippings about their father.

I must also thank Arthur J. E. Child, a Canadian businessman and philanthropist whose outstanding business success was surpassed only by his care and concern for others. Arthur and his lovely wife, Mary, became good friends along the way. Arthur graciously made available gifts to the Air War College Foundation (now the Air University Foundation) that allowed the extensive interviews for this book to be conducted. Sadly, he died before the project was completed. Arthur Child was an amazing man of many talents who did many good things for the people and the military services of several nations. This book would not have been possible without Arthur's support, both personal and professional.

Finally, I must thank my family for their patience and support. My wife, Caroline, and my daughters, Sage and Dana, had many frustrating times when Dad took an inconvenient trip, stayed on the phone with John for hours, or pored over research material instead of giving them more time and attention. My family's patience and understanding have been absolutely essential for this project. It is as much theirs as it is mine. Thank you, ladies, for your love and encouragement.

# 1.                    The Man and His Mind

Boyd has personally spent hours briefing (tutoring would be the better word) most recent members of the Joint Chiefs of Staff, many of their senior officers, and several recent top civilian defense officials, up to Secretary Cheney.

Gregg Easterbrook, "With Enemies Like These," *Washington Monthly*

This nation lost an incredible array of talent during the second week of March 1997. One of its premier fighter pilots—a man of legendary skill and scholarship who wrote the first manual on jet aerial combat, developed tactics against Soviet planes and surface-to-air missiles, and thereby saved innumerable lives in Vietnam—died that week. So too did one of the nation's premier aircraft designers, whose work on something called energy maneuverability theory changed the way aircraft were designed and tested. He was largely responsible for the development of the U.S. Air Force's premier fighters, the F-15 Eagle and the F-16 Fighting Falcon.

That same week saw the passing of one of the more original students of military history. This was a man whose views on war and warfare through the ages did much to change how the U.S. armed forces went about preparing for war in the last quarter of the twentieth century. His views on maneuver warfare helped change the U.S. Marine Corps and the U.S. Army. Another who labored behind the scenes succumbed that week. For more than a decade he had waged a campaign to change how the U.S. military went about the business of defense, changing the procurement process and helping to improve a variety of weaponry in the U.S. arsenal.

A man of great thought and originality, whose views on how we learn and think in order to survive and prosper in a complex world have infected American business and education, also passed from the scene. His notions of competition and time cycles — observation, orientation, decision, action (OODA) loops — have followers around the world who study his insights and employ them in a variety of ways and professions.

Last, a paragon of virtue who was loved by many in politics, business, and the military for his character and integrity, who shunned personal wealth and private gain for service to his country, died that week. That the nation is less for the passing of these men should be obvious. That they were little honored during their lives is regrettable, but perhaps understandable. None was a published author, decorated hero, high-ranking government official, or an academician of renown. More startling still is that they all were really one man, Col. John R. Boyd, USAF (ret.).[1]

This book is about John Boyd, his life, times, and accomplishments. Most important, it is about his ideas on winning and losing. It does not do the man or his ideas justice. No single volume could. It tries, however imperfectly, to give some sense of the man, his thought and his importance to the nation. It can in no way substitute for the sheer dynamism of his personality, the intensity of his thought, the richness of his intellect, the breadth of his conversation, the warmth of his friendship, or the wrath he inspired in those with whom he disagreed. Nor can it convey the insight, imagination, and innovation contained in his ideas and the verbal give and take that was an eclectic conversation — a discourse — with Boyd and his ideas. John Boyd was a man both loved (called "Christ-like" by the head of one branch of the U.S. military) and vilified as "a 24-karat pain in the ass" by other senior general officers. There is merit to both descriptions.

This is an effort to introduce the man and his work to a wider audience. For a variety of reasons, Boyd never published his ideas. This book begins a discourse on his massive 327-page briefing entitled "A Discourse on Winning and Losing." It is an explanatory presentation, not a critical analysis. It is a first step in the extension of his discourse. Detailed scholarly assessments of his ideas will follow later, but his views must first be made known before they can be debated.

John Boyd's death on 9 March 1997 was the occasion for a rather extraordinary outpouring of tributes. There was a lengthy obituary in the *New York Times*, and his life and accomplishments were celebrated at length in *U.S. News and World Report* and *Defense Week*.[2] Yet, it is likely that 99 percent of the readers of those publications, save perhaps for *Defense Week*, had never heard of John Boyd. Why should they? He was one of thousands of USAF colonels who did not make general officer, and he had been retired for more than twenty years at the time of his death. He was unknown to most but vitally important to a few. Who was John Boyd? Why was he so important?

## An Honorary Marine

Some hint of the answers to those questions is contained in a glowing tribute written two days after his death and published in *Inside the Pentagon*.

To the Editor:

I was deeply saddened to learn of the passing of Colonel John Boyd, USAF (Ret.). How does one begin to pay homage to a warrior like John Boyd? He was a towering intellect who made unsurpassed contributions to the American art of war. Indeed, he was one of the central architects in the reform of military thought which swept the services, and in particular the Marine Corps, in the 1980's. From John Boyd we learned about competitive decision making on the battlefield—compressing time, using time as an ally. Thousands of officers in all our services knew John Boyd by his work on what was to be known as the Boyd Cycle or OODA loop. His writings and his lectures had a fundamental impact on the curriculum of virtually every professional military education program in the United States—and on many abroad. In this way, he touched so many lives, many of them destined to ascend to the highest levels of military and civilian leadership.

Those of us who knew John Boyd the man knew him as a man of character and integrity. His life and values were shaped by a selfless dedication to Country and Service, by the crucible of war, and by an unrelenting love of study. He was the quintessential soldier-scholar—a man whose jovial, outgoing exterior belied the vastness of his knowledge and the power of his intellect. I was in awe of him, not just for the potential of his future contributions but for what he stood for as an officer, a citizen and as a man.

As I write this, my mind wanders back to that morning in February, 1991, when the military might of the United States sliced violently into the Iraqi positions in Kuwait. Bludgeoned from the air nearly round the clock for six weeks, paralyzed by the speed and ferocity of the attack, the Iraqi army collapsed morally and intellectually under the onslaught of American and Coalition forces. John Boyd was an architect of that victory as surely as if he'd commanded a fighter wing or a maneuver division in the desert. His thinking, his theories, his larger than life influence were there with us in Desert Storm. He must have been proud of what his efforts wrought.

So, how does one pay homage to a man like John Boyd? Perhaps best by remembering that Colonel Boyd never sought the acclaim won him by his thinking. He only wanted to make a difference in the next war . . . and he did. That ancient book of wisdom—Proverbs—sums up John's contribution to his nation: "A wise man is strong, and a man of knowledge adds to his strength; for by wise guidance you will wage your war, and there is victory in a multitude of counselors." I, and his Corps of Marines, will miss our counselor terribly.

Sincerely,
C. C. Krulak
General, U.S. Marine Corps
Commandant of the Marine Corps[3]

To understand how extraordinary such a tribute is, one should remember that one has to earn the right to be called a Marine. There are few honorary Marines. Retired Air Force Col. John Boyd was one.

What did he do to earn such accolades? What made him different? Why is he a hero to the Marine Corps and not his service, the U.S. Air Force? Like many others of Tom Brokaw's "greatest generation," he lived through the Depression, World War II, and the Cold War. Conflict and war were a part of his existence. He studied war, both tactically and strategically. If one had to fight, he wanted to know how to do it faster and better than an opponent. John Boyd played many roles in the course of his life: a student, an athlete, a mathematician, a teacher, an engineer, an aircraft designer, a military historian, a strategist, and a fighter pilot. But it is the last of these roles that was the most important. Out of the experience of aerial dogfights in Korea flowed most of what he came to learn.

Boyd (or more often "that fucking Boyd," "the Mad Major," "Genghis John," "the Ghetto Colonel," or "the Ayatollah," as he was referred to at various times in his career) was anything but a typical military officer. A colonel in the U.S. Air Force who retired in 1975, he had entered the military out of high school as the Battle of Okinawa raged in the Pacific. He served as a private in the U.S. Army Air Forces from 1945 to 1947 with the occupation forces in Japan. While attending the University of Iowa, he joined Air Force ROTC and was commissioned in 1951. His adult life was synonymous with the first fifty years of the independence of the U.S. Air Force. His military career spanned the thirty years from the fall of Berlin to the fall of Saigon. It was, as the Chinese curse says, "an interesting time."

### The Making of a Strategist

Taking his cue from what he learned in air-to-air combat in Korea, the essence of Boyd's thought is rooted in something called the OODA loop, or Boyd Cycle. OODA stands for observation, orientation, decision, action. The first element, observation, is sensing yourself and the world around you. The second, orientation, is the complex set of filters of genetic heritage, cultural predisposition, personal experience, and knowledge. The third is decision, the review of alternative courses of action and the selection of the preferred course as a hypothesis to be tested, and the fourth is action, the testing of the decision selected by implementation. The notion of the loop, the constant repetition of the OODA cycle, is the essential connection that is repeated again and again (see p.190 for his final schematic). This and Boyd's study of military history led to the theories he presented in his "Discourse on Winning and Losing."

It is a significant contribution to strategy. As Colin Gray describes it:

Boyd's loop can apply to the operational, strategic, and political levels of war as well as to tactics for aerial dogfights. Boyd's theory claims that the key to success in conflict is to operate inside the opponent's decision cycle. Advantages in observation and orientation enable a tempo in decision-making and execution that outpaces the ability of the foe to react effectively in time. This seemingly simple tactical formula was duly explained and copiously illustrated historically by Boyd in many briefings within the U.S. defence community over the course of twenty years. The OODA Loop may appear too humble to merit categorization as grand theory, but that is what it is. It has an elegant simplicity, an extensive domain of applicability, and contains a high quality of insight about strategic essentials, such that its author well merits honourable mention as an outstanding general theorist of strategy.[4]

That is high praise from one of the premier students of strategy. It places Boyd and his ideas in a rather select circle of strategists whose theories transcend temporal, cultural, geographic, historical, and technological contexts.

Totally self-taught, Boyd's strategic odyssey was an odd one that flowed from the tactical experience of air-to-air combat in Korea and then branched out in myriad directions. How did he do it? Boyd read. He read military history, studied mathematics, learned about evolution and geology, and delved into formal logic and thermodynamics. He developed a taste for theoretical physics, quantum theory, and cosmology. He studied the mechanics of flight, the essence of aerodynamics, and engineering requirements for designing aircraft of different types, at different speeds and performance envelopes and how to compare them. He taught himself calculus and computer programming, studied history and politics, biology and how the brain works, economics and international relations, psychology and human development. He tried to summarize what he had learned from those different pursuits about how the world works, what life was all about, and how an organism should behave in order to survive and prosper.

Boyd talked with people. He talked with defense contractors, engineers, politicians, journalists, historians, people in other services (a taboo in his era for many officers), scientists, mathematicians, bureaucrats, consultants, other pilots, German war heroes from World War II, businessmen, academicians, and writers. In the 1980s, he had regular conversations with people as disparate as James Fallows of *Atlantic Monthly,* John Fialka of the *Wall Street Journal,* and business guru Tom Peters on the one hand and politicians such as Dick Cheney, Sam Nunn, Gary Hart, and Newt Gingrich on the other. He gave briefings to the President's Scientific Advisory Board, the School for Advanced Military Studies of the U.S. Army at Fort Leavenworth, Kansas, the Institute for Advanced Studies at Princeton University, Navy pilots at Cecil Field, Florida, and the congressional Military Reform Caucus. For five years, a retired Air Force colonel taught every young lieutenant who went through the Marine Corps basic course at Quantico, Virginia, about maneuver warfare. He taught them how to think about combat, how to develop a *fingerspitzengefühl* ("fingertip feel"), as the Germans call it, for war, and to seize the initiative to shape the battlefield.

Boyd made a difference in how the U.S. military prepares to fight its wars, in the aircraft the U.S. Air Force has to fly, and in the cost of military procurement. He tried, with less success, to change how many political leaders think about war. He improved how well U.S. pilots of all services flew in combat, and his ideas have been used to help businessmen compete. He taught people how to synthesize complex ideas across different disciplines. His "Discourse on Winning and Losing" has made a difference while leaving Boyd himself in relative anonymity, known only to a few thousand cognoscenti interested in defense, air-to-air combat, and his brand of synthetic thinking. His accomplishments were made with no expectation or receipt of great financial reward, fanfare, or fame (except in isolated cases) and virtually no publication of his ideas, a rare circumstance for a person deemed so important in certain circles in the last decade of the twentieth century.

## The Making of a Maverick
An iconoclast and self-proclaimed maverick thinker, Boyd was hated by many, admired by some, respected by most. Arrogant, brash, cocky, bright, articulate, profane, he was always testing the limits—of airplanes, people, science, the military, and, most especially, bureaucracies. Although he was consumed by the importance of time, Boyd was always late for meetings, not by ten or fifteen minutes but usually by much more. On first meeting, people (even those who admired or respected him or his reputation) thought Boyd crazy or brilliant, perhaps both. Unkempt in his appearance, unruly in his behavior, and unpredictable in his thinking, Boyd hardly inspired confidence. He was frequently dismissed as a crackpot. That's the way he wanted it. If people thought he was "bright but screwy," as Boyd said, that meant they underestimated him, and that gave him an edge.

To his admirers, he was a superb pilot, a brilliant thinker, and a premier strategist of the twentieth century. To his detractors, he was loud, brash, a foe of new technologies, and an irreconcilable pain in the ass. Boyd was known as someone who regularly bucked the system. Many knew of him by reputation, but few really knew him. To some, he was not much different from many good pilots, just a hard-driving type who usually went too far to get his way. To many, his greatest skill and damning sin was in pushing his ideas and end-running the system. He disregarded the chain of command with impunity and cared little about the rank of those he crossed or those who agreed with him. The hierarchy that counted was the one based on sound ideas. He did what he had to do to push his ideas; others did not. He was called simply "Boyd." Controversial, routinely; memorable, always; John Boyd was truly an unforgettable character. He was a maverick—a wild, unbranded stallion, owned by and beholden to no one—and proud of it.

From such personal preferences emerged a brilliant fighter pilot who helped shape air combat training for the Air Force and other services. He literally wrote the book—*Aerial Attack Study*[5]—on jet combat fighter tactics. He knew almost instinctively how to get the most out of an airplane and to fly it better than anyone else, but he needed to explain why and how to do it for others. So, as a young captain at Nellis Air Force Base, Nevada, he taught himself calculus at night and flew during the day. He sought to understand the mathematics and the physics of what he was able to do with an airplane. Nellis and the Fighter Weapons School were the basis for the education of John Boyd. Everything he knew flowed from the insights he had while flying the F-86 in Korea and thinking about and refining those ideas at Nellis after the war.

It was at Nellis that he first achieved fame within the Air Force. He was simply the best instructor pilot at the Fighter Weapons School, and everyone knew it. The secret to air-to-air combat was to get inside the other guy's OODA loop. Get your opponent in a position where he was already reacting one or more moves behind what you were able to do; fling him out in front of you by quickly changing speed, altitude, or direction. Then nail him. The key was the speed with which you could change and adapt to the changes ("fast transients"). Do it well, and you would win. At Nellis, Boyd earned the nickname "40-Second Boyd" for a standing bet against all comers, including any USAF pilot or Navy or Marine aviator from Miramar Naval Air Station in California, later the home of the Navy's Top Gun school: if he couldn't outmaneuver you in a dogfight and get on your tail in position to shoot you down in 40 seconds, he'd pay you 40 bucks. In six years, he never lost the bet.[6] It was usually over in 10 to 20 seconds.

Boyd needed not only to understand but also to explain to others what he had learned and why. He began treatises on air combat maneuvering in 1957 and kept working on them. The result, in 1960, was the first comprehensive manual on jet aircraft combat, the *Aerial Attack Study* that Boyd produced while at Nellis. Though *Aerial Attack Study* was the basic manual for fighter tactics used by the Air Force, Navy, and Marines, he went farther. At Eglin Air Force Base, while working with Tom Christie for the Systems Command of the USAF in the early 1960s, Boyd developed his ideas on energy maneuverability (EM) theories that revolutionized fighter design.

In typical Boyd fashion, he and Christie sketched out their ideas at the Officer's Club bar on cocktail napkins and pursued them with stolen computer time in dummy accounts. He had an idea that the performance characteristics of an airplane could be plotted in terms of the trade-off in the relationships between altitude and energy expressed in terms of maneuverability. Doing this for several aircraft, he could plot one against the other and determine the precise conditions of speed, altitude, and g forces at which one aircraft, handled by a knowledgeable pilot, would have an advantage over another. Luckily, the work to develop the EM concepts was completed before an Air Force audit discovered the subterfuge. The results were so profound that the manner in which the data were developed was forgiven in an effort to share the insights with Tactical Air Command and senior Air Force leadership. Boyd and Christie won several Air Force awards for their work. The energy maneuverability concept and subsequent refinements revolutionized U.S. air superiority tactics, doctrine, and equipment.

## Taking on the System

After his work on EM theory at Eglin, Boyd was assigned to the Pentagon to work on the Air Force's new fighter project called the F-X (Fighter Experimental). After reporting for duty, he was shown the current plans and projections for a 60,000-pound plus, swing-wing follow-on to the F-111 fighter-bomber and asked for his opinion. After spending two weeks reviewing all the materials, Boyd (a major at the time) was called into Gen. K. C. "Casey" Dempster's office with his boss Colonel Ricci and asked what he thought. His reply? "Hell, I've never designed an airplane before, but I could f— — up and still do better than this."[7]

He gradually convinced the powers-that-be that the performance differential was not worth the extra weight and complexity of the pivot for a swing-wing fighter or the increased financial cost over a more conventional fixed swept-wing model. The F-15 Eagle, the U.S. Air Force's premier fighter, was the result. Along the way, Boyd and his colleagues Pierre Sprey (a Department of Defense analyst) and fellow Air Force officer Rich Riccioni decided that the F-15 was too expensive and not agile enough. They thought what the Air Force really needed was another fighter that was simpler and cheap enough to be bought in large numbers to insure air superiority through both quality and quantity. Joining forces with others of similar insight—fighter pilot C. E. "Chuck" Myers,

Jr., General Dynamics engineer Harry Hillaker, and a bevy of others—they worked behind the scenes, outside the rules, and inside the Pentagon to push their ideas. Thus was born what came to be known as the Fighter Mafia, their quest for a lightweight fighter, and a conceptual mutiny within the Air Force.

Convincing others of the merits of what became the F-16 was an epic five-year struggle inside the Pentagon. The Air Force senior leadership did not want the F-16 and worked hard to kill it. Ultimately, a bunch of upstarts centered in the Tactical Air shop took on the system and won. Perhaps most remarkable was the creation of a fighter that cost less than its predecessor, a record likely to stand in perpetuity.[8] Boyd reveled in the role of David against Goliath. He managed to change the way the Air Force and Department of Defense designed aircraft and, at least for a while, how they procured and tested new weapons systems. In the process, he made adversaries as well as friends. Spies were assigned to his office. He was followed at work. His phone was tapped. His close associates and allies were transferred, or nearly so, to remote assignments in Korea and Alaska. This was hardball.

That the Air Force would not only tolerate but also promote one such as Boyd—who challenged the ideas and decisions of superior officers, who questioned tenets of institutional culture, or who spoke his mind and gleefully took on the system—is rather miraculous. Without a senior officer patron or two along the way who remained behind the scenes, it couldn't have happened. Many in the Air Force were appalled by Boyd's ideas and even more by his actions. He was not a team player; he defied authority and told others in detail what he thought of their "dumb-ass ideas." As one author has put it, "Almost more than his theories, the Air Force's brass hated Boyd. They perceived him as overbearing, arrogant and conceited. Boyd said he simply suffered no fools; that, said Boyd, included both pilots and generals."[9]

But he was tolerated, however grudgingly. Being a "good stick" (a superb pilot) and helping to design the Air Force's premier fighters counted for something. John Boyd did all that and more. As a retired Air Force officer, he worked with a small group of devoted military and civilians who met at senatorial staffer Bill Lind's townhouse in Alexandria for Friday-night seminars on maneuver warfare. He helped set the stage for a complete revision of U.S. Army doctrine that eventually became known as "AirLand Battle" and, along with other mavericks in and out of the service, helped the Marine Corps to embrace maneuver warfare. When he retired from the Air Force, he worked as a consultant for an additional thirteen years (albeit it for only one day's pay per pay period, the least he could receive and still have routine access to the Pentagon). While doing so, he helped to run what became known as the military reform movement of the late 1970s and early 1980s from inside the Pentagon. Boyd proved even more adept at guerrilla warfare in the policy debates in the Pentagon than he was in air-to-air tactics at the Fighter Weapons School. He is still having an impact on how the U.S. military thinks about strategy, doctrine, tactics, and decision-making.

## To Be or To Do?

Along the way, he set out to implement his personal credo—philosophic and strategic—in everything he did, every job he held, and every decision he could influence. Simply stated, it was more important to do what was right than to be promoted. As he put it in talking with younger officers: Do you want *to be* promoted to general officer or *to do* what is right? On active duty, Boyd delighted in finding the very best officers the Air Force had (Air Force Academy graduates, promoted below the zone two or three times and thus several years ahead of their contemporaries) and challenging them. They were the epitome of company men, team players who wouldn't rock the boat and who wanted desperately to become Chief of Staff of the Air Force. Anything else would be a failure, despite the very long odds against it.

One such example was Jim Burton, then a lieutenant colonel recommended to Boyd by a colleague because he was bright. Boyd hired him, and they became close friends. Burton would go on to occupy a critical post in Test and Evaluation and to blow the whistle on rigged tests in the Army's procurement of the new Bradley Fighting Vehicle. He recalls the Boyd "To Be or To Do" speech as follows:

Jim, you are at a point in your life where you have to make a choice about what kind of person you are going to be. There are two career paths in front of you, and you have to choose which path you will follow. One path leads to promotions, titles, and positions of distinction. To achieve success down that path, you have to conduct yourself a certain way. You must go along with the system and show that you are a better team player than your competitors. The other path leads to doing things that are truly significant for the Air Force, but the rewards will quite often be a kick in the stomach because you may have to cross swords with the party line on occasion. You can't go down both paths, you have to choose. So, do you want *to be* a man of distinction or do you want *to do* things that really influence the shape of the Air Force? To be or to do, that is the question.[10]

Burton's decision and his personal, Boyd-inspired crusade are documented in his book *The Pentagon Wars: Reformers Challenge the Old Guard*.

For doing what was right, Burton's career was sabotaged. The Air Force tried to have him reassigned to Alaska with no notice, and several officials lied under oath to Congress regarding the Bradley and the Army's testing of it. Burton, schooled in guerrilla tactics and strategy *a la* Boyd, countered with powerful congressional allies, media contacts, and stories (*Washington Post, Time,* and *60 Minutes*), all orchestrated by Boyd. He didn't shrink from a fight and wouldn't desert those who challenged the system.

A whole coterie of junior officers, most of whom left the Air Force rather than compromise or put up with the system, have gone on to do important work in a variety of fields: Chuck Spinney, Ray Leopold, Barry Watts. Others, like Jim Burton, stayed and even attempted to outdo Boyd in taking on the system and making it do what was right. A few profited from the association and went on to senior rank; Gen. John M. "Mike" Loh, a four-star general who became head of the Air Combat Command, was the most notable example. All grew immensely in the process and looked on John Boyd with awe and respect. Ray Leopold, from his position as a senior engineer at Motorola, recalled, "I had a Ph.D. in electrical engineering at twenty-seven, but my education began when I met John in 1973." He was a mentor for all of them, a father figure for some, and a demigod for a few. To his detractors he was a troublemaker whose harebrained antitechnology ideas caused enormous problems for the Air Force in particular and the U.S. military in general.

To do what he thought right, Boyd didn't care how high he had to reach or how many senior officers' feathers were ruffled in the effort. His influence always exceeded his rank, a damning sin in a military hierarchy, particularly when he did end runs on the system. And influence others he did, from the Office of the Secretary of Defense and the U.S. Congress in the 1970s to a *Time* magazine cover story (1983) and a supplement on technology and defense in *The Economist* (1995).[11] The terms "OODA loop," "cycle time," and "Boyd Cycle" had meaning not only in the U.S. military but also in American business, as articles in *Forbes* and the *Harvard Business Review* will attest.[12] Though he wrote only a handful of Air Force studies (some of which are still classified) and never published anything commercially, John Boyd is mentioned in scores of books, journal and newspaper articles, and dissertations by those fortunate to know him or his work. His reputation is global. Business school students in Denmark; military officers in Australia, Holland, and Thailand; graduate students in Canada; and businessmen throughout the United States know of John Boyd and use his teachings. As one author characterized it, "John Boyd is a national asset, but the public does not know him. He prefers it that way."[13]

## The Man and His Mind

For Boyd, thinking—thinking differently—came naturally and defined his very existence. His study of chemistry, physics, and biology, his investigations about how the brain works, the nature of memory, how one learns, thinks, and questions, were central to his worldview. These combined with a moral sense of the highest order and a belief in a hierarchy that ranks people first, ideas second, and things third made him a force to be reckoned with. He had a rare but effortless and intuitive capacity to collect disparate pieces of information over a period of days, months, or years and to connect them. He could interpolate among and between these disparate bits of information and create sweeping insights. More important, they were generally correct, though often abstract and flowing from seemingly unconnected sources. These intuitive leaps were frequent and allowed Boyd to paint broad-brushed understandings of complex issues that others could grasp only in pieces.

Most men possessed of Boyd's contacts and insights would have become multimillionaires by writing, consulting, and advising others on putting these ideas to work. Not Boyd. He found money to be corrupting and wanted no part of the temptation. He told his family—a wife and five children then living in a basement apartment in Alexandria, Virginia—that they should get used to living on a retired colonel's pension early because that's all they would have. When the children complained about some of the strictures this caused, Boyd went out and bought a copy of Darwin's *On the Origin of Species* and told them to read it. Other than token honoraria (a couple of hundred dollars from time to time, and that under duress), Boyd made no money from his rather considerable intellectual talents in the 22 years after he retired from the Air Force.

The reason was simple. John Boyd did not view knowledge as a proprietary commodity. He wanted to share his insights, not charge for them. And he has. Despite not publishing his "Discourse on Winning and Losing," there are businessmen, officers in all branches of the U.S. military and in other militaries around the world, aircraft designers and engineers in aerospace defense firms, politicians in Washington, students, academics, and journalists who regularly use John Boyd's ideas.

This is really quite extraordinary, that near the end of the last decade of the twentieth century, a man is known mainly by word of mouth and the passing of his insights from one person to the next. The knowledge of his accomplishments more resembles something out of the Middle Ages, 997 perhaps, but not 1997. But Boyd and his accomplishments are well known to those whose knowledge and opinions count. This is true even though he did not appear on television, did not publish anything (even within the Air Force in more than 30 years), and retired from military service more than 25 years ago. Boyd was still a significant force until shortly before his death. Up until 1996 Boyd still briefed consulting firms, military classes, and groups inside and outside the Pentagon interested in the nation's defense.

In his last 22 years, Boyd delved deeper and probed more widely and connected more completely insights from a variety of disciplines to improve his understanding of thinking, strategy, and time. He delivered his famous briefing "Patterns of Conflict" nearly 1,500 times. (It grew into "A Discourse on Winning and Losing" in nineteen different versions ranging from one hour to almost fifteen hours in length.) Originally, it was called simply "The Green Book" because of the green paper cover on its 327 pages. (In recent years, after Boyd's partial rehabilitation within the Air Force, "A Discourse" has been distributed with a light blue cover, more befitting its origins and heritage.) Boyd would distribute it to nearly anyone who wanted it, telling him or her to make as many copies as you like and spread the word. Indeed, as a colleague tells the story, the first time Boyd saw a copy machine his eyes lit up and he grinned with Machiavellian glee. "Now," he said, "there are no secrets!"[14]

Until the mid-1990s, Boyd was adamant about giving the whole briefing and would not give pieces of it. As the master teacher of his own ideas, he "had to take people through it" so they would understand the full implication of what the words, maps, diagrams, and such could only imperfectly represent. Gen. Edward Meyer, Chief of Staff of the U.S. Army, once called Boyd: "I hear you've got a briefing that I should hear. I've got an hour or two later this week I could use to hear it. Can you do that?" Boyd replied, "Sorry, General. The briefing is four hours long. You get the whole brief or no brief."[15] General Meyer somehow found the time for the whole briefing. Eventually, after one version ran for nearly fifteen hours over two days, Boyd consented to give that part entitled "An Organic Design for Command and Control" or "The Conceptual Spiral" as stand-alone presentations that could be delivered in far less time than the magnum opus itself. But it was done reluctantly and infrequently. It hurt to discuss only pieces of his vision, to share only the fragments of his fleece.

## Integrity and Intensity

In the dozens of interviews conducted for this book, the most consistent theme and nearly universal comment was that John Boyd was the essence of an honorable man and incorruptible. All men may have their price, but Boyd's was apparently never offered. He refused consulting opportunities, avoided asking for speaking fees even when he and his family could have used them, rejected jobs, expensive dinners, and other blandishments to change his mind for defense contractors, senior officers, and high-ranking political officials. Indeed, after his death, when archivist Janet Kennelly from the USMC Research Center was collecting his papers prior to taking them to Quantico where they are housed, she found stacks of government checks for travel expenses, honoraria, and reimbursements of various kinds that Boyd had never cashed. They amounted to thousands of dollars. Even if it was legitimate, Boyd did not want to feel beholden to anyone. Besides, he was retired and didn't work for the government anymore.

Boyd lived modestly, with few clothes, no cable TV, in an apartment. He had owned a home only briefly in the early 1960s. His life style was less than modest. His nickname "Ghetto Colonel" referred to his basement apartment in Alexandria, in a rather rundown area. (His youngest son, artistically and scientifically inclined at an early age, is said to have filled a sketchbook with 70 different kinds of insects he found in and around the apartment.) Boyd often read large portions of books and magazines (if not whole volumes) at local bookstores. He drove old cars, ate out rarely, and instead spent wild amounts of money on his one extravagance, the telephone. Boyd didn't write many letters, didn't have a computer to use e-mail; he talked on the phone. He talked frequently—at least weekly and sometimes daily—with a circle of a dozen or so close associates and less frequently with a secondary realm of another two dozen contacts. His passion for discussion and what he learned in the active interchange of ideas was nearly boundless, as were his monthly phone bills.

Boyd was a complex combination of intense intellect, dedication to high principles, deep friendships, and focus on fundamental, serious issues confronting the Air Force, the military, and the nation. He was also a kid at heart at times, fun loving and possessed of an infectious laughter that could sweep away nearly any other emotion. Though rarely shown, he had a tenderness of concern for others that is uncharacteristic of many fighter jocks but an important part of his essential humanity. His key ability was his intensity, his ability to focus, to shut out everything while he solved a particular problem, human or mathematical. It was almost frightening to behold.

That a mind could concentrate so intensely to the exclusion of all else—noise, temperature, food, sleep, time, and place—was astonishing. To see him do so conjured up images of a hypnotic, trancelike state in which the brain's instruction is all consuming. It was his essential mental characteristic. When his mind was seized with a problem, he could shut down everything else to concentrate on finding a solution, actually an array of alternative solutions in most cases, until he was satisfied that he had exhausted the possibilities. Colleagues tell of Boyd going for hours almost in a trance, doing formulae in his head until he solved a particularly vexing problem. He could go for days focused on just one element of a complex problem.

John Boyd was, as the subtitle of Murray Gell-Mann's book *The Quark and the Jaguar* states, a set of "adventures in the simple and the complex." Coming to understand him, his ideas, their implications and significance on a variety of levels, has been no easy task. I am under no illusions that the task is complete, that either he or I have everything right, or that the insights, debates, and issues with which he wrestled are resolved. This volume is a beginning of a continuing discourse that will no doubt follow on Boyd, his ideas, and the military reform movement.

## Boyd's Way

What I call Boyd's Way, his thought and vision, is a sort of Western Zen, oxymoron though that is. It is a state of mind, a learning of the oneness of things, an appreciation for fundamental insights known in Eastern philosophy and religion as simply the Way. For Boyd, the Way is not an end but a process, not a state of mind but a journey. It is kaleidoscopic in its effect, with new patterns emerging from the same colored stones of insight and reflection mirrored in constantly changing patterns. The connections, the insights that flow from examining the world in different ways, from different perspectives, from routinely examining the opposite proposition, were what were important. What one takes to be the question may be the answer and vice versa. The key is mental agility and the ability to sort through the "windmills of your mind."[16]

All of this came naturally to Boyd. A single comment that he found intriguing for its richness fueled his mind for hours and was revisited over weeks and months until he fully appreciated the insights contained in the compression of a few words and what they signified. He was not satisfied until he could wring out the totality of an idea or concept. Alternatively, he strove to compress complex ideas into their most elemental formulation. In this sense he used words as a mathematician uses numbers and symbols. The very concept of algorithmic compressibility fascinated him. The height of elegance was the simplest representation of the most complex phenomena. Boyd's equivalent of $E = MC^2$ is OODA loops. That to Boyd is the sum total of life. All organisms seek to survive and prosper. They do so by enhancing their freedom of independent action or establishing symbiotic relationships through timely adaptation to a constantly changing environment. Those who adapt will survive; those who do not, die. Those who do survive do so by being good at doing OODA loops. Though abstract, this was an important concept to a fighter pilot who had only seconds to make the right decision or perish.

Boyd's trinity was a synthesis of the breakthrough thinking of three major scientific concepts. They are linked by the mathematical compressibility of complex events into simple truths. These three concepts form the theoretical basis for Boyd's view of the world. The irony is that he knew these things before he discovered them. He was aware of their importance before he knew the provenance of his insights. The three elements of Boyd's Way in a scientific sense are taken from the second law of thermodynamics, Werner Heisenberg's indeterminacy principle, and Kurt Gödel's incompleteness results. Collectively, they underpin Boyd's Way with a scientific gravitas. The second law implies that working within a closed system, over time, the amount of confusion and disorder will increase. Heisenberg's uncertainty principle states that there is a limit to the precision with which even physical values can be known. Gödel's results show that the concept of truth is not coextensive with provability in formal systems. "Taken together, these three notions support the idea that any inward-oriented and continued effort to improve the match-up of concept with observed reality will only increase the degree of mismatch."[17]

This is heavy stuff and not the usual sort of reading or thought processes for a fighter pilot, but for Boyd it was necessary. He was a bird of prey circling his domain, constantly alert and surveying his environment. He processed an immense amount of data, selected carefully the bits that he needed at the moment, remembered where he had seen other pieces that might be needed later, and swooped in for the kill. His talons were his neural network, his mental ability to grasp instantly and hold complex ideas, seemingly unrelated, and synthesize some new construct. He fed on ideas and maintained, "When there are no new ideas or I am unable to think, I'll be dead because that's my life's sustenance."[18]

## An Anomaly

Boyd's contributions to the military and the country did not stop after his retirement. He continued to talk with people on the phone, give his briefing, consult with think tanks and politicians, fighter pilots and academics, business people and journalists. Talking on the phone was raised to a high art with Boyd. During the work on this book, Boyd and I would talk several times a week, sometimes several times a day, for anywhere from three to twelve hours a week. I was continually astounded by his contacts among defense intellectuals, senior military and political leaders, and journalists. He had access to a large number of high-profile, influential people.

Jim Burton, now a retired Air Force colonel, recalls that he and Boyd talked so much by phone for a period of three years that his teen-age daughter complained. He got a second phone line just for Boyd's calls, which his daughter christened "the Boyd phone." Gen. Mike Loh, long before he became commander of Air Combat Command, worked with Boyd as a major in the Pentagon in the early 1970s—surreptitiously. Unbeknownst to his superiors, he was feeding information to Boyd at night that his boss at the Pentagon had tried to use during the day to defeat Boyd's latest initiative. He later became the system project officer for the F-16. Interviewed as we flew from Maxwell Air Force Base to Langley, General Loh said he spent so much time on the phone with Boyd at night that his wife resented it. Twenty years later, Loh could still recite Boyd's telephone number from memory.[19]

With such gifts, contacts, and talents, why isn't Boyd better known and why didn't he write anything other than a few Air Force tracts? First, Boyd came from a culture that is, though technically competent, essentially anti-intellectual. You don't earn fame and promotion by thinking and writing but by flying, leading, and doing. Second, most information is presented and distributed in the military through the briefing. A briefing is a set of overhead projections, 35mm slides, or, more recently, Power Point programs presented in a darkened room to a group of usually superior officers. Its purpose is to convince them that whatever is supposed to be happening is—preferably on time and under budget. If not, it presents the necessary excuses for the delay and cost overruns. Oral, not written, communication and conviction, not accuracy, still rule in military culture. It was not a part of Boyd's culture to write, and when he wrote, it was done in briefing format.

Third, his ideas were always imperfect, always being refined, connected in new and different ways. If one's understanding is always imperfect, it can't be committed to print because revision is imminent, or so it seemed to Boyd. Hence, he read, discussed, refined and polished ideas, and kept synthesizing and reexamining. His thoughts would never be complete, fixed, or perfect. He was caught in a spiral of unending OODA loops. The possibilities were limitless. Although he came to understand the importance of his insights and the need to share them with others, he did not necessarily hit upon the most efficient and effective way to go about doing that.

We have the anomaly of an individual known very well to a few thousand important people who share his concerns about war, about winning and losing, about thinking, strategy, and time, and yet who is unknown to the general public. This book is an effort to remedy that in some small way and to make his insights available to all who might benefit from them. It is belated, incomplete, and not nearly the same as if Boyd had written it himself, but he didn't and somebody should. Boyd's Way is not the only or the easiest way to come to grips with problems and their solutions, but it is a way of thinking, connecting, learning, synthesizing, solving, and surviving. Immersing ourselves in it cannot help but improve our ability to cope—as all organisms must—with a complex, unknown, constantly changing environment. So begins a more detailed examination of John Boyd and his way.

# 2.　　　　　　The Making of a Maverick

John Richard Boyd grew up with flight and came of age as aviation did.
He was born on 23 January 1927. The year was significant. Later that
same year—in May—Charles Lindbergh would make his famous solo flight
across the Atlantic. As a young boy growing up in Erie, Pennsylvania, Boyd
was entranced by flight and the exploits of the pilots of the era. He followed the
adventures and derring-do of Wiley Post, Douglas Corrigan, Howard Hughes,
and the Air Trophy races with enthusiasm and awe. As a youngster, he was fascinated not only by aviation and advances in technology (highlighted by the
New York World's Fair) but also by what Winston Churchill called "the gathering storm" of the approach of World War II.

His young life was marked with the milestones of aviation's horrors and dis-
asters, the breakdown of peace, and the onslaught of war. He was only nine
when German bombers raided Guernica in the Spanish Civil War. When he was
ten, the USS *Panay* was strafed and bombed by Japanese aircraft in the Yangtze
River, Amelia Earhart was lost in the Pacific, and the huge airship *Hindenburg*
burned at Lakehurst, New Jersey. The Munich Crisis occurred in his eleventh
year, and despite Neville Chamberlain's declaration of "peace in our time," to-

ward the end of the summer of his twelfth year, World War II began. The blitzkrieg attack against Poland consumed the beginning of seventh grade for him. Almost exactly a year later, the Battle of Britain was fought over the skies of southern England. The fate of Britain hung in the balance. Boyd remembered the Edward R. Murrow reports from London on the radio. When he was fourteen, Japanese torpedo planes and bombers attacked Pearl Harbor. Franklin Roosevelt's "Day of Infamy" speech was broadcast over the radio at his high school. During the summer of his fifteenth year, the Battle of Midway was won. The radio, newspapers, and the *Movietone News,* as well as many movies themselves, were full of the images of aerial battles and the war.

After Pearl Harbor and the German declaration of war on the United States, the entire country was soon mobilized for war. Auto factories made tanks and planes, not automobiles. Gasoline, nylon, rubber, and countless other goods were rationed. There were Victory gardens, recruitment posters, war bonds, men going off to war, and women off to work, all as constant reminders at home of the war that was being fought across both the Atlantic and the Pacific. The Doolittle Raid on Tokyo, accomplished by flying B-25 bombers off the deck of the carrier *Hornet* in April 1942, rallied the nation with a militarily insignificant but psychologically important strike against the Japanese. Boyd's favorite movie as a kid was *Dawn Patrol,* the 1938 classic about aerial combat. Even the sports he enjoyed and the heroes who played them—baseball and football— were interrupted by war. It is not surprising that with this sort of socialization, his life would be dedicated to both flight and war.

John Boyd grew up with several strikes against him. He never really knew his father, he was raised by a single mother, and they were poor. He was able, however, to use the hardships as a crucible in which to form character. The day Boyd turned three, his family buried his father, Hubert Boyd, a Hammermill Paper Company official, who had died of pneumonia. That event would color birthdays for the rest of his life. His birth day was his father's death day, at least symbolically. His mother, Elsie, had five mouths to feed, no husband, and not much to fall back on in the winter of 1930. The year his father died, more than 1,300 banks would fail. Unemployed fathers sold apples on the street to buy food for their families. Boyd's mother got a job in telephone advertising, sold baked goods, and did whatever odd jobs she could to earn a living.

Until his father's death, the Boyds led a fairly genteel, upper middle class existence. After it, they had to scrape to get by. They went from being socially well connected and economically comfortable to wearing hand-me-down clothes and scrimping to make ends meet. His mother had to spread herself pretty thin among the children and the ever-present need for income. Boyd said that as the youngest boy in the family, he "was able to be a little more curious, to explore and do things at a younger age than most. I had a lot of freedom to do things as long as I tended to produce."[1] A tough taskmaster that Boyd remembered fondly despite her stern Germanic discipline, Elsie always had a basic optimism about the future. From her, Boyd learned to be independent and the value of being strong-willed and working hard. He was to practice all of them with a dogged tenacity.

As a youngster, Boyd was fascinated with flight and airplanes. He used to doodle and draw rather modernistic monoplane aircraft in an era still populated essentially by biplanes. Jack Eckerd, of the family who started the drugstore chain, befriended Boyd as a youngster. Through Elsie's friend Hazel, Jack's sister, Boyd got to know the Eckerd family. Jack had a Stimson biplane and was a licensed pilot. Boyd longed to go for a ride and finally did so in 1941. It was Jack Eckerd who gave Boyd his first two flights. Boyd was hooked. Flying was fantastic. When he went into the service, it would be into the Army Air Forces.

## Sports and School

Like many boys, Boyd was not a bad student, but his real interests lay elsewhere. He enjoyed what he enjoyed—sports—and paid little heed to books and grades, relatively speaking. Regardless of the game or sport, the point was to win. Boyd was tall, slender, athletically inclined, quick, and very competitive. "I only went to school because I had to, but I was, even back then, tremendously fascinated by athletics. I have always carried a fantastic fascination for sports. . . . The experience made me, I would say, very competitive. I know that I liked to win and I liked the attitude. The feeling brought something out of me." As a youngster he played baseball, football, basketball, and hockey. He is the only person I have ever encountered who gave as an example of his competitiveness early reminiscences of dodge ball during recess in elementary school. His competitive streak may well have been caused by an incident in which he was sent home from school for being too shabbily dressed in hand-me-down clothes. It was humiliating for him, but he transformed his embarrassment into a desire to become somebody. Later in life he visited Erie regularly in part to prove that he had indeed become something more than the kid who had been sent home from the third grade for being poorly dressed.[2]

He didn't really start to apply himself as a student until the sixth grade. He started out slowly, sometimes poorly, and then did very good work at the end of a course. Boyd said he always had the feeling that he learned differently from others, although he didn't know why or how until much later. Boyd liked putting things together (synthesis) better than analysis (taking things apart), but he learned to do both well. He used a learning style that would trip over an insight and then try and find the question for which it was an answer. He was equally comfortable with induction and deduction. Far from the traditional elementary school approach of proceeding from near to far—building bridges from what you do know to what you don't know—often as not Boyd would make leaps into what he didn't know and proceed backward to what he did. He was adept at making connections, be they forward or backward. Nobel laureate Murray Gell-Mann has accurately described Boyd's cast of mind: "Nietzsche introduced the distinction between Apollonians, who favor logic, the analytical approach, and a dispassionate weighting of evidence, and Dionysians, who lean more toward intuition, synthesis and passion. These traits are sometimes described as correlating very roughly with emphasis on the use of the left and right brain respectively. But, some of us seem to belong to another category: The Odysseans, who combine the two predilections in their quest for connections among ideas."[3] Boyd was interested in how things fit together in a general sense.

Academically, Boyd was competent but inconsistent, undisciplined, and occasionally just not interested. He was good in some subjects he liked (math and science in particular) and average in others that he didn't really care for much, such as history. He wasn't overly concerned about studying and grades. The first time he discovered that he could really concentrate, compete against the best, and succeed academically was in an eleventh-grade chemistry class where he and the school valedictorian competed for the highest grade in the class. Boyd won. That, he said, was the first time he derived real satisfaction from intellectual, as opposed to physical, competition. The experience was illuminating but not transforming. He slowly began to like the learning. He was still inconsistent as a student, but he had gotten a taste of intellectual challenge.

He did like to read. Fiction was an escape from less than exciting immediate personal surroundings. He was a hopeless romantic at the time. As a child of the Depression, he would escape with Natti Bumpo in James Fenimore Cooper's *Last of the Mohicans*. As an adult, he loved the movie and saw it several times. He resonated with Jack London's *Call of the Wild*. Despite his reputation as a coldly calculating adversary, he was rather emotional. Asked to recall his teenage years, Boyd remembered early outbursts of anger or emotion. He would let his feelings get the better of him. He was more transparent in his youth, too quick to show others how he felt, and hence vulnerable. He learned over time that he had to suppress those basic characteristics to accomplish his goals. He slowly realized that when he became emotional, he lost control and things didn't work out well. He began to try to exercise some self-discipline.

## Water World

For a man who dedicated his life to the Air Force, it is strange that Boyd owes so much to water. Though he wanted to play football, his mother was afraid of the medical costs of injury for their Depression-era household; the family budget was already on a knife-edge of subsistence. Boyd was not happy about this, but he respected his mother's wishes and went looking for other challenges. He settled on swimming and swam and played water polo for Erie Strong Vincent High School. He swam the 220-yard freestyle and 220-yard backstroke on the swimming team and played center forward—the playmaker—in water polo. The 220-yard events were the longest in high school swimming at the time. Water polo was a rough and tumble contest, a team sport that required great individual effort. It was much like a hockey game played in a pool, without sticks but with plenty of contact. Both his swimming events and water polo required strength, stamina, and endurance.

Through swimming in high school and college, Boyd learned the discipline of mind over matter. Competitive swimming led him to the other levels of competition that became so important in his life. A swimmer first competes against an adversary (Did you beat him? By how much?). Second, he competes against the clock (Was it your best time? Could you have done it faster?). Finally, he competes against himself (Could you have done better? Was it your personal best effort? If it was not your personal best, why not?). Having to defeat an opponent in a faster time and do your best in the process was good training, as they say in the military.

Swimming led him to appreciate the discipline of mental as well as physical preparation. He learned the sheer force of human will and what it could accomplish. Concentration and focus are all important. It is the athlete's own skills and ability, not those of the opponent, that are most important. As the young swimming phenomenon Amanda Beard learned at an early age, "The swimmer in *your* lane is the one that matters."[4] It's an insight anyone who has pursued an individual competitive sport can understand readily, and one others often cannot comprehend. It helped mold Boyd's character. He was always his sternest taskmaster. His personal best became the standard, and he looked on the whole exercise of winning and losing somewhat differently as a result.

Art Wieble, the swimming coach at Strong Vincent High School, was Boyd's most important male mentor. "He had the biggest influence on me. He gave me a good sense of self-discipline. I learned you have to do things right. Being an athlete, you realize you have to work hard if you want to be good at whatever you are doing." Apparently both Wieble and Boyd succeeded, for the 1945 Erie Strong Vincent High School team won the Pennsylvania State Championship his senior year. Boyd placed second in the 220 freestyle. It was a good showing but not the first-place prize he had hoped for. He decided he didn't like finishing second.

The discipline he got from swimming was important, but what he learned from water polo was also essential in shaping his character. A little-known sport, save at the time of the Olympics every four years, water polo encapsulated tendencies that were to characterize Boyd in later life. It required stamina, bursts of raw energy and power, strategy, the ability to change from offense to defense and back again with precision, and a sense of teamwork as well as individual prowess. Played well, it demands carefully rehearsed tactics, a concern for the geometry of attack while moving and shooting, and knowledge of when to abide by the rules and when to break them. In this sense, it shares much in common with piloting a fighter. It is the essence of maneuver warfare in athletic competition, for it requires continuous movement—players are not allowed to touch the sides or bottom of the pool throughout the match.

Players learn to test the limits and the rules. There is only one referee who is out of the water, watching seven players on each team, and he can call only what he sees. The holding and underwater fighting for advantage are as much a part of water polo as the surface swimming, passing, and shooting. Much of the splashing that occurs is for cover and concealment, not mere thrashing about. What better preparation could a future fighter pilot and theorist of maneuver warfare want? Boyd learned at an early age to push the envelope, study tactics and strategy, and focus on how to win. He was good at all of them. Most important, it became almost intuitive.

Another influence on Boyd in those early years was Frank Pettinato, chief lifeguard at Presque Isle State Park near Erie for many years. Boyd worked summers as a lifeguard for Pettinato when he came home from college and even after a stint in the service. Serving as a lifeguard on the shores of one of the Great Lakes was demanding. There are currents and storms, unpredictable weather, and a lot of people over a large area. But, it was a good job for a young man. It was not stressful most of the time, he was outdoors, and he got to swim, meet girls, and have a good time. Pettinato took an instant liking to Boyd, thought he had leadership qualities, and put John in charge of some of the beaches. They stayed in touch throughout Boyd's life. "Frank ran those beaches with discipline. There you are talking about human life. He had rules, and he expected people to abide by them."

Their friendship was enduring, and John would return to Erie over the years to visit. On one occasion in the 1950s he wrapped up a visit in Erie, having left his plane in Buffalo, and promised Frank he would say good-bye before leaving. He did.

"When I first saw him," Frank recalled, "his plane was a little speck way out over the lake. I was on the jetty. It had rained that day, and there was no one on the beach." Boyd's jet screamed in low toward Presque Isle—very low. "He roared over and wiggled his wings. He came in so fast it startled me, and I jumped off the lifeguard tower I was on."

Boyd said simply, "I thought it was about time Frank got a thrill." Boyd was flamboyant and a newly minted fighter pilot who wanted to show off for the folks back home. It just seemed like the thing to do.

## The First Confrontation with the System

Boyd often daydreamed of becoming a fighter pilot and engaging enemy planes in the skies over Europe or the Pacific. For a young man about to graduate from high school with a world war going on, there was only one thing to do—join the Army. Boyd did. He enlisted in the Army Air Forces in the spring of 1945 and arranged to go in the service as soon as he graduated, but the war ended before he could join the fray. As World War II ground to a close, first in Europe and then in the Far East, there was a scramble to get the troops home and to rotate new recruits for occupation duty in Germany and Japan. At the age of eighteen, Boyd found himself part of the occupation forces at a former Japanese airfield halfway around the world. Though disappointed that he didn't get to flight school before things shut down, he enjoyed himself and even swam on the Far Eastern Forces Swim Team. It was in Japan that Boyd learned a fundamental lesson that was to color his whole career.

As Boyd recalled the event, it went something like this. He and his fellow privates guarding a former Japanese air base were sleeping outside in the cold and snow of a Japanese winter without tents and with little cold-weather gear as well. Meanwhile, the officers were sleeping inside old wooden barracks with a coal-fired stove to keep them warm at night. Boyd and a few of his compatriots decided there was no reason they should freeze their ass off and took matters into their own hands. They started systematically to disassemble two old wooden hangars, one board at a time. They placed the wood in an old 55-gallon drum with some holes cut in it, posted fire guards as required by regulation, and slept around a fire that gave more warmth than they would have had otherwise. This worked reasonably well until February 1946, when the Army decided to survey the base. The noncommissioned officer assigned to do the survey asked Boyd what had happened to two hangars shown on his map. Boyd cheerfully replied that they had been disassembled and used for firewood over the last few weeks.

The NCO quickly departed to report to his superior. It did not take long for the appropriate charges to be filed—destruction of government property—and an investigation to be launched. Boyd and his compatriots were called singly into a room with three rather grim-faced officers seated behind a table. "It was not quite the single bare lightbulb hanging overhead," Boyd recalled, "but the effect was the same. You knew you were in trouble, being interrogated and about to get hammered."

Boyd was asked, as were the others, if he realized the seriousness of the charges against him. He did. The charges were explained in perfunctory fashion. He was asked if he had anything to add. Boyd asked if he was permitted to ask questions. They said he could.

"Were the Principles of Leadership for the U.S. Army in effect?" Boyd was assured they were.

"Well," said Boyd, "one of those is that an officer should look out for the welfare of his men. Since the officers were sleeping inside a heated building, and the troops were literally out in the cold, it seems there might be a violation of some kind. The guys discussed it and I thought instead of writing to our congressman or something like that, we could probably take care of the problem ourselves. That's how we came to burn the hangars for heat."

There was a hurried conference among the officers, and Boyd was dismissed. The next day, the base commander called all enlisted personnel to a meeting to explain why appropriate tents, winter sleeping bags, and other supplies were not available and what would be done to rectify the shortages as soon as possible. Boyd and his buddies not only solved their heating problem but they had also taken on the system—and won. It was a valuable lesson for an impressionable eighteen-year-old. The system—any system—never looked quite so large, immovable, and all-powerful ever again. Rank had its privileges but also its responsibilities, and Boyd had learned he could manipulate the system. "If they had court-martialed me then and put me in jail, they would never have had to put up with me later."[5]

Boyd laughed at the thought of a career that might never have been. If he could take on the system and win as a lowly private at eighteen, imagine what he might be able to do later. It was a real confidence-building experience for a young man half a world away from home, freezing his butt off in a Japanese winter, who longed to fly but couldn't. Save for this incident, Boyd's first brush with military service was as uneventful as it was uninspiring, but knowing he could buck the system and win—if he was right and willing to stand up for what he believed—was a powerful experience and insight.

## College

Boyd returned home from Japan in January 1947. He hung around home, worked at Presque Isle State Park again, and enrolled at the University of Iowa the following September, largely on the recommendation of Art Wieble, his mentor and swimming coach in high school. He was not a bad student, just an uninspired one with no real focus. Boyd drifted through his college courses and enjoyed the swimming team, girls, and parties. His college roommate Bob Busch, himself a high school swimming star from Illinois, recalls that Boyd rarely studied and cracked few books while an undergraduate. Though they had a study room in the fraternity house where they lived (Phi Kappa Psi), the only thing Busch remembers that he and Boyd did in the study room was to paint it one year. Academics were not a high priority.

Boyd and Busch were fortunate to become friends with a legend in American swimming, Doc Councilman. Councilman, then an assistant coach at Iowa, would later go to Cortland and eventually become the head swimming coach at Indiana University. There, in the 1960s, he established a swimming dynasty. Because Boyd and Busch did not particularly like the swimming team coach, they gravitated toward Councilman. Boyd and Councilman were close. It was from him that Boyd learned the importance of style and technique in swimming. A swimmer does not have to move his arms faster and flail at the water to gain speed. He can move more slowly than most, but if he has perfect technique, he will go faster because he is more efficient. It takes less energy to do things right. Wasted motion, however forceful, was simply of little use. How he did things was as important as what he was trying to do. It was an insight regarding form and function and an important lesson. Doc Councilman was the second important mentor in John Boyd's life, another substitute father he looked to for advice, and the most important aspect of his college days, save for his introduction to his future wife.

Boyd had many fond memories of swimming practice, meets, and trips with Doc Councilman, including one trip to Florida in 1948. They were on a limited budget and hungry, driving all night to go to a meet in Fort Lauderdale. They stopped and climbed over some fences to liberate some oranges from the numerous groves along the highway. Boyd recalled living on oranges on that trip. He was deeply moved when he and Councilman visited and spoke by phone many years later; that Councilman would remember him after all that time, given the numerous swimming stars he had coached and mentored over the years, meant a lot to Boyd.

It was not only the friendship that was important but what he learned as well. It was because of Councilman that Boyd refined his appreciation and understanding of competition and the importance of sheer will, of mind over matter. He also came to appreciate the routine practice and repetition that was required to become really good at something and to overcome the boredom by focusing on minute improvements. These were lessons that he was to practice many times in later years and from which he always profited. If you want to truly excel, you have to work hard to do it. Hard work—and lots of it—would characterize Boyd's Air Force career.

Even in college Boyd had a rather strong sense of propriety. Certainly no prude, Boyd took his sense of what was and was not right seriously. The swimming team used to elect a Miss Dolphin, named for the Dolphin Club of swimmers. One year a particularly fetching Miss Dolphin took a liking to Boyd and invited him home with her for Thanksgiving. On the second evening at her parents' home, Boyd was somewhat startled to hear Miss Dolphin enter his room and then his bed. Boyd demurred and asked her to leave. When asked if he found her unattractive or he was not a red-blooded all-American guy, Boyd said it was no reflection on her or their relationship. Rather, it was just that it was inappropriate. He was a guest in her parents' home and to sleep with her under their roof was simply not something he could do. Maybe they would later and elsewhere, but not then and there. It was an early example of Boyd's willpower—or won't power. Self-denial was to become a characteristic of Boyd. It was also the end of his relationship with Miss Dolphin.[6] Years later, after reading Musashi, Sun Tzu, and others, he would appreciate the Eastern view that every want is a weakness.

Boyd was bored in college. He was an average student in most courses. Because he liked math and science, Boyd considered majoring in engineering. It seemed a good fit. He actually started the engineering program, but one of the curriculum requirements at the time was drafting, and he hated it. When he was told that drafting was likely to be his first job in the field, Boyd said no way and dropped that idea. There were a few classes he enjoyed, one in philosophy in particular, but he decided he needed to make some money, and one didn't do that with a philosophy degree. He then decided to major in economics to insure that he could escape his childhood experience and steel himself against the poverty of the Depression. Though the classes were not terribly inspiring, becoming a Wall Street broker held a certain appeal, even if he knew little about it or how to accomplish it. His vague image of the career held some attraction and seemed competitive; he could keep score with money.

That never quite happened as intended. Along the way, a couple of other things intervened. First, somewhat by accident, he stopped by a booth on campus and was asked if he would like to join the Air Force Reserve Officer Training Corps (ROTC). There were strong incentives to do so. He loved airplanes. He had enjoyed his brief experience of flight with Jack Eckerd as a kid in Erie and had longed to become a fighter pilot during World War II. Having watched all the war movies and propaganda of the era, he had been more or less programmed into a love of both aviation and war. Besides, he hadn't minded military service, unglamorous though it had been. So here at last was something he was interested in and could do in college. When the folks in ROTC told him they would pay him $27 a month as well, he figured he'd died and gone to heaven. He could really use the money. It launched his Air Force career.

### Marriage

The second big event at college that changed his life was meeting Mary Bruce, his future wife. Mary, a native of Ottumwa, Iowa, was majoring in home economics. She met John during her junior year, and they took an instant liking to each other. They began dating and eventually became rather serious about each other. They married on 23 December 1951. As she explains it, he was ruggedly handsome, an athlete on the swimming team, and a nice guy. She thought he was great, "a good-looking guy who didn't think too much."

"Look what I got!" she would say later.

It was a strong marriage, despite some rocky stretches. It was hard on Mary and later even harder for the children. There was Steven's battle with polio and long drives to Warm Springs, Georgia, for treatment for their oldest son. Life with John Boyd was not easy. It couldn't be. He was gone a great deal and, over the years, put in long hours on the job and became increasingly preoccupied (some would say obsessed) with his work. His commitment and focus did not include his family in the same way that he seemed always absorbed by ideas, tactics, battles, and intellectual insights.

"Nobody told me it would be easy. I complained some but got used to it. He was gone a lot," but "we understood how important his work was to him," Mary recalled. "It was a mission he was on. We all know he is very loyal and will be there for us." She added, "He's a very interesting person. It's been a challenge, but we're proud of him."[7]

A private man with a close family, Boyd did not talk much of their children, and neither did Mary; they kept their private lives out of the political strife in which he frequently found himself. Their children have their own lives and follow disparate pursuits. Steven, the oldest, suffered a bout with polio. He was born in 1953, was always interested in electronics, and had a rough go of it. Confined to a wheelchair, he made his own way until he too succumbed to cancer a year after his father. That was particularly hard on Mary and his siblings. It just didn't seem fair. John Scott, born in 1958, is a gifted programmer and works with computer software. Jeffrey, born in 1959, was always interested in nature and animals as well as art. Kathy, born in 1955, lives with Mary in Florida. Mary Ellen, born in 1961 and the one "most like John," has been married and divorced but had the apple of her father's eye, his granddaughter, Reba.

All of Boyd's close friends agree that Mary was a saint for putting up with him and his intensity. There were the long workdays, the interminable telephone calls, the incessant strategy sessions, his voluminous reading, and a life of the mind that exacted a heavy toll on his time with his family, whether on active duty or in retirement. Still, their adoration for each other was strong. Though Boyd did not often talk about such things, the tenderness in his voice and the moist corners of his eyes belied his true feelings. John and Mary were vastly different in demeanor, attitude, and preferences. Like an intellectual tesla coil, full of electrical energy, John was constantly sparking with ideas at random intervals. Always restless and never still, at least mentally, John never really relaxed, constantly making analogies and insights, explaining connections. Mary, on the other hand, is quiet and subdued, but then, anyone would be in comparison to Boyd. She likes to go to Audubon Society meetings and watch old movies or just stand on the balcony and take in the sunset—things John would do with her only grudgingly at best. Perhaps it was their very differences that made their marriage successful.

Everest "Rich" Riccioni, a retired colonel and coconspirator in the development of the lightweight fighter, doesn't know how Mary Boyd coped all those years. He readily admits that their careers were hard on their families and confesses that he and Boyd shared the same mistress for years—the country.[8] That relationship demanded great sacrifices from their families and themselves, but he thinks the cause was well worth it. The effort was no more than they should have given, no less than they had to make. That attitude toward one's work (viewing it as a vocation or calling, not merely a job) is increasingly rare in many professions, but it is, however, shared by most in the military. In that, the country is well served.

## Pilot Training

The day the Korean War began, 25 June 1950, Boyd was on a train on his way to ROTC summer camp between his junior and senior years in college. As a recruit with prior service, Boyd was hardly the typical college lad facing his first encounter with the real military. Since the trainees are not officers yet, NCOs have been known to get their digs in early and make sure the ROTC guys learn something about the way the military really works. On his return, Boyd was told he would probably be called to active duty, which for him meant being a fighter pilot. He was genuinely excited and afraid. He was afraid not of going to war but that once again the war might end before he could get into it. All the heady talk about having the boys home before Christmas after MacArthur's successful Inchon amphibious landing did not bode well. Boyd ached to become a fighter pilot and see combat.

After graduation and initial testing in Omaha, he got his wish. Sent to Columbus, Mississippi, Boyd learned to fly the T-6 Texan, the venerable World War II plane that was a trainer for air forces around the world. Almost immediately, Boyd started to test his limits and those of the airplane. As usual, he soon got into trouble. Having learned to solo fairly quickly, Boyd started reading books about flying. He was impatient, a character trait later tempered with a sense of timing and a willingness to let some things take their course. It was typical of Boyd, though, to want to push the envelope. If he learned the basics, he wanted to learn more. Then he wanted to test what he had learned, make adjustments, and learn some more.

In flight school Boyd started to practice and refine some traits he had exhibited before but not really honed to perfection. He not only understood what we call the scientific method, but he also practiced it and lived it. His thought and action became an unfolding set of hypotheses, a flow of connected "if-then" statements, followed by testing to confirm or deny his hypothesis. A part of the scientific method is the specification of the conditions under which a given result will occur. Boyd, almost intuitively, started to specify conditions for maneuvers in flight. Speed, altitude, g-forces, intertwine to make certain maneuvers possible under one set of conditions and impossible under others.

There was great value in learning well what the plane could not be made to do under certain conditions, and the same held true for determining the pilot's skills. Learning both, however, risked death. It was a necessary set of experiments. Boyd just tended to push them a little farther than most. Exploring the fit of plane and pilot, what they can do and what they cannot, was a necessary exercise in learning to fly well. He was merely perfecting his flying skills (all pilots feel that way to some degree), but Boyd was also honing his mind to a much sharper edge. He observed very carefully. Through trial and error and extension building on a base of what he had learned, he progressed rather rapidly to absorb new concepts. It was the beginning of the development of a method of inquiry on which he would rely.

Another thing happened in pilot training in Mississippi: Boyd learned to learn for himself. He was autodidactic, self-taught, in almost everything he did. Years later he would emphasize this and tell people his education had consisted of going to a "cow college" in Iowa (the University of Iowa) and a "trade school" in Georgia (Georgia Institute of Technology). He had undergraduate degrees from both and never earned a master's degree or attended any professional military education other than Squadron Officers School in the Air Force. The great majority of what Boyd learned, he learned on his own. He began the practice in flight school by reading books about flying and going beyond what he was learning in the formal program.

At the base library he checked out books on aerobatics. Tired of gliding turns and other such basic "nonsense," Boyd taught himself to do Immelmann loops in both directions and then point roll-outs, barrel roll-outs, and snap roll-outs, all to either the right or left, along with low-speed loops and high-speed turns. He learned how to do lazy eights and a snapdragon eight and then a snap roll at the top of a lazy eight. He had a ball, but he never practiced gliding turns. Then his instructor took him up to check him out on some of the basics, including gliding turns. "It was a disaster. I couldn't even begin to do them correctly."

The instructor was furious. This guy was obviously incompetent if he couldn't do the simple basics as required. Boyd asked, "Hey, can I show you something else? Since I did so badly on the gliding turns, you probably want to know what I have been doing."

Luck was with him, for the instructor agreed, and Boyd proceeded to do his repertoire of hotshot tricks: rolls, loops, and such. The instructor demanded to know who had taught him. "I read it out of a book. I kept trying until I got it good." The instructor was impressed.

Boyd's final check ride came a few days later. During the intervening time, he practiced gliding turns and the other basic routines on which he knew he would be graded. After a few preliminaries, the instructor doing the check ride said he understood Boyd knew how to do Immelmanns. Boyd said yes and showed him.

"Show me the rest of your stuff," the instructor ordered. Boyd again went through his repertoire. Suitably impressed, the instructor said, "Okay, let's head for home. You pass." Boyd got his pilot's wings, instead of washing out of flight school.

## Honing His Flying Skills

Boyd was sent to Williams Air Force Base, in Arizona (known as Willy), for fighter training. There Boyd was introduced to the F-80 Shooting Star, America's first jet fighter procured in any numbers. Boyd was ecstatic about being a jet pilot, but he was not enamored with the regimentation and what he considered the slow pace of the flying training. He wanted to push the limits of what he did know and learn more about what he didn't know. That agenda did not include the many boring cross-country flights to test his navigational skills; he wanted to see what he and the airplane could do. Once again, Boyd nearly got into trouble for breaking the rules. Long before Tom Wolfe's book *The Right Stuff,* fighter pilots were known as a breed apart. You either had it or you didn't. Guys who were good sticks (first-rate pilots) were respected and could get away with a lot. Boyd quickly set about becoming a good stick.

Far ahead of fellow students at Willy in his ability to fly, Boyd hated the cross-country flights that were required. Some of his friends who already had their wings were flying out of nearby Luke Air Force Base doing air-to-air practice. "I had heard that they were going down to Ajo and that they were going to do some of their air-to-air stuff, so rather than go on my cross country, I decided to fly down there and join in on their air-to-air practice."

Air-to-air combat was another eye opener for Boyd. What looks to others like a confusing and disorderly fur ball of a fight among swarming planes in the air was really a delight to Boyd. There was more order to the process than one might think, and Boyd would spend years deriving order from the chaos of air-to-air combat. What initially excited him was that it was limitless. It could start or end at any altitude, from any direction. It was all azimuth and multidimensional. It was, he would realize, the best way to think about a problem. Years later, after refining his skills and trying to teach others how to do air-to-air combat, Boyd would realize he had simultaneously developed a new and different way to think.

Boyd sneaked off to taste the delights of air-to-air combat not once but on several occasions, and finally he got caught—by an instructor from Willy who was doing the same thing. Boyd figured out that the instructor wasn't supposed to be there either. He immediately solved the problem by outlining the dilemma: The guy who caught him could not turn him in. To do so would mean that the instructor would expose himself. Boyd offered a deal. Neither would rat on the other, and each would continue the practice. They made a pact that they would both keep their mouths shut about their extracurricular activities.

## The Air Force: Old and New

Boyd then went to Nellis Air Force Base for further training. Little did he know that it would later be his home for six years. On his arrival, he was rather taken aback by the condition of his quarters. According to Boyd, the room could be described at best as rather Spartan. It had an old metal bed with a wire rack and thin mattress, the sort of Army issue that had served millions in World War II. There was a single light and a broom-handle dowel in a niche in the wall for a closet. A hole in the wall was roughly the size and shape of a window, though slightly larger, but there was no window frame or window, just a hole where the window should be. Boyd thought this a bit odd and inquired about it at billeting. He was told he was lucky to have a room, window or not. Things could be worse, you know.

"Are you flying airplanes, Lieutenant Boyd?" the billeting sergeant asked. Boyd said he was and he sure enjoyed it, but the hole in the wall in his room where the window should be was a bit of an annoyance. If he turned the light on at night after he got in, his room immediately filled with every flying insect known in the desert. If he left it off, he was reduced to doing everything by Braille. The clerk at billeting finally consented to give Boyd an Army blanket and some nails so he could cover the hole in the wall. Throughout his initial stay at Nellis, he never did get the window and window frame installed. But he was flying, and he was deliriously happy to be in the Air Force and to be a fighter pilot. Any sacrifice to achieve that was well worth it.

Boyd used to tell that story and contrast it with his first visit to the Air Force Academy in Colorado Springs. He was brought out there to lecture by a fellow who used to work for him, Ray Leopold, who was then teaching at the academy. When Boyd saw the facilities the young cadets had — the beautiful setting amid 10,000 acres of Colorado countryside just below the mountains, the imposing cathedral, the classrooms and athletic facilities, their dorm rooms, all with windows — he was amazed and saddened. He understood, he said, the difference between his generation in the Air Force and those who came after.

"I was so happy to be flying," he would tell people. "The living conditions were just not that important. But now, we take the cream of the crop, the best and brightest the U.S. Air Force can attract, and start them out with such a high level of creature comforts and such plush surroundings that they come to expect it as their due for their entire career." He was right, and it reflects the difference in service cultures in the U.S. armed forces. Visiting officers, indeed colonels, in the Army get a cot and share a bath down the hall in bachelor officer quarters at certain installations. In contrast, the average Air Force officer on temporary duty at another Air Force installation expects his minibar in the room, air conditioning, and cable TV. Boyd thought it a most unhealthy and unnecessary state of affairs. Worse, it coddled America's air warriors.

Boyd spent the first half of his accelerated training, from September to December 1952, in the F-80 Shooting Star and the last half in the F-86 Sabre Jet. In the 80 hours of flying time in the program, Boyd continued to sharpen his skills and learned how to do high-g rolling maneuvers, high-speed breaks, when to do reversals in hard turns, and other refinements to his repertoire. He found that he could beat his instructors at air-to-air combat rather handily most of the time. He was good, he knew it, and wanted others to as well. This was competition with a purpose, and he loved it.

Sidney Woods at Williams Air Force Base and Clay Tice at Nellis were

Boyd's role models and pilot mentors. They were wildmen who flew hard, partied harder, and introduced young Mr. Boyd into that elite circle known as fighter pilots. Boyd soaked up the ethic and entered into that fraternity of devil-may-care risk takers who are hotshot pilots. He was on a team again. He was competing. He was flying. He was learning and having fun at the same time. The fellowship among fighter pilots was even better than a jock fraternity in college.

He was gloriously happy. Others, however, were not. John was about to go off to war in Korea, leaving behind his young wife and a mother who didn't understand why he had to do this. He had already served a hitch in the military, and his mother was grateful it had been after World War II ended. Elsie Boyd could see no reason for him to do it again. Until her dying day in June 1976, despite his successful career and all he had accomplished, she was unhappy that John had gone into the Air Force. She chewed out Mary Boyd for letting him go to Korea, as if she had any say in the matter.[9] Boyd simply could not and would not give up on the opportunity to fly and go to war. That the women in his life couldn't understand that was their problem, not his. He had missed out the last time around in World War II, and he almost missed out again in Korea. Timing—it really was everything.

# 3.                                              **Air-to-Air Combat**

In battle, this ability to rapidly pass through the observation-orientation-decision-action loop (the Boyd cycle) gave American pilots a slight time advantage. If one views a dogfight as a series of Boyd cycles, one sees that the Americans would repeatedly gain a time advantage each cycle, until the enemy's actions became totally inappropriate for the changing situations.

Robert Leonhard, *The Art of Maneuver: Maneuver Warfare Theory and AirLand Battle*

**B**oyd was sent to Korea in the winter of 1952–1953, assigned to the 51st Wing, 25th Squadron. What Boyd learned and did there constituted the basis for nearly everything he thought and did later. It was a truly transforming experience and provided the foundation for all of his later contributions, not only in air-to-air tactics, energy maneuverability, and aircraft design but also in his development of OODA loops, his thinking on strategy and maneuver warfare, and ultimately his thought on time and thinking itself. Boyd's thoughts were grounded in empirical observations and data. He was a true scientist, always testing hypotheses and refining them before constructing a theoretical compression of what he had learned. The serendipitous connection between the data and observations on the one hand and the imagination, insight, and innovation on the other is what made him unique. It is no overstatement to say that it all flowed from his experience in air-to-air combat in Korea.

Boyd was intrigued by the observation that even though the MiG-15 was faster, had a higher operational ceiling, and could turn tighter than the F-86, the

kill ratio was 10:1 in favor of the F-86 during the Korean War. True, it fluctu-
ated wildly (from 4.9:1 when Russian pilots flew the MiGs to 20:1 in the last
six months of the war after the Russian pilots were pulled out in January 1953),[1]
but why, wondered Boyd, did the F-86 do so well? According to information
supplied by Col. Jim Hagerstrom, USAF (a triple ace from World War II and
Korea), Col. C. E. "Chuck" Myers, and others, the factors most responsible for
successful air-to-air kills are several. "In order of importance they are (1) obtain
the first sighting, (2) outnumber the enemy in the air, (3) outmaneuver the adversary to gain firing position, and (4) have the ability to achieve split-second kills."[2]

The F-86 had a bubble canopy that allowed superior visibility compared with
the MiG-15 pilot's view, which has been likened to "looking through a Coke
bottle."[3] Hence, the F-86 provided much better visibility and a decided advantage in aerial dogfights with MiG-15s. Though the USAF was at a distinct numerical disadvantage at the war's outbreak, by the end of the war it enjoyed
superiority. Still, in many engagements the F-86s were outnumbered but scored
superior kill ratios. They had superior pilots with superior training, many having
had combat experience in World War II, but there were many new pilots like
Boyd flying in Korea too. The lopsided kill ratio seemed to involve something more.

It is true that on paper the MiG-15 surpassed the F-86 in some performance
characteristics, but there are some subtle differences that must be considered.
As Boyd was to prove later, an aircraft's capabilities are not merely a question
of how high, how far, and how fast it goes. The MiG was the superior high-
altitude plane, but the F-86's ability to transition from one maneuver to another,
in particular to roll and transition from left turn to right or vice versa, was better than the MiG-15's. The F-86 could do a horizontal scissors causing the MiG
(usually diving from behind and above) to overshoot and find the F-86 in firing position. An added capability was attributable to the ability to move the entire horizontal surface of the tail, the so-called flying-tail power system first operational in the F-86E. This advantage, utilized effectively by American pilots,
meant that they could more easily outmaneuver the MiG-15. Their advantage
was reinforced by a combination of the F-86's full-power hydraulic flight controls, much better visibility, and superior pilot training.

The injunctions of air-to-air combat are simple. Don't be predictable, and end
the engagement as quickly as possible. You are most likely to be shot down by
an adversary you don't see who takes advantage of a random opportunity while
you are occupied elsewhere. This is so important that the Navy Fighter Weapons
School developed a nine-second rule: never fly in one direction for more than
nine seconds in an aerial engagement.[4] The quality of pilots is as important or
more important than the quality of the plane. Compared with the North Kore-

ans, U.S. pilots were better trained, and many had combat experience from World War II. Surviving long enough to get the experience to enable one to survive was a "Catch 22." Many did, some did not.

As James Burton puts it: "Fighter pilots in those days were wild, aggressive, irreverent, self-confident and independent—they had to be in order to survive. The training was so aggressive and realistic that pilots killed themselves left and right."[5] What was true of the group in general applied to Boyd in spades. Boyd never thought he'd reach his fortieth birthday because he would die in a plane crash "doing some wild-ass maneuver." In the 1950s, an era when scores of fighter pilots died every year in plane crashes while training, that outlook was a fair assessment of the risks.

Training has evolved considerably. Visibility was critical, but it expanded over time into what is now called "situational awareness." Historically, at least through the Vietnam War, most sightings were visual, not by radar. The great majority of downed pilots did not see their attackers before they were hit. In Vietnam especially, the majority of those hit (by missiles and gunfire from the ground as well as the air) didn't even know they were under attack until hit by enemy ordnance. Several improvements over the years changed that considerably. The technology of attack warning indicators (showing that a missile had locked on to you as a target) improved situational awareness, and more realistic training of aircrews (with the founding of Top Gun and Red Flag) greatly improved combat skills and competence from the early 1970s. The whole business of air-to-air combat was changed by those factors, the introduction of far more sophisticated radar, air-to-air missiles, and surface-to-air missiles.

### Air-to-Air Combat in Korea

Despite U.S. claims to the contrary and United Nations assurances that U.N. and U.S. forces would not cross the Yalu River border with China, Boyd and a great many others frequently went north of the Yalu to find MiGs and mix it up. Many of the U.S. pilots shot down in the Korean War were lost over China, not North Korea.[6] So much for national niceties in war and precedents in international politics regarding the sanctity of borders and sanctuaries for the enemy. Individual pilots did the same thing later in Southeast Asia, flying over supposedly restricted airspace in Cambodia, Laos, and North Vietnam. Press reports are one thing. Realities of war are another.

One of Boyd's best days in the war was one in which no shots were fired in the engagement. He and Jock Maitland, an RAF exchange officer, decided to sneak across the border so Jock, who was about to return home, could see if he could get a kill. Off they went. As they crossed the Yalu, they turned off the IFF

(Identification, Friend or Foe). They knew MiGs were in the area, and they went high to look for them. No MiGs. Then they went low. Coming down through 19,000 feet, they found them. Eager for combat and ignoring the odds, Boyd and Maitland in a two-ship formation dove into fourteen to sixteen MiGs. The purpose of the effort was to get Maitland a kill; Boyd was to protect him while he did. Maitland swooped in on an enemy MiG with Boyd covering him. He was only 200 feet off the MiG's tail and hadn't fired. Boyd called on the radio, "Damn, Jock, why don't you shoot? Goddamn, Jock, those other guys are coming, you have to hose that guy!" No response.

"I figured, Oh-oh, I goofed. He must have switched channels and I missed that goddamned channel change." Boyd called Communications Operations and asked them to try and raise Maitland and call him back so he could switch to the right channel. "We cannot pick him up," was the reply.

"I figured he had a radio failure. Meanwhile, guys are whistling in from behind and were shooting, so I hooked fast and rolled over to get them off Jock. Jock was still chasing the same guy! I thought, What in the hell is he doing? We are both going to get hosed down." What Boyd didn't know was that Maitland had suffered not just a radio failure but a complete electrical failure—his guns couldn't shoot.

"Boy, was I pissed," Boyd recalled.

Maitland waggled his wings, and Boyd thought, "Oh, my God! Somebody has snuck in on me. I thought he had made a break and someone had snuck in behind me. What I did not know was that Jock was trying to get me to take the lead and hose the guy."

Soon, a lot of antiaircraft artillery fire came up, and the MiGs just took off. Low on fuel, Boyd and Maitland headed for home.

"We did not get anything, not one kill! That was terrible."

That was one of the last times that Boyd was to have such an opportunity. He had only three other missions after that encounter. The war was winding down, and the truce would be signed that summer. Boyd never got to fly lead, because the standard operating procedure was 30 missions under your belt before you could fly lead instead of wingman. Boyd had only 22 missions when the war ended. Not much, but he made the most of it and developed important tactical insights from his limited experience.

### Nellis and the Fighter Weapons School

As the war ended, the guys in the 51st practiced against each other. Boyd could beat them all, regardless of rank, age, or experience. They made him the wing tactics officer. Some told him he should lay out all his tactics stuff and teach it to others. Unintentionally, those now nameless compatriots changed the course of history.

"I had never really thought much about it before," said Boyd, "so I kind of mulled it over in my mind, then I began to make notes on different things, putting briefings together, etc. I really got into tactics, along with some gunnery."

At the beginning of 1954, Boyd was assigned to Nellis Air Force Base, Nevada. There, his career almost came to an end before it really got started. Soon after arrival, Boyd was told he would be assigned to a maintenance squadron. He raised hell.

"Bullshit on maintenance. I don't want anything to do with it." He was a pilot, not a maintenance officer, and though the Air Force in its infinite wisdom would keep trying to put him in maintenance, Boyd never condoned the idea. Unlike many USAF pilots who served tours in maintenance, he always managed to beat the system. He was to end up with some of the best flying one could get in an Air Force career, for the next five and a half years.

Boyd continued to push the limits of rules and the Air Force's tolerance for breaking them, and he created a larger-than-life image, in keeping with the fighter-pilot mystique of the era. It was a different Air Force from the one we have today. Life was a bit wilder than it is now until well into the 1980s, when women became an increasingly larger portion of the U.S. military. In many ways, it resembled a college fraternity party. The officer's clubs routinely had strippers (men for the women and women for the men), wet T-shirt contests, wild parties, and lots of cheap beer and booze at happy hour as a part of the weekly schedule. Fighter pilots were supposed to work hard and play harder. They had an image to maintain. Pushing the limits and breaking the rules—and sometimes their necks—came with the territory, both on duty in uniform and off duty and out of uniform. It was part of the ethos of being a fighter jock.

Eventually Boyd was assigned to the 97th Squadron, the Thunderbird Squadron, as an instructor. It was then he started to develop his repertoire of tactics and techniques. After a year there, he was assigned to the Fighter Weapons School, where he stayed as an instructor until 1960 (with the exception of one brief interlude). Boyd flew and studied for nearly six years, refining his tactics and teaching for air-to-air combat. He accumulated hundreds of hours of mock air-to-air combat. No one proved himself better. Boyd's experience and questioning of air-to-air tactics were the guts of his real education. Through a series of accidents, the first of Boyd's revolutions began. It resulted in the first comprehensive manual on jet aircraft combat, *Aerial Attack Study*.

Boyd was appalled that the Fighter Weapons School in 1954 was largely a gunnery school. Pilots spent much of their time shooting at a 6-by-30-foot banner towed for target practice. It hardly resembled air-to-air combat. He thought the school should combine flying skills as well as gunnery. He continually revised his notes and developed outlines for four additional courses of study and application. At the time, the Fighter Weapons School was divided into three sections: Academics, Operations, and TR&D (Training, Research, and Development). In the scale of assignments, everyone wanted to be in TR&D or Operations. No one wanted to be in Academics. Boyd went to Col. John Giraudo, commander of the school, and said, "I have a bargain for you. You need a guy over in Academics, right? I will honestly volunteer if you will allow me to try one thing. With your approval I want to put tactics in the Weapons Squadron."

Giraudo, familiar with Boyd's work and reputation, agreed. Remember, Boyd had only been commissioned in 1951, and now he was a first lieutenant making radical suggestions to a full colonel for how the Air Force should train fighter pilots. Call it confidence or arrogance, he took on the system to change it.

Boyd laid out his courses, developed mission cards, taught mock classes, and prepared. "Most mission cards said how we taxied out and how we would come back, with only about five minutes of what we could do in the air. Bullshit! I wanted five minutes clocking out, five minutes coming back, and fifty minutes on a preflight briefing to discuss what was to be done on the mission and how well the guy was trained to do all these different things."

He didn't stop there. Boyd made an even more radical proposal. "Instead of flinging a guy in a four-ship flight where nobody knows what the hell is going on, I wanted to have one instructor and one student in the initial flight. That was a hard fight; they just did not want to do that. I said I want to give these guys individual attention. Those first few rides are so important. From there on, it becomes easy. If they were taken in formation, it would go much faster. The sorties would not be wasted either."

Adding flying hours was a concern. Each unit got so much money for so many flying hours. Additional hours didn't necessarily mean more money. Usually there wasn't enough money to pay for the flying hours the commander thought necessary, so commanders became expert at not spending money on other things in order to fund their flying hours. Finding more money would be hard to do. Boyd came up with a second-best solution: "We will just take the guys up and have two guys stand off and work with one guy, then work with another guy, and then with a third guy. In other words, have the guys watch what is going on rather than have everybody just mix it up."

## Flying the F-100

Individual attention and the chance to observe were both critical to improving flying skills, but first they needed a cadre course to upgrade the skills of the instructors. They were going to be teaching new things, in novel ways, and with a new aircraft, the F-100 Super Saber, which had entered service in 1955. The F-100 was a very difficult plane to fly and maintain. Though it was the first USAF fighter to go supersonic in level flight, it was nearly twice as heavy as the F-86 (18,185 pounds empty versus 10,890 pounds), and its nickname was "the Lead Sled." Nearly one fourth of the total number of F-100s produced were lost in accidents resulting from maintenance problems or pilot error.[7] Learning how to fly it well and milk all the performance one could get out of it in such a short time frame was a tall order.

Once again, it was Boyd's flying skills that backed up the boasts and changed the Air Force's way of doing things. Boyd figured out how to get the most out of the F-100 in only four rides. He learned how to use something called opposite stick to cope with an annoying tendency of the F-100 to exhibit negative yaw. Under certain conditions, the pilot had to move the stick in the opposite direction from the way the plane was supposed to go. The plane was unforgiving, and it took good pilots to fly it well. Boyd was one of the best.

"I figured out how the ailerons worked. I figured out how they rolled off one way. I thought about it in the classroom one day and said: I am moving the aileron this way and if it goes all right, that means it is acting as a speed board. All I have to do is use a cross control technique for the goddamn thing to really hook around or just neutralize the aileron, the rudder being the primary control. So I went up and tried it, and sure enough, it actually worked. I practiced a number of times and took a couple of guys up with me. We did it in rolls and everything else. Anyway, I was the first guy to accomplish that, to develop those techniques. The company engineers said it could not be done."

North American, the company that built the F-100, sent someone down to the school, and he came back convinced that Boyd and company knew what they were talking about and began rewriting the manuals. Boyd also made believers out of others by showing off with the F-100 in other ways. Ron Catton, a former student of Boyd's at the Fighter Weapons School and later a pilot with the Air Force demonstration team the Thunderbirds, contributed this curious accolade to the reflections at Boyd's memorial service at Arlington: "John Boyd could fly an airplane slower, faster than anybody else in the world."[8] Boyd could go from 500 knots to stall speed, practically stopping the plane in midair, which would force any aircraft on his tail to overshoot him and thus gain the advantage for Boyd. In another trick, he would stand the F-100 on its tail and slide down the pillar of its own exhaust. Fire would come out of the intake in the nose of the aircraft and the tailpipe simultaneously. A seemingly impossible feat, it was challenged by others. Boyd went to Edwards Air Force Base in California, where NASA had two fully instrumented F-100 aircraft, and demonstrated it and other techniques to a series of nonbelievers. The test pilot at Edwards who challenged him at the time was a fellow by the name of Neil Armstrong.[9]

## The Human Dimension

Boyd's relationship with Thunderbird pilot Ron Catton bears review. It shows another side of Boyd, not only as a brash, bold, and capable pilot but also as an insightful leader, a good teacher, an important mentor. Catton, a pretty good stick himself, had come to Nellis to attend the Fighter Weapons School on the recommendation of his wing commander (who was sticking his neck out by recommending him, knowing that Catton was sometimes undependable and had a drinking problem). Catton arrived at Nellis—a hot young fighter pilot driving his new Corvette—determined to use this opportunity to turn his career around and make something of himself. Unfortunately, the first week he was there, a bunch of guys from his old unit came through town and invited him to a party at the officers' quarters. He accepted. Later that evening, Catton was stopped by the police for driving under the influence and thrown in jail until the next morning.

After being released, he was called before Col. Ralph F. Newman, the commander of the Fighter Weapons School, along with his flight instructor, the director of Operations, and Boyd as head of Academics. He had a hangover, was humiliated, and was at the end of his rope as Colonel Newman filled out the court-martial forms. When Catton gave the name of his commanding officer at his old unit, as required on the form, Newman stopped, leaned back in his chair, and told Catton this was the luckiest day of his life. In World War II, Catton's wing commander had chased an ME-109 off the tail of his flight leader, the very same Colonel Newman who now held Catton's Air Force career in his hands. In partial payment of a debt to Catton's former commander, Catton got a second chance. He was forbidden to go into Las Vegas, and he had to turn in the keys to his Corvette. If he was seen in a taxi or accepted a ride from anyone, he would be court-martialed. He also had to lay off the booze. It would be tough going for Catton.

After that meeting, Catton went to see Boyd. He recapped his career and his problems, the difficulties he had had with alcohol and his passion for flying. He knew he was a good pilot and wanted desperately to complete the course and to have the chance to become an instructor at the Fighter Weapons School. Catton explained that his attendance at the school was to have been the occasion for his resurrection, for turning his career around. Now, with a single, thoughtless act, he had blown everything. Was there anything, he asked Boyd, that he could do?

Catton was bright, a good pilot and a nice guy. He was worth saving for the Air Force, if it could be done. Boyd liked him. Boyd could have lectured him about taking responsibility for his life, getting a grip on his drinking problem, shaping up, accepting his circumstances like a man, resigning himself to what he had done, or dished out countless other conventional forms of advice, but he didn't. Realizing Catton's sincerity and commitment to becoming a truly exceptional pilot, Boyd made a single suggestion, with just the right inflection: "Well, you might go through the school with 100 percent in academics. Nobody has ever done that before. That might get their attention."

It was all Catton needed to hear. With Vegas and the officer's club off-limits, no car, and no partying or drinking, Catton had plenty of time for intense academic study, and he jumped at the chance to save himself. He was the first and the only (as of the time Boyd left Nellis in 1960) student to get a 100-percent rating on the extremely demanding academic portion of the school. He also finished third in the class in flying skills, second overall. It was an amazing turnaround. As far as Ron Catton is concerned, he owes his life, his Air Force career, and his success as a financial adviser to that encounter with John Boyd and his mentoring and tutelage at Nellis.[10] He was probably the first but certainly not the last to feel that way.

Shortly thereafter, Boyd was told he would be moving from Academics. He assumed he would go to TR&D, but instead he was assigned to a new shop called Training Analysis and Development (TA&D). Boyd was appalled. "A headquarters weenie! No way."

He was told that another officer whom he respected, Maj. Leroy Clifton, would join him to start the section. After learning more about the opportunity before him, he cooled down a bit. They would review all the lesson plans, check on the training, and see that the programs fit together appropriately. It was essentially curriculum development for the entire Fighter Weapons School. Boyd agreed. He accepted the assignment with renewed zeal, and his influence increased accordingly.

### Teaching, Learning, and Writing

In 1957 Boyd wrote up some of what he had been working on in his courses and notes developed from Korea and at the Fighter Weapons School and published it in the *Fighter Weapons School Newsletter* under the title "Air Combat Maneuvering."[11] There, disdaining the rigid choreography of the aerial dances known as dogfights, Boyd laid out what he called "fluid separation." It was one of the first TA&D reports.

The problem, as with most military bureaucracies, was that the system wanted to standardize everything, to have a checklist of reactions for every action, a school solution for every circumstance. Boyd wanted to show people a variety of moves and countermoves to have in a repertoire and let them decide when and how to do what they thought needed to be done in a given situation. Hence, he developed terms for formations such as "fluid separation" to give latitude to the individual pilot. It was the first time he used the term "fluid" in his thinking about tactics or strategy. It would not be the last. It became one of his favorite analogies.

It was also in 1957 that Boyd met Vernon "Sprad" Spradling. Sprad was a World War II pilot and former schoolteacher who had moved to Las Vegas for his son's health; he worked at the Fighter Weapons School as a civilian. They became good friends, and Sprad helped Boyd put ideas on paper, formalize lesson plans, write up his insights, and produce *Aerial Attack Study*. Sprad remembers Boyd as a naturally gifted teacher, someone who could explain very complex things in ways most could understand, a master in the use of analogies to clarify concepts for his students. He was also a strong disciplinarian who didn't suffer fools gladly. Sprad recounted a classroom incident when a student asked a series of three stupid questions. The guy was pretending to be serious but wasting class time as a joke, showing off by jerking the instructor's chain. Boyd stopped, glared at the fellow, and then said, "Look, you silly S.O.B., we're here to learn. You are not helping our efforts. You keep asking stupid questions. You can shut up or get out." The class broke into applause. Boyd never had any problems of that sort again.[12]

Later in 1957 Boyd went to Maxwell Air Force Base for a few weeks of training in officership at the Squadron Officers School (SOS). Group activities, sports, and competition play a big part in the SOS experience, which is a combination of classroom study and carefully selected team-building activities. Boyd loved the athletic competition and thought the classroom instruction a waste of time. Lessons were scripted for the instructors and moved in lock-step fashion. It was boring. Each flight (seminar), however, played all the others in various competitions and accumulated points for all that they did (academics, athletics, inspections, etc.), competing to be the best flight in that class.

Volleyball was one of the sports. Tall, limber, and a ferocious competitor, Boyd was good at it. The instructor heading the seminar took a lot of heat from the class members for the way he coached and substituted during the games. When the flight asked him to let Boyd run the games, he agreed. Boyd played the same six men in the next matches without substituting anyone, contrary to the ethic of participation by all members of the flight.

The instructor called Boyd on it, which led to a rather public row. "I thought you wanted to win and get the most points," said Boyd. "If you want to win, let me do it my way. If you want to make everybody participate while they lose, then do it your way." The instructor blew up, saying he had had just about enough of all these hotshots from Nellis and Boyd would be put in his place. From that day on, he went out of his way to make life difficult for Boyd. Boyd put up with it and persevered but eventually got his revenge. When the instructor tried to embarrass him at a social function at the end of the class by remarking on his lackluster academic performance, Boyd turned the tables. Noting that he had put up with this instructor's crap with reasonably good grace, all things considered, Boyd said he would not be lectured to in public about how to perform as an Air Force officer and pilot when the instructor was the one who had washed out of flight school. It would become a trademark of Boyd's: no unnecessary fights, but if someone pushes too hard or too long, bury the S.O.B., preferably with public humiliation.[13]

After the interlude at Maxwell, it was back to Nellis. There, nobody seemed to know quite what to do with the Fighter Weapons School within the Air Force organization. Should ATC (Air Training Command) or TAC (Tactical Air Command) run it? People were being raided out of the school, and the whole operation was in limbo. *Captain* Boyd went to see *Colonel* Hinton and told him of his concerns. "Damn, here you have a wonderful school, and you are going to let the whole thing go down the tubes. Well, you know, once it is gone, you will never get it back again. It would take too long a process to build it back to where it is."

TAC eventually took over the operation. A new commander, Lt. Col. Floyd W. White, made Boyd head of Academics. It was then, in 1958, that he really began to work on integrating all his notions about air-to-air combat. He had a draft of his "Air Combat Maneuvers," but it was episodic, insightful but incomplete. Boyd and others redid the curriculum and training, mission cards, and courses. For the next two years Boyd also worked on what would become *Aerial Attack Study,* first published in 1960 and revised in 1964, the basis for most of the air-to-air combat manuals for the Air Force since then. Many a fighter pilot, whether he knows it or not, owes his life to Boyd and the development of the tactics and maneuvers explained in that manual. Though not an ace, 40-Second Boyd was regarded by many as one of the best pilots this country produced.

Spradling recalled one incident in particular from among the numerous challenges to Boyd's "forty seconds or forty dollars" bet. A certain Marine Corps captain, Hal Vincent, came up from China Lake, California, while flying a mission near Nellis and challenged Boyd to an aerial duel. "I hear you've got some standing bet about being able to slam someone on your six in forty seconds or less," Vincent said. Boyd said it was true. "Well, I don't have time or fuel on today's mission, but let's make a date and see how good you are."

At the appointed time and place, Vincent in his F8U Crusader met Boyd in an F-100. Boyd allowed Vincent to get on his tail and try to stick with him. It was over in less than 10 seconds. Boyd was on Vincent's tail. They repeated the game three times with the same results each time. "You've convinced me," said Vincent. "I'll apply for a slot in your school."

He eventually went through the Fighter Weapons School at Nellis and proved to be a superb pilot—after the course and Boyd's tutelage. He finished number one in air-to-ground, number one in air-to-air, and number one in academics, quite an accomplishment.[14]

## The Aerial Attack Study

Boyd would be reassigned in the summer of 1960. Before he could go, he had to convert all his notes into a curriculum for the Fighter Weapons School, a mammoth task, especially for someone who wanted to fly as much as possible in his remaining months at Nellis. Boyd didn't see how he could get it all done, so he went looking for the colonel in charge. In the base coffee shop, Boyd asked for time off to complete the task. When the colonel said no, Boyd became livid and launched into a heated exchange in front of the coffee-shop crowd. It ended when Boyd got right in the colonel's face and screamed, "God damn you, I'll do it on my own time!" Fortunately, he didn't get court-martialed for his behavior.

His good friend Sprad had the solution. Boyd could dictate his notes and thoughts and the section secretary, Mrs. Sugars, would transcribe them and then cut and paste as required before typing the final product. They put it on mimeograph forms, and then Sprad, one chapter at a time, bootlegged it through the base print shop. The process was by no means fun, but it was a godsend to Boyd, who was always more verbal anyway. It took Boyd a month just to outline the project and several months of dictating. Relying on Navy manuals, formulae from math books he was reading, and his own ideas for how to illustrate the maneuvers, he synthesized it all into the final product, giving credit where it was due for all the other material he had utilized. It was his first great synthesis, and he loved it. Thus was born what became the essence of the Fighter Weapons School curriculum and the *Aerial Attack Study*. Sprad still has some of the transcripts of the tapes.

*Aerial Attack Study* is an impressive piece of work, detailing every maneuver possible for a pilot to use in a dogfight. It is meticulously researched, explained, and illustrated with old ribbon diagrams that had to be painstakingly drawn on mimeograph forms for reproduction in the manual. It has been described as the first comprehensive logical explanation of all known (and some hitherto unknown) fighter tactics in terms of moves and countermoves. Previous tactics manuals were just a bag of tricks, without the logic of move and countermove. Boyd did not advocate one maneuver over another but represented the options (and the logic for selecting them) available to a pilot to counter any move his opponent made. The study represented the first time that anyone had based fighter tactics on three-dimensional, rather than two-dimensional, maneuvers.[15]

It was all Boyd knew about air combat maneuvers and remains the core of what is known today, despite tremendous improvements in fighter aircraft, avionics, and computer-assisted fly-by-wire designs. As Air Force major Barry Watts put it: "The moves and countermoves laid out in this study formed the basis for all fighter tactics used by the Air Force, Navy and Marine fighter pilots in Southeast Asia. It is still the basis for tactics used in all jet fighter air forces today. . . . According to the Navy Fighter Weapons School journal *Top Gun*, since Boyd's 1960 treatise 'not even one truly new move has been uncovered.'"[16]

It was a tour de force, 147 pages of single-spaced manuscript that covered all jet fighter air-to-air tactics. There were sections on virtually everything one needed to know, including Fighter versus Fighter; Maneuver, Counter Maneuver; The Overhead Attack; How You Execute the Attack; What the Advantages Are in G, High Side, Underside; Non-Maneuvering Targets; Flight Tactics; Basic Limitations of the AIM-9 against Maneuvering Targets; Defending Turns; Procedures for Adverse Yaw—everything. All were laid out and supported by diagrams, calculations, and precious advice drawn from years of experience. But the work almost didn't survive.

First the Air Force classified it. Then, his superiors thanked Boyd and told him they would be using another manual. Boyd exploded on both counts. "It was classified. They classified the damn thing! I got madder than hell and said I don't want to classify it, I want it unclassified. They said, 'No, you have to have it classified because you are talking about the damn tactics we are going to use in combat.' I said, 'Hell, if you classify it, then nobody will get to use it. So, damn, what good is it?'"

Before the classification process was completed, however, a number of copies disappeared. Then some 600 copies were printed without the Fighter Weapons School logo or documentation—just the author's name, Capt. John R. Boyd. Copying an unclassified document was not a violation of regulations. I have met several retired fighter pilots who have copies of the 1960 and 1964 versions in their homes. Though not a solution, it was what the military calls "a work around."

Much of *Aerial Attack Study* eventually became part of Air Force Manual 3-1 (now Major Command Manual 3-1), on air-to-air tactics. Many a pilot who flew in Vietnam owes his life to Boyd, and several, from each of the services, called to tell him so over the years. It was perhaps his greatest satisfaction. Given the thousands of allied pilots trained in the United States from scores of nations, Boyd's dedication in conveying what he learned to others has created a lasting legacy to pilots the world over. He accomplished it as a captain at age 33 and, in many ways, against the wishes of the U.S. Air Force.

The adoption of the manual was a bit trickier. As Boyd recalls the process in his Air Force oral history, after completing *Aerial Attack Study* he took the manual to Colonel Newman. "Here's your new manual."

"Well, we're not going to use your manual."

"Why not?" retorted Boyd. "You're not going to find a better one."

He was informed that they would be using a 15-page manual from TR&D because they had a charter to produce one and Boyd did not. Boyd decided he could play that game too. He contacted Maj. Leroy Clifton, his cohort at Nellis earlier. Clifton, now stationed at TAC in the tactics shop, was to visit Nellis shortly, and Boyd arranged for him to review his manual and the TR&D one. Clifton thought Boyd's clearly the superior product, but Boyd didn't want to use his friendship with Clifton in that way. Instead, he asked Clifton to arrange an independent review of the two manuals. A TAC panel was convened. A while later, Colonel Newman received a message stating, "We are going to publish Boyd's. We have decided to use his as the training prospectus at the Fighter Weapons School for students coming in, or for any other squadron that might want to use it."

Boyd went to see Newman and told him, "You ought to be glad. This way you end up with a better book. It is a reflection on you as commander. Why are you protecting a goddamn bunch of losers over there who cannot even do their homework? You know they did not do as good a job as me."

Newman threw Boyd out of his office. The next day he called Boyd back. "I want to apologize to you. I really never read your manual until last night. Yours really is much better than the one from TR&D."[17] Boyd respected him for having the honesty to admit he was wrong. More important, he had the courage to tell Boyd that face to face. Meanwhile, the guys at TR&D had their ass chewed by Newman for producing a lousy product and telling him Boyd's was lousy when it was far superior. Boyd had won all his air-to-air battles and most of them on the ground as well. He could now leave Nellis with a sense of genuine accomplishment.

## The Legend and Legacy

The first set of legends about John Boyd dates mainly from his years at Nellis. A hotshot fighter pilot who loved to fly and teach his students to beat the other instructors, Boyd was wild, daring, sometimes reckless and arrogant. Despite having a wife and four children, he was a leading member of the older but still adolescentlike fraternity of fighter jocks who worked hard, played hard, drank long and hard, and never shrank from a dare. For better or worse, much of that ethos (especially the drinking) has been banished from the Air Force, or at least is no longer officially sanctioned. But the attitude persists. If you want a good fighter pilot, you want someone who is bright, cocky, self-confident, aggressive; someone who pushes the performance envelope, and takes calculated risks. That attitude combined with exceptional aptitude makes an ace.

Even the drinking played an important role. Alcohol took a toll on one's body, and the problems it caused no doubt were severe, but it provided a medium and a place—the officer's club bar at happy hour—for learning about the Air Force and being socialized into the fraternity. The young officers could mix with senior officers easily and routinely. The lore of the colonels could be passed to the captains, and the bonding and socialization that are so important to military units could take place. Given the health-kick, diet-watching, weight-conscious, workout-oriented military today, this no longer happens. It's hard to imagine the boys swapping yarns, true or not, over carrot juice in the weight room. The golf course has become even more important as a result, at least for the Air Force, but it still lacks in both quality and quantity compared with the happy hours of yore.

Even then, Boyd was making a name for himself as a character on the ground as well as in the air. Seized with an intensity and concentration unimaginable to most, he was known for a gaze that could burn holes in the eyes of the person he stared at. People in the academic section told students to "Boyd it," meaning to focus and concentrate until the task was done right. Boyd didn't go looking for fights necessarily, but he never backed away from one, in the air or on the ground, physical or mental. He so loved competition, and once in a contest, he would destroy an opponent. The great prizefighter Jack Dempsey was once asked, "When you are about to hit a man, do you aim for his chin or his nose?" "Neither," Dempsey replied. "I aim for the back of his head." So too with Boyd: he always, mentally and physically, drove his point, or his fist, all the way home.

Boyd always pushed the envelope and bucked the system. On 1 June 1960, just before leaving Nellis, he was flying an F-100 that lost all hydraulic pressure, including backup. Rather than ride the plane down with no controls, Boyd punched out and the plane crashed. Brig. Gen. John N. Ewbank, the commander at Nellis and not a Boyd booster, immediately grounded Boyd for losing an airplane. Boyd protested, saying it wasn't his fault, that he was flying within the plane's performance envelope and that there was a design flaw in the plane that caused the crash. General Ewbank was convinced otherwise. Boyd pleaded his case and offered to run an experiment to demonstrate what he believed to be the problem. Under certain stresses during certain maneuvers, the pop-off valves in the hydraulics system would be under so much pressure that they would do what they are supposed to do—pop off—but both the primary and secondary systems could be blown simultaneously, something that wasn't supposed to happen. Boyd offered to demonstrate. Ewbank didn't want to lose another airplane. Boyd said the circumstances could be demonstrated on the ground. Ewbank, still suspicious, said okay, they could do a test, but Boyd was not to be in the cockpit. A crew chief would run the test.

The day for the test came, and rather than doing it with a plane Boyd had selected, General Ewbank walked out on the flight line and picked the tail number of the plane to be used. As luck would have it, students from one of the classes were assembled nearby, where they watched the demonstration. The crew chief started the engine and then maneuvered the power and controls as Boyd had instructed. The hydraulic system failed exactly as he had predicted, and the fluid drained out on the tarmac. To insure that he hadn't been set up, General Ewbank selected another plane and had the test repeated, with the same results. "All right, Boyd," he snarled, "you're reinstated to flying status," and stalked off. Present in the class observing this were two future chiefs of staff of the Air Force, Mike Dugan and Merrill "Tony" McPeak.[18]

What Boyd left behind was much more substantive than the stories of his run-ins with authority and the skills he displayed in flying. He changed the Fighter Weapons School. He changed the way flying skills were taught. Students mixed it up in group encounters as well as one-on-one, and others observed in the air what happened and how it occurred. On the ground, they studied why it had happened. Boyd changed the emphasis from gunnery alone to aerial tactics. He changed the way students were taught, both in the air and on the ground, theoretically and practically.

Boyd had changed himself, too. He learned to teach others and found that he liked it and took satisfaction and pride in doing so. He began to write, something that he had never done before. He wrote articles for the *Fighter Weapons School Newsletter* and *Aerial Attack Study*. He learned that he was different in how he thought about things and how he solved problems, and he started to think about that. Thinking about thinking and how one learned certain things was a novel and intriguing pastime. He would devote more time to such insights over the next 30 years than he ever imagined possible at Nellis. He had established a remarkable symbiotic relationship, the first of many he would uncover. Boyd had transformed air-to-air combat, and air-to-air combat had transformed him.

# 4.                    Energy Maneuverability

There were a lot of aerodynamic types of analysis on how to design aircraft. These evolved from a standpoint of analyzing the ability to fly at certain speeds or pull so much g, but energy maneuverability doesn't limit itself to these factors. As far as the factors that we can address now, yes, other types of analysis are now obsolete. You have proof of that when you know that just about every aircraft company in this country, and most other countries, now applies these techniques.

                                    Tom Christie, U.S. Air Force Oral History Interview

**B**oyd's departure from the Fighter Weapons School was about as atypical as his arrival. He seemed to be a walking example of unorthodox inclinations. He had applied to the Air Force Institute of Technology (AFIT) to go back to school, paid for by the Air Force, at a civilian institution. Since Boyd had an undergraduate degree in economics, AFIT wanted to send him to graduate school in economics or business administration. That was entirely reasonable and the way the system worked, but it didn't suit Boyd. He wanted to learn what he thought he needed to know to appreciate fully and explore further the implications of what he had begun at Nellis. He needed to start over. Boyd told AFIT, "I want to go back to undergraduate school and get a degree in engineering."

AFIT's reply was "We don't have any provisions for that."

It was a standoff. AFIT didn't do what Boyd wanted to do, and Boyd had no use for a master's in business administration. He wanted to study mathematics and engineering. Then, fate intervened. Boyd got a call from AFIT in the fall. "Remember that letter you sent a few months ago stating that you wanted to do undergraduate work in engineering? Well, we can give you a waiver on that now because people are needed in that field. We normally do not do this, but in your case, we will give you a waiver. We have your records, and the general has already approved it. All you have to do is tell us yes by letter that you are willing to go."

Boyd was ecstatic. He had originally considered going to Edwards Air Force Base in California and getting into test and evaluation as a test pilot, but the more he worked at Nellis, the more he knew he needed formal training in mathematics or engineering to understand what he had discovered. He would have preferred math, but engineering was acceptable. Boyd decided on industrial engineering because he could learn a lot about several different fields. He remembered thinking at the time, "It covers physics, math, production lines, et cetera. I really like this; it really appeals to me."

So in the summer of 1960, Boyd, Mary, and their four children moved to Atlanta, Georgia, where John would spend the next two years getting a degree in industrial engineering at Georgia Tech. Here his earlier experiences and insights would be synthesized and refined in ways that would color nearly all his later work. Boyd was excited, ready for a change, and more than a little out of place compared with his fellow students. A good fourteen years older than most, he should have been in graduate school, not getting another undergraduate degree. Adding to the stress, his fifth child was born in the midst of the two-year program. Going to school and working late hours on homework projects while raising five children was no picnic, but he loved what he was learning.

The work was alternately tedious and exhilarating. Boyd still had some bad habits from his high school and undergraduate days. Instead of working harder on what he didn't like, Boyd apportioned his effort by spending more time on what he liked and sloughing off what he disliked. Academically, he had always started slowly and finished fast. Several times he failed a first test and then did consistently better throughout the course, much to the astonishment of his teachers. He didn't exactly revel in learning, but studying how and why things worked as they did and being in a place where he could find new ideas and formulate new syntheses was interesting. He gravitated toward the big ideas, the general concepts. The mathematical details were not fun for him as they were for others. What he relished were the concepts.

At Tech, Boyd encountered the usual: a few good professors, a few also-rans. Boyd was fortunate, though, to be taken under the wing of two professors, Dr. Ewalt and Dr. Jacob Mandelker. Mandelker, a physics professor and a refugee from war-torn Germany, became his mentor, the first real one since his swimming coaches Art Wieble and Doc Councilman. He worked with Boyd, encouraged him, talked with him about his ideas, and guided his study. Ewalt taught thermodynamics and saw in Boyd something other students didn't have.

Boyd really worked hard on Mandelker's first test and scored only a C. When he went to talk to the professor about his difficulties, Mandelker praised his performance. Most of the students had failed the test. Mandelker told Boyd that he worked through things differently, that compared to others he did them backward. He reasoned by selective analogies and then tested and refined them. This, he told Boyd, provided a richer and deeper understanding of physics and was a real asset. Synthesis was not only okay, it was a better way of thinking. Thus reinforced, Boyd redoubled his efforts and pursued his study of physics with real dedication.[1]

A nineteen-year-old fellow student named Chuck Cooper hung around Boyd and helped him with thermodynamics and other course work in exchange for a steady stream of war stories about Korea, flying, and the Air Force in general. Young Chuck Cooper idolized Boyd. Loud, profane, worldly, Boyd had countless stories to relate to those who wanted to listen. As Cooper recalls, "He was a nut. He was the most profane man I ever knew. I loved the hell out of him, but I wouldn't introduce him to my mother."[2] Though brilliant on some subjects, Boyd struggled at times and was, according to Cooper, an average student at Tech in those years. He grasped material better discussing it with students after class than he did listening to lectures in class. Much of the work was just something that had to be accomplished, an instrumental goal for a higher purpose later. When the lightbulbs came on, though, everything changed. It was in the spring of 1962. Boyd was busy studying for finals and worrying about his next assignment.

### Thermodynamics, Burgers, and Beer

"For some reason, I just did not like double E [electrical engineering]. I was bored by all those circuits and fields, and trying to get that stupid eight-digit answer after looking at the problem for a whole goddamn minute. Bullshit!"

An easy sort of camaraderie developed as the guys helped each other through the hard slogging of detailed course work. Some were better at thermodynamics than double E, others the reverse. They held group prep sessions for the exams. After a session one night, they decided to take a break and go get a hamburger and a beer. Over their beers and burgers (nearly all of Boyd's major insights seem to be associated with bars and scribbling on cocktail napkins and tablecloths), the flash of insight that became the energy maneuverability theory occurred. It started out innocently enough, and Boyd didn't even realize what was happening until it was almost over, but it was a transforming event. Someone in the study group asked Boyd what he did before coming to Tech. Boyd always wore civilian clothes, so his classmates did not know he was an Air Force officer. They just thought he had waited a long time to go to college. He explained that he was a fighter pilot and the Air Force was sending him to school so they could use the skills he acquired later in his career. Over their beer, they were discussing the transfer of energy from one form to another and what it was like to be a fighter pilot. Suddenly, the two fused as Boyd tried to match his frame of reference with what they were studying. He was looking for the right analogies to explain flying to them.

"Let me explain it this way," he began. "We've been talking about the transfer of energy from one form to another, whether it's chemical, mechanical, or electrical—there is always some kind of energy transformation. . . . Now, when you are in the air, what is altitude? Isn't that potential energy? What about airspeed? Isn't that kinetic energy?"

"Right."

"Fine. Let's maneuver. You might have to give up a little altitude, a little airspeed, or both. If you have a lot of power and you soften a maneuver, you can gather in altitude, gather in airspeed, or both."

Then it hit him.

"Jesus Christ, wait a minute! I can look at air-to-air combat in terms of energy relationships. I can lay out situations, I can do it formally now. . . . You guys don't know what you have done for me!"

A casual effort to answer an offhand question had led to a startling discovery. "After they left, my mind was really buzzing, going every which way. After I stabilized, I went over to the library and took notes for the rest of the evening. Then I went home and wrote down more notes. At three o'clock in the morning, I was deriving equations, laying the whole thing out. I said, Goddamn, this thing is right. I just know it." He was on a roll and kept on working.

He was feverishly extending the initial insight, testing the relationships mathematically and thinking through this set of relationships. Boyd stayed up and wrote down a list of questions that his insights raised while his mind was still active. He made a list of ways to test pieces of his emerging theory. After filling three or four sheets of a yellow legal pad, at six in the morning he called Sprad Spradling, his friend in the Academic Section of the Fighter Weapons School at Nellis. It was 3 AM Sprad's time, but that didn't matter. "Hey Sprad, I've had a breakthrough. Listen to this." For the next hour and a half, Boyd described the mathematics underpinning what would become the energy maneuverability theory. Poor Sprad hung on doggedly, trying to follow what John was laying out. He knew Boyd and understood what was happening. Boyd had a breakthrough and had to share it with someone. "I'll do some graphs and send them to you so you can use it at the school," promised Boyd.[3] He crashed and got some sleep before his exam that day. Then he hit what he called his drawdown period.

Boyd felt a sense of contentment in that he had figured something out on his own, but he no longer believed his insight was unique, because it was too logical and simple. Surely somebody else must have done this before. It was interesting but not pathbreaking. It couldn't be that good, that novel. There had to be a precedent of which he was unaware.

"Then all of a sudden my dumb brain said, Wait a minute, if that had been done before and had been related to tactics, that means I would have had access to it at Nellis. That kind of information would have had to come through there; it would have grabbed everybody's attention. I know it was not used there at school, so it probably has not been done before, otherwise I would have seen it. If it has been done, it has been done in such an obscure fashion that it has never surfaced."

The next quarter started, and Boyd had to focus on the tasks at hand, getting through his courses. Plus, he had to worry about his next assignment. Boyd had wanted to return to Nellis, but he received orders assigning him to Air Force Systems Command, not the Tactical Air Command. Once again, he was not at all happy about the system's plans for him, and he set about trying to do something about it. He got into a big skunk fight trying to change his assignment. As he recalled it, a general in Systems Command telephoned him to say, "You are going to get court-martialed unless you stop that shit. You are going to Systems Command. Drop all that other goddamn hanky-panky you are playing. Now, we want to be fair about this assignment. If you can choose the base you want, will you stop all that crap you are pulling?"

"Yes, I would like to go to Eglin."

"You have it. We will send a message out there. Now is it all over?"

"Yes, sir. Fine."

"Glad to have you onboard."

## Eglin, Tom Christie, and Energy Maneuverability Theory

Boyd was ready to leave Atlanta and move on. Many over the years were impressed with Boyd's intellectual breadth and depth, assuming that he had at least one if not more graduate degrees, probably a math and physics background with a degree in engineering or aeronautics and perhaps even military history. Few schooled in economics and industrial engineering are nearly as eclectic in their interests, as capable in their reasoning, or so widely read. For Boyd, however, being autodidactic (largely self-taught and exceptionally well read) was a life-long condition. There was little time to explore knowledge during his Air Force career, given the nature of his assignments and the detailed examinations of specific problems that they entailed. It was not until later in life that Boyd really came alive intellectually. Most of his real education occurred after he retired from the Air Force. His expertise developed slowly over a long period of time and was the result of a huge synthesis of nearly everything he learned, formally and informally.

So Boyd and his family moved to Eglin Air Force Base in the panhandle of Florida. He was out of school, and his two-year civilian respite was over. There would be some difficulties as he went back into the Air Force; it would take some readjusting to get used to uniforms, regulations, and the ways of the bureaucracy. As soon as he reported, his unhappiness and the disagreements over assignments started again.

"When I arrived at Eglin, they put me in maintenance again. People love to put John Boyd in maintenance, and John Boyd does not like maintenance. I said, Wait a minute, I've been through this once before."

Boyd was told that after a two-year stint as a civilian student funded by the Air Force, he should be grateful. In return, the Air Force would do with him what the Air Force thought best; he owed the Air Force, not the other way round. He now had a controlled assignment for the next four years, and it was in a maintenance billet. The Air Force would exact its pound of flesh whether he liked it or not. Boyd went looking for his superior and told him what he was going to do. "I am going to get out of this job in six months, and I am going to get the job I want. I want to let you know it so that you will know ahead of time. If you write me a bad OER [Officer Effectiveness Report], it makes no difference to me. I am going to show you how to get out of a job if it is controlled or not."

That was Boyd. He had an in-your-face form of vendetta, which he announced as "not professional, just strictly personal." In his case, "in your face" is not merely the use of the vernacular. As James Fallows describes him, "John Boyd laughed often, yet when he turned serious, his preferred speaking distance was three inches from your face."[4] Boyd's confrontational style of argument was to corner someone (literally if possible), get as close as possible, and dare him to argue, or even fight, by asking sarcastic questions and demeaning his intellect, credibility, and character in the process. With words and spittle flying, decibel level rising, and eyes glaring, Boyd would bore in for the kill. Combined with the smoke from his foul-smelling cigars, such encounters were bound to be unpleasant physically, and they were often intellectually and emotionally distressing as well. No wonder he made so many enemies, particularly since he won most of the battles and usually got his way. Boyd did his first job during the day and his second one at night until he got out of the maintenance billet and into another job.

From then on he worked on creating what became the energy maneuverability theory. EM, as it came to be called, was a way to plot not just the basic characteristics (how far, how fast, how high) of a given airplane but also the mathematically plotted maneuverability of it at different altitudes, g forces, turning radii, and so on. He could plot a graph for each plane and specify the conditions. Furthermore, he could compare the graphs of different planes and determine at what points (altitude, g force, speed, etc.) one plane had an advantage over another. Such information would obviously be valuable to pilots in air-to-air combat. It was also a new way to compare capabilities between nations before the actual encounters took place in air-to-air combat. By using these diagrams, designers could see exactly where, when, how, and under what conditions one plane could gain an advantage over another. It was the sort of breakthrough thinking that could revolutionize fighter design.

Then, in early 1963, Boyd was at another happy hour on Friday at the officer's club bar when, once again, fate intervened. Some friends introduced him to Tom Christie, a civilian mathematician working at Eglin. Quiet but also bright, he and Boyd were to become fast friends and even partners in crime over the next two years. Boyd proceeded to explain the basics of his ideas, covering a tablecloth with equations and formulae. Christie's response was low key but positive. "That makes sense. I think you are right, but we're going to have to run all that stuff out."

Then Boyd began talking about curves and data on aircraft performance and such. Christie had access to an IBM 7094 computer, a large one at the time. He and Boyd began to write the necessary computer programs, debug them, and start to work on the data they collected. They became very close and formed an almost symbiotic relationship. Boyd learned a lot about mathematics, computers, and programming from Christie. Christie learned a lot about air combat, fighter performance, and a host of other topics from Boyd. Christie gained a respect and admiration for Boyd that only grew over the years. Each went out of his way to pay homage to the other for the relationship they had, the significance of their shared insights, and what they accomplished. Whenever Boyd talked about EM in public, he always mentioned Tom Christie. Christie maintains that what he learned from Boyd was more important than what Boyd may have learned from him. It was Tom Christie who hosted a long and rather liquid gathering for Boyd's friends and family at his home following Boyd's funeral. There were many anecdotes, memories, tears, and laughter that afternoon. One was struck by the genuine affection that so many people of diverse backgrounds had for Boyd.

After working on the EM project for some time, Boyd and Christie decided it would be good to get data on foreign aircraft to compare with American planes. So Boyd grabbed a T-bird (a T-33 jet trainer) and flew up to Wright Patterson Air Force Base in Ohio, home of the Foreign Technology Center, to collect data on foreign (Soviet) aircraft. He had some friends from Nellis there, and they collected what he needed, despite thinking he was a little off the wall when he told them what he was up to. He flew back to Eglin, where he and Christie started reviewing the data and crunching the numbers—again.

"I expected to see our airplanes, like the F-4 and all of those, look a lot better than the Soviet airplanes. I was really convinced in my mind—the way the writing went—that we were much better. Then we ran our first plots off. I said, Gee, Tom, wait a minute. The Soviet airplanes are better. I think we made a mistake."

Not able to accept the contrary findings, Boyd called the Foreign Technology Center people and double-checked the data he had been given. He and Christie checked and rechecked their programs. Boyd went back to Wright Patterson and reviewed the Soviet data with the people there. Christie went through the entire program again. They kept getting the same results. Unknown to anyone else, working offline on a project that didn't really exist, Boyd and Christie had stumbled onto the indisputable but highly controversial conclusion: Soviet combat aircraft, all of them, were better—in the sense that they were more maneuverable—than their American counterparts. So much for vaunted American military technology. Boyd and Christie knew their data were correct, but they still found it hard to believe. The implications were huge.

Still with a good reputation in TAC and some contacts there, Boyd informally briefed some people from TAC who were visiting Eglin. They liked it and were excited about it. That was a relief to Boyd, because others he had tried to discuss it with at Eglin, with few exceptions, thought he was nuts and wasting his time. They didn't appreciate the degree to which fine-tuning these concepts would allow them to plot the comparative performance envelopes of different aircraft against each other. They could then derive the tactics for successful engagements by utilizing those performance areas and characteristics inherently advantageous to their own planes, not the adversary's. He kept pushing and refining his ideas, crunching the numbers, checking the programs, and sifting the data. It was just like being back at Nellis, in terms of figuring out comparative combat advantage so he could teach it to others. Boyd was spending long hours but having a ball.

Boyd's competitive juices flowed routinely, and he took out his frustrations during allegedly touch football games at lunchtime at Eglin. He played as he worked: fiercely, competitively, and with abandon. Occasionally, the guys he played with would try to stack the deck against him by insuring that he had the losers on his team. Boyd would rant and rave and then threaten to quit because the game had been rigged. Often as not, he would just play harder, turning touch into a more brutal game of tackle without the benefit of pads and helmets. Tom Christie recalled that "as a major, John was hell. He would challenge everybody on everything. To Boyd, competition is the milk of life, and if there wasn't enough routinely, he'd go make some more."[5] Hard work and hard play filled most of his days and nights, including some drinking at the Eglin Officers Club. Christie has a collection of more than 2,000 cocktail-napkin cartoons drawn at those sessions by different participants; it was bound and presented to Christie as a going-away present when he moved to Washington.

In the midst of all this, there was nearly a family tragedy. Boyd's oldest son, Steven, who had had polio while they were at Nellis, developed appendicitis. For several days, it was touch and go, and they didn't know whether he would live or not. For that period, Boyd was human in his concern for his son, but he focused on his son's illness with the same intensity he had devoted to his work. It consumed him for nearly a week. He and Mary were taking care of the children or at the hospital with Steven. It was a difficult time for Boyd, a situation over which he had absolutely no control. There was nothing he could do to save his son. Luckily, Steven rallied and survived. When it was over and Steven returned home, Boyd turned his laserlike concentration back to his work, rather than his family. It was just the way he did things. He had two speeds, on and off. It was only the target of his concentration that varied from time to time.

## The Importance of Energy Maneuverability

What was so revolutionary about energy maneuverability? It was a fundamental definition of maneuverability, expressed in mathematical terms using physics constructs. The term had been used for years without being precisely defined in scientific terms in the aircraft business. Boyd's approach plotted the ability to change altitude (potential energy), airspeed (kinetic energy), and direction (turn rate, radius, or g) in any combination for each airplane in the U.S. fighter inventory. More important, Boyd devised a way to compare them with each other and against any Soviet aircraft or other plane one wished. According to Jim Stevenson, energy maneuverability theory was "the first quantitative global analysis by which one could accurately compare one aircraft against another throughout their performance envelopes."[6] Maneuverability could be measured, but Boyd figured out how to measure it in a manner that allowed uniform comparisons, with precise graphs and pictures of where in the performance envelope one plane could outmaneuver another.

We should pause for a moment and realize what has happened. Boyd became interested in flying. Once he learned to fly, he became interested in air-to-air tactics. Because of his interest in aerial tactics, he wrote the *Air Combat Maneuvering Manual* and *Aerial Attack Study* while teaching at the Fighter Weapons School at Nellis. He went back to school to learn more math and physics to understand more fully what he had been able to demonstrate at Nellis. He and Tom Christie then developed energy maneuverability, which led him ultimately to aircraft design. From the perspective of many people, that was backward. Boyd did things in the reverse of the way they are supposed to happen. One should begin with the theory, learn the relationships it uncovers, and apply them to specific needs and problems. Most learn about aircraft design to appreciate handling characteristics that would lead in turn to training and doctrine appropriate for that aircraft. Boyd, rarely the traditionalist, managed to do this upside down and outside in. It was odd, but it was characteristically Boyd.

On one level, EM was basic physics, not much more than the application of equations of motion; but conceptualizing those sets of equations as aircraft performance maps was genius, for it created another way to assess aircraft performance and compare it. In that sense, EM was truly revolutionary, not only as an assessment tool but also as a design parameter in the development of tactics and doctrine for combat engagements. It could not have been done before because there were no large high-speed computers to handle the computational matrices that constructed the plotting for the visual representation of performance envelopes. True to form, Boyd insisted that every time a new dimension of EM was discovered or refined, all the computer programs and the findings be turned over to the aircraft companies. It made other types of analysis obsolete. The outcomes were both undeniable and shocking. Higher, farther, faster—the traditional benchmarks of aircraft performance—do not necessarily translate as better. Maneuverability is critical, and the ability and speed with which a plane and pilot can transition from one maneuver to another may well hold the difference between life and death, between winning and losing in an air-to-air engagement. EM was fundamental and profound.

EM provided dynamic rather than static analysis pictures of aircraft performance across a range of altitudes, g forces, and turning radii and gave a composite scorecard of its maneuver capabilities. It did not assess a pilot's skills, but it did add to them by telling the pilot exactly where his aircraft's performance profile gave him an advantage against a particular adversary. As Tom Christie explained it: "The point is that EM theory provides you with a way of at least designing certain factors into the aircraft which will permit you to have better hardware to outperform the other aircraft in a maneuvering situation, in a fuel conservation situation, or whatever your 'measure of merit' is. A better pilot with better hardware is certainly going to beat a better pilot with inferior hardware."[7] EM provided the way to understand how to give American fighters an edge, and Boyd had produced the data to explain it to them and the tactics to teach them how to utilize it. It was a truly revolutionary way to assess capabilities and to teach tactics.

Crucial to the briefing of these complicated ideas and comparisons was the manner in which they were presented. Here, Boyd had a stroke of genius. He plotted the characteristics of maneuver performance of one aircraft against another at certain sectors of the performance envelope. Turning rate and g forces might be plotted at a certain altitude and speed. Boyd decided to show U.S. aircraft in blue and enemy aircraft in red, a fairly standard approach, but where they overlapped, he used purple. The visual presentation made explicit in an instant what it might take hours to explain in scientific detail. Simply stated, the larger the area of purple on a given vu-graph, the less the advantage of one plane over the other. Ideally, what he wanted were graphs with large blue areas, small purple zones, and no red areas of superior maneuverability. What the U.S. aircraft often got were graphs with large red areas, small purple areas, and almost no blue areas of superiority. Thus complex mathematics, computer programming, physics principles, equations of motion, and comparative data in carefully specified conditions could be reduced to the relative sizes of color on a graph. No one had to understand all the science to appreciate the outcome, and size and color were the perfect graphic medium to express the results. Even those with little knowledge of or appreciation for aeronautical design and flight characteristics could see the results of these comparisons and understand what was being portrayed.

Boyd and Christie went back to Wright Patterson to talk with the Foreign Technology Center about their findings. According to their data, the U.S. planes (F-4, F-104, F-105, and F-106) were inferior in maneuverability to the Soviet ones (the MiG-17, MiG-19, and MiG-21). The people at the Foreign Technology Center went back and scoured the data again and came up with some changes. Boyd and Christie ran the data again. The Soviet planes were still better. "The margin was still huge, but not quite as huge as before," Boyd recalled. The outcomes were still surprising.

## Sorting Things Out

Now what? Boyd's colleagues in TAC had an inkling of what was going on, but nobody in Systems Command knew what he was doing. The guys in TAC, contrary to Boyd's instructions, had started talking about his work at Eglin, which eventually resulted in a request from TAC for a briefing on EM. When the word got out, everyone in the Air Force would be shocked by the results. How was Boyd to break the news, and to whom? How was he to explain how he came up with these results? Boyd did not have much time, and he would have to come clean to his superiors. The effort to do everything quickly and in the right order was reminiscent of the Keystone Kops. The story goes like this.

More folks from TAC showed up at Eglin, and Boyd and Christie showed them their study. All agreed that when the senior brass heard about this, they would come unglued. Shortly thereafter, Boyd got a message from Gen. Walter C. Sweeney, commander of TAC, saying he wanted to hear Boyd's briefing on energy maneuverability. Boyd went to his boss, a Colonel Ryan, and told him what had happened. It was Thursday, and he had just been ordered to brief a four-star general at Langley Air Force Base in Virginia on the following Monday. Unfortunately, no one in Systems Command, save Colonel Ryan, had been informed of what Boyd and Christie had done or the results of their work. Ryan was convinced they would all be fired. Boyd suggested that he brief Gen. John W. Roberts and his staff in Systems Command as soon as possible the next day. "Tell him it's vitally important that he hears the briefing before it is presented to TAC. If they want to chew me out, fine. I will take the blame. But they have to hear it. Tell the general it is very urgent. Otherwise, he will not know how to respond to some nasty phone calls he may start receiving from TAC after I brief them."

The general and his whole staff assembled, and General Roberts was not in a good mood. Nor were the other officers in the room (all senior to Boyd) pleased to be called to an urgent, "must attend" briefing by a major. It was a Friday afternoon, no less, with the usual end-of-week gatherings and social engagements to attend. After Boyd explained how he had gotten into the fix he was in, the general complained that he didn't see what all the fuss was about. As Boyd proceeded with the briefing, however, the color on the general's face changed perceptibly, and his blood pressure and displeasure rose apace. The implications of the findings, military and political, began to dawn on him and the others in the room. First, the direction in which Systems Command and TAC were going was wrong. Their planes were not good enough. Years of effort, cherished assumptions about aircraft design, confidence in the caliber of the Air Force, all were being trashed. Second, if Boyd had briefed Sweeney at TAC first, he would have gone to Gen. Bernard Schriever, head of Air Force Systems Command, and heads would have rolled quickly.

Brig. Gen. Allman Culbertson said he wanted to check out the data and called the people at Wright Patterson to confirm what Boyd had just told them. He came back into the room even more pissed off than before. They had confirmed the data and Boyd's conclusions. Then Culbertson began looking through his project books to find a listing for the energy maneuverability study with its budget and description. It wasn't there. Boyd told him so. He was incredulous. "What are you trying to tell me, the project is not here? I just heard you say a few minutes ago about the computers you had to use, the resources you had to get, et cetera, to make this thing go, but there's no way you can get those computer resources without having a project number and a budget for it."

Boyd answered, "Do you really believe that now? I can steal computer time on any computer you have in this whole command and you would never know it if I did not want you to."

General Roberts intervened. "Everybody except Boyd leave the room."

Roberts proceeded to tell Boyd that what he had discovered was important, but how he had done it was wrong, and he sure hoped he was right in his findings. If wrong, he would be court-martialed. Boyd agreed on all counts: "That sounds fair. I knew when I first began that I would not get any support, that the risk was totally mine, but we believed in the theory and had to move with it, so we just grabbed what fucking resources we could."

General Roberts told Boyd that he could be destroyed for doing what he had done, but he also paid Boyd a compliment. "You know, I didn't know we had many officers like you left in the Air Force." Unfortunately, what was true then, in 1964, is even truer today. Few people buck the system to do what is right. Messengers with bad news are metaphorically shot with some frequency. In most cases, data that do not support conventional wisdom, service policy, or current funding priorities are buried anonymously. There are even fewer officers who test the system routinely. Those who do have a very tough time unless they have some sympathetic top cover to assist them in their efforts. As things turned out, Boyd did.

Boyd's briefing to TAC was delayed. In the meantime, he briefed the Systems Command hierarchy. It was a terrible meeting, and Boyd recalled being called nearly every name in the book by nearly all those present. The implication was that Systems Command didn't know how to design its planes, was wasting money to buy a second-rate air force, and wasn't even aware of how poorly it was doing. Then some colonel told Boyd that this sort of thing had been done before, and it was wrong theoretically. Boyd gave him enough rope to hang himself and then asked where and when the work had been done. The reply was "at Edwards Air Force Base a few years back." Boyd then asked for the source document. There wasn't one. Another general officer who had been at Edwards for years admitted no such study existed at Edwards. The EM theory was novel.

The TAC reaction to Boyd's briefing was the same as Systems Command's. People canceled meetings, called the Foreign Technology Center at Wright Patterson, called in other experts, and reluctantly concluded that Boyd's data were correct. As the analysis slowly penetrated the system, people began to see the full implications. The Air Force had purchased planes with poor maneuverability and was designing future aircraft without proper attention to maneuverability. Ultimately, Boyd's data suggested that we had and were continuing to build an inferior air force. There had to be a better way of designing new airplanes, or the Air Force would be in trouble in a head-to-head engagement. It was a shocking revelation, not what anyone wanted to hear in the depths of the Cold War.

## Taking Care of People

A minor incident during all this reveals Boyd's commitment to others and his willingness to buck the system to get things done. During one of his trips back and forth to the Pentagon, Boyd ended up with the wrong data from Eglin and needed to have a complicated set of graphics plots redone, photoreduced, and colored for his presentation—on a weekend. A woman named Betty Jo Salter in the graphics section of the Pentagon was the one to help get this done. On a Friday, Boyd tried to see her boss to arrange the work. He was playing golf. Boyd told her if she would make the emergency fixes, he would see that she got paid for the overtime. They worked all weekend and redid the whole briefing.

Come Monday, however, Salter came to Boyd in tears. She said her boss, a certain Colonel Lawson, had just told her that not only would she not get the extra pay but he was also considering firing her for doing work he hadn't authorized, and then he chewed her out in front of her coworkers. Boyd's request for overtime pay was denied. Boyd went to Lawson's boss, Col. Red Grumbles, a friend from his days at Nellis. Grumbles told Boyd not to worry, he'd take care of things. He did. Briefings to four-star general officers were serious business, and Lawson's action had been less than supportive. Lawson was told if he didn't authorize the overtime pay, he could pay Salter out of his own pocket. Furthermore, he was instructed to gather those who worked in the section and publicly praise Salter for her selfless devotion to duty. If he did not, he would be fired.

Lawson did as instructed, and overtime pay was authorized. Just to make sure that there would be no retribution against Salter, Boyd took the matter up with General Roberts, who had been the commander at Nellis and was now head of the Proving Ground Command at Eglin. Roberts thought the treatment of Salter shabby and Lawson arrogant. Colonel Lawson was transferred in less than a month. Following what was later dubbed "the Kennedy maxim of politics," Boyd did not get mad; he got even.[8]

The typical USAF service culture allowed two responses to what Boyd had done. The first was to bring him up on charges and court-martial him for stealing computer time to prepare his energy maneuverability study. If he hadn't lied, he hadn't exactly told the truth either. He had technically misappropriated government funds, filed fraudulent records in charging work to other programs, and engaged in conduct unbecoming an officer. All three are serious court-martial offenses under the Uniform Code of Military Justice. On the other hand, the significance of the work was such that he should be recognized for brilliant insights, hard work (much of it on his own time), and a major contribution to the Air Force in the form of improved design and assessment of aircraft performance. He and Tom Christie had performed a valuable service to the nation. A package was prepared to present him an award for that contribution. Initially, the system pursued both paths simultaneously: to court-martial Boyd, punish him, and force him from the service and to reward him with a medal and commendation attesting to contributions that "reflect great credit on Major Boyd and the United States Air Force." He may not be the only man in the Air Force to have found himself in the circumstance, but it was an extremely rare situation. The award paperwork went forward. The court-martial proceedings did not.

Boyd, after being persona non grata for a while, was hailed as a hero and presented with the customary awards and citations. Systems Command presented him and Tom Christie with the Air Force Systems Command Scientific Achievement Award for developing the energy maneuverability theory in the fall of 1965. In 1966 Boyd was awarded an Air Force Research and Development Award in aeronautical engineering. Today, some of the work he did on the theory more than 35 years ago remains classified, but not by the Air Force. (It was declassified years ago in an Air Force review.) Some nameless, faceless bureaucrat at the Department of Energy, no doubt acting on well-intentioned but idiotic instructions, classified the energy maneuverability theory and related reports by Boyd because the documents had the word "energy" in the title—just part of the protection and security we get for our tax dollars.

As Boyd prepared for his next assignment (in the Plans and Requirements Office of Air Force headquarters in the Pentagon), an enterprising young first lieutenant did a story for the base newspaper with the catchy and prescient title "Remember the Name."[9] It began, "Major Boyd, who has been referred to as personable and at the same time outspoken, will be concerned with advanced systems, an area he literally lives for, and will probably fight for in the future." That was a bit of an understatement. One is reminded of Dorothy Parker's retort after listening to an interminable boor. A friend said to Parker, "Well, she certainly is outspoken," to which Parker replied, "By whom?" The article continued: "Boyd's credo is simple: do your homework—present your views—then be prepared to defend them with the facts. To date, his batting average is pretty impressive." The lieutenant concluded, "There is no disputing Major Boyd has made major scientific contributions to the Air Force. And judging from his enthusiasm and positive ideas, he doesn't plan to stop contributing for a long time." He was right on all counts.

As Boyd moved to Washington, his career, the future of the Air Force, and the nation's military were to change dramatically. The next three decades of post-Vietnam experience would be hard for the American military and the country. The nation still has not recovered fully from the triple blows of civil rights upheaval, the defeat and deception practiced by the government regarding Vietnam, and the erosion of faith in our own political processes and institutions occasioned by Watergate. The trials that Samuel Huntington has called "the S&S Decades" of the 1960s and 1970s, especially the period from 1965 to 1975, were a tough time for America. Even the end of the Cold War and the false euphoria of the Gulf War have not entirely erased their pall.

In the midst of these troubled times, Maj. John Boyd left Eglin Air Force Base and was reassigned to the Pentagon. While in Washington, D.C., he would do great things over the next 23 years, in and out of uniform. He owed nearly all of his insights to the experience of air-to-air combat, reflection and learning about basic science and mathematics, and the opportunity to apply those to his craft as a member of the profession of arms and an officer in the U.S. Air Force. A series of chance encounters combined to create an utterly transforming set of circumstances that permitted all of this to fall into place. He had not washed out of pilot training for failing to perform gliding turns. He had not been punished for practicing air-to-air combat instead of cross-country training at Willy. He had not gone into maintenance, twice. He had been able to change things at Nellis. He had talked AFIT into sending him to Georgia Tech. And he had learned the math, science, and computer programming he needed to know to put it all together.

Just what were the key events in the culmination of these last steps in the chain reaction of circumstances that led to even greater accomplishments in the future? The chance meetings, flashes of insight, and great ideas all came while eating hamburgers and drinking beer at Georgia Tech and the Eglin Officer's Club bar. It just doesn't get any better than that.

# 5.                        Designing Fighters: The F-15

The situation was saved by an aggressive young Pentagon action officer, Major John R. Boyd, who led the effort to redirect F-X development to a highly maneuverable aircraft optimized for the air superiority role. . . . His precepts led to a demand for the F-X to have the capability to outturn and outaccelerate enemy fighters under all conditions encountered in a dogfight.

> **Walter J. Boyne,** *Beyond the Wild Blue:*
> *A History of the United States Air Force, 1947–1997*

Things were looking up for Boyd, or so he thought. He had won several prestigious awards instead of being court-martialed for stealing computer time. His work was hailed as important and had caused the Air Force to pause and reconsider how it designed and procured new aircraft. He had personally briefed many of the top brass (three- and four-star generals) in the Air Force on his findings as a young major. Not bad for a guy with no advanced degrees, little in the way of aeronautical engineering experience, using stolen computer time. But he had broken the rules and screwed with the system. Military bureaucracies in general and the Air Force in particular don't like people who aren't team players and who, as the saying goes, "color outside the lines." The Air Force, in its infinite wisdom, decided to send Major Boyd to Okinawa, one of the few places where his rather considerable talents would not be used effectively. It was also halfway around the world and really out of the way. It would be hard to rock the boat there.

Fate intervened once again. Col. Chuck Myers, a successful test pilot, persuaded his friend Tom Cheatham, in the Directorate of Defense Research and Engineering (DDR&E), to help him undo the original assignment. Myers knew of Boyd's EM work and convinced Cheatham that they needed someone with his talents in the DDR&E system, where his work on aircraft design could be properly utilized. After they combined forces to lobby Air Force Chief of Staff John P. McConnell, Boyd's orders for Okinawa were rescinded, and Boyd received orders to report to the Pentagon to work on the evolving F-X project.[1]

Boyd left Eglin in the fall of 1966 and was assigned to the Operational Requirements Team in the office of the deputy for Research and Development at Air Force headquarters in the Pentagon. It ushered into Boyd's life a series of big changes. Save for his stint at Georgia Tech, when he was a civilian student, this was the first time in his career when he was not on an Air Force base. He would now fly a desk, not a fighter. Instead of the intricacies of air-to-air combat, he had to learn the ways of the Pentagon. With only a brief interruption for service in Southeast Asia in 1972–1973, it would be Boyd's home for the next 22 years, 9 in the Air Force and 13 in retirement. The hotshot fighter pilot with bright ideas would learn to change the system. He would also find others who shared some of his maverick views and could assist him in pushing them. Once again, a series of serendipitous accidents prepared the way for Boyd.

Other than flying, it was the best part of his career. Win or lose, he was in combat, and the heat of a different battle was every bit as exhilarating intellectually as the real thing. You had to think quickly and well, or you were dead, at least metaphorically speaking. One is reminded of Winston Churchill's comment about the difference between politics and war: "Politics is almost as exciting as war, and quite as dangerous. In war you can only be killed once, but in politics many times."[2] Although not as deadly, the stakes were still high: promotions, early retirement, reassignments, public humiliations, and the winning and losing of contracts and policy decisions. The warring parties kept score, but the victories were of a different sort, and so were the defeats—and the engagement was continuous.

Boyd had been reassigned to work on the design of the next-generation air superiority fighter for the Air Force, the project known as the F-X, for Fighter Experimental. Through a series of insights and initiatives over the next nine years, the F-X became the F-15, and the work on the F-15 led Boyd and a coterie of others to push for the development of the lightweight fighter (LWF) that became the F-16. Before one can fully understand the story of the F-X's transition to the F-15, which in turn spawned the F-16, one needs to understand the context of the debates that these planes and the groups of supporters and detractors represented. To do that, one needs to look at the Air Force between Korea and Vietnam.

## In Search of Air Superiority

The last air superiority fighter the Air Force had designed and used in war was the F-86 designed in 1948. In the intervening years it had designed the century series, but they were not air superiority fighters per se. The Air Force had been forced to accept the F-4 II Phantom, designed by the U.S. Navy, and the Navy's A-7D Corsair was forced on it by the circumstances of the war in Vietnam. Having to make do with two Navy-designed planes in the early 1960s stuck in the throats of all Air Force pilots. The Air Force was dedicated to the proposition that it would not happen again. To make matters worse, the USAF-designed F-111, son of the McNamara-ordained TFX (Tactical Fighter, Experimental), was to be a joint Air Force–Navy fighter-bomber.[3] The Air Force procured its version, the F-111A, but the F-111B for the Navy was eventually canceled. The leadership of the Air Force vowed that the Navy would not sucker them again. They would design their own air superiority fighter.

Meanwhile, making do with the F-100, the F-105, and the F-4 in Vietnam proved less than satisfactory. The loss ratios against both North Vietnamese and Soviet pilots were not good. In fact, they began at 1:1 in 1965 and overall were far less than the 10:1 ratio in Korea. From 1 April 1965 to 1 March 1968, despite some interludes of great success, the United States had an exchange ratio in air-to-air combat of 2.4:1.[4] Why were U.S. planes and pilots performing so poorly?

That is a complicated story requiring detailed analysis that cannot be fully explored here. Numbers, tactics, capabilities, and rules of engagement changed on both sides throughout the air war in Vietnam. Making summary judgments of much breadth or over a long time frame invites serious error. There were several general reasons for lack of success early in the war. First, many U.S. pilots were not being taught maneuvers to elude surface-to-air missiles (SAMs). Second, aerial dogfighting was for many a lost art. Third, the F-4 Phantom originally had no gun, and the pk (probability of a kill) ratio of air-to-air missiles was far less than had been hoped. The missile pk rate (combined for Falcon, Sparrow, and Sidewinder) from 1 April 1965 to 1 March 1968 was only 11.8 percent.[5] This situation improved dramatically as the war progressed. The United States also developed better missiles with improved seekers, greater BVR (beyond visual range) range and accuracy, and increased front-aspect capability leading to the solid performance with the AIM-9L after Vietnam. Vietnam represented an important testing ground on many fronts.

Fourth, as Boyd's energy maneuverability studies had shown, U.S. planes were at a disadvantage in certain encounters against their Soviet counterparts. They simply were not as agile as the enemy's lighter, quicker fighters. Fifth, we were not permitted to take out the North Vietnamese bases and continued air strikes with large packages into North Vietnam regardless of risk and loss. Sixth, the enemy proved adept at developing tactics that virtually guaranteed U.S. air losses. These included selective defense in mass, MiG-17 use of low-altitude wagon wheels to eliminate the threat from the Sparrow missile, use of ground control intercept radar for MiG-21s to attack U.S. strike packages from the rear at high speed, and a variety of other tactics, techniques, and procedures that made life difficult and dangerous for American pilots.[6]

Throughout 1965, as Vietnam heated up, so too did concern for the next fighter for the U.S. Air Force. The F-4 Phantom was the primary air superiority fighter of the 1960s and 1970s, but there were problems with it. It began life in 1953 as the Navy's proposed fleet air defense plane. When it entered service in 1963, the Air Force had been ordered by McNamara and company to buy it to save money. No Air Force pilot worth his salt was going to have another Navy plane as an Air Force fighter, just on principle. The F-4 looks nasty, not graceful or elegant at all. It looks like the brutish war machine that it is. It is big and heavy (nearly 30,000 pounds empty, almost 60,000 pounds gross weight). Original versions had no gun, and it had to rely solely on missiles for its kills. It had poor visibility, and its engines gave off plumes of heavy black smoke, making it easy for enemy pilots and ground gunners both to detect it. It was the antithesis of today's quest for stealth. It entered combat in Vietnam in 1965 and, through January 1973, was credited with downing 107.5 enemy aircraft, more than 40 of which were obsolescent MiG-17s and 19s. In the same period, there were 362 F-4 losses, nearly 300 of which were lost to SAMs.[7] The plane had been a disappointment, the design was old, and the Air Force needed a new fighter—soon.

### The Air Superiority Society (ASS)

In 1967 the newest plane about to enter the Air Force inventory was the F-111. It was a curious plane that had variable-sweep wings: straight for range, swept back for speed. It emerged from the McNamara-inspired TFX concept but came to be more of a nuclear bomber in the interlude before the Advanced Manned Strategic Aircraft (which became the B-1) would come on line. It had a gross weight of 92,500 pounds and a range of 3,400 nautical miles unrefueled. It was nearly four times as heavy as the F-5 and nearly five times as large. The follow-on to the F-111, the F-X was presumed to be similar in design. That is, it would be a large, two-seat, two-engine, heavy (80,000 pounds gross weight), variable-sweep wing, multirole fighter-bomber. Just why that should be so was not really questioned. There were problems in the early design phase, however, and because of his work with energy maneuverability, Boyd was called in to review the project and assist in the design of the F-X. His response to the challenge was noted in the previous chapter. Now he had to make good on it.

In his quest to make the F-X a better fighter, Boyd was aided by a group of others who held similar views and had done much to prepare the ground that he then plowed. Chief among them was the almost equally flamboyant fighter pilot Chuck Myers. Myers and a series of others, both military and civilian, inside and outside the Pentagon, Air Force and Navy, who believed in the need for a true air superiority fighter, were active in the period 1961–1965, before Boyd ever got to the Pentagon. They formed an alliance that became known as the Air Superiority Society, ASS for short (female associates were known as ASSETS). They used to meet at the Windjammer Club on the top floor of the Marriott Hotel, just off the Fourteenth Street Bridge and across the highway from the Pentagon in Arlington.

Myers, a rough and ready sort who cuts to the chase and minces no words when asked for his opinion, is rare among pilots. In World War II he flew B-25s for the Army Air Forces. During Korea, he was in the Navy and flew F9Fs from the carrier *Bonhomme Richard*. He then became a professional test pilot and flew helicopters as well as the most advanced fighters and attack aircraft for General Dynamics and Lockheed. Few could match his range of flying skills, his combat experience, and his considerable insight into the requirements for successful air-to-air combat.

While with Lockheed, he became involved in marketing as the company competed with General Dynamics for the TFX (F-111). Myers became convinced of the need for an air superiority fighter for a nonnuclear war. As he explained, "The DOD requirement produced an airplane that was pushing 80,000 pounds—almost two and a half times heavier than a World War II B-17—and was expected to perform five separate missions: air superiority, close air support, all weather attack, nuclear attack, and all weather intercept. What's more it was going to do it for two different services."[8] It was only logical that a single aircraft could not perform all these missions as well as five different airplanes each designed to accomplish a single mission. The problem was that the Air Force couldn't afford to buy a separate plane for each mission. Hence, aircraft tended to become multirole so that one aircraft could perform multiple missions. Worse still, under the systems analysis and micromanagement regime of Secretary of Defense Robert McNamara, the TFX was supposed to be used by both the Navy and the Air Force, requiring further trade-offs. Following those injunctions, both services were likely to get a plane that could perform all the missions marginally, but none of them really well.

In doing interviews for his book *The Pentagon Paradox,* Jim Stevenson tells of interviewing Myers. Stevenson asked Myers why he thought it was wrong for a contractor to provide what a military service requested. After all, Stevenson queried, why is it up to the contractor to tell the military what kind of aircraft it should have? He likened the relationship to that between a customer and a prostitute: although the prostitute may not approve of the request, her job was to provide the customer with whatever services he wished to purchase. Myers shot back that the analogy was flawed: "A hooker can do all that," the implication being that a defense contractor could not.[9]

Myers, along with J. Ray Donahue (another legendary character who then worked for Litton) and others, began proselytizing for an air superiority fighter. J. Ray had access to God and everybody, or so it seemed, and after schmoozing a bit with senior Air Force leaders about the wife and kids, he'd turn and introduce Chuck and tell whomever the victim of the day was that he should listen to what Myers had to say. Some listened, some didn't. One who did was Maj. Gen. Arthur Agan, at the time the assistant deputy chief of staff for Plans and Operations. Myers persuaded him to convene a panel of World War II and Korean War aces in December 1964 in an attempt to specify the most important characteristics for a fighter. As a result, a paper was produced in 1965 that underscored the need for an air superiority fighter, not some multimission hybrid.

### The Search for an Air Superiority Fighter

Early in the Vietnam War, two older MiG-17s used gunfire to shoot down two USAF F-105s, the newest planes in the Air Force inventory, during a bombing run on the Than Hoa Bridge on April 4, 1965. Despite the tactical rules of engagement in the operation and the extenuating circumstances, it was a shock to the Air Force. For such obsolescent planes in the Communist inventory to take out two F-105s was unacceptable. General McConnell, Air Force Chief of Staff, issued a document entitled "Air Force Doctrine on Air Superiority."[10] The paper laid out in detail what was required to achieve air superiority and what capabilities a fighter should have to accomplish that mission. Among other things, it stated:

1. The air superiority element of airpower needs to be more clearly understood and more positively considered in our plans, our definition of force characteristics, and our conduct of operations. The following Air Force doctrine on air superiority is provided as guidance to all members of the United States Air Force.

2. *Definitions*
   **a.** Air superiority is "that degree of dominance in the air battle of one force over another which permits the conduct of operations by

the former and its related land, sea and air force at a given time and place without prohibitive interference by the opposing force."
**b.** Air supremacy is "that degree of air superiority where the opposing air force is incapable of effective interference."

Contained within this document are the seeds of the controversy surrounding the ill-fated F-X and what eventually became the debate over the lightweight fighter. Often misconstrued as a simple quality versus quantity debate, or high technology versus low technology, the issues are more complex, the nuances more subtle, than such statements suggest.

One small group of smart, well-connected, and knowledgeable advocates sought to design what they thought the Air Force most needed: a small, fast air superiority fighter. They based their arguments on paragraph 8 of McConnell's air superiority paper: "To assure that we can gain air superiority, we must provide and train the proper forces. We must be prepared to win air superiority. We must not assume it. We need at least one—preferably two or all three—of the following interdependent advantages: numerical superiority, tactical superiority (including training), and technical superiority (e.g., aircraft performance)." Boyd wanted to meet all three criteria. His work at Nellis on *Aerial Attack Study* had focused on superior training of pilots for attaining combat skills. His work on energy maneuverability had focused on carefully measuring aircraft performance. He could determine the technical design features and the comparative performance characteristics through careful trade-off analyses needed to customize the combination of attributes desired. He would come to believe that large, heavy, two-engine, advanced, radar-dependent fighters were simply too expensive to be purchased in sufficient quantity to guarantee air superiority. If the Air Force wanted sufficient quantity, the planes had to be cheaper than the F-111, F-X/F-15 aircraft on which it was now focusing. This was the essence of the argument made by what came to be known as the Fighter Mafia, the group that championed the lightweight fighter that became the F-16.

The other group, far larger and representing the conventional wisdom of Air Force leadership at the time, sought a large twin-engine, multirole aircraft based on the design of the F-111. Bombing the enemy into submission was the only appropriate way to win. This group sought to emphasize paragraph 10 of McConnell's letter: "Enemy airpower is destroyed in two ways: in the air and on the surface. Both methods are essential parts of counter-air operations and should be carried out concurrently." This argument is as old as airpower itself, going back to Douhet's 1921 contention in *Command of the Air* that it is better to kill the birds in the nest than in the air. The faith expressed by British prime minister Stanley Baldwin in 1932—"The bomber will always get through"—

remains undiminished despite evidence to the contrary. On the other hand, the combination of stealth, precision, and stand-off capability has greatly improved air-delivered ordnance in the 1990s.

What was really at issue were assumptions about how to achieve air superiority. Was offensive counterair to be accomplished by bombing enemy aircraft on the ground or by dogfights in the sky using air-to-air strategy and tactics? To the first group, destroying enemy forces on the ground was preferable to wresting air superiority in the skies over the battlefield. To the second, virtue lay in designing air-to-air fighters primarily to destroy aircraft in the air. The latest edition of the *Historical Dictionary of the U.S. Air Force* characterizes the debate this way: "One school contends that the mission [air superiority] can be accomplished on the forward edge of the battle by tactical strikes of more numerous but less expensive aircraft. The other suggests the more traditional deep penetration attack against enemy airfields and staging areas. This would require fewer, highly sophisticated fighters capable of surviving in a high threat environment. Recent designs suggest a balanced force capable of both approaches."[11]

The debate continues, though the bombing faction maintains that the Gulf War has determined the victor. The experience in Kosovo shows mixed results, with the bombing of infrastructure highly successful but the destruction of fielded forces decidedly less so. The crux of the matter is that the justification for the existence of the U.S. Air Force has been built on strategic bombing.[12] There has been a shift, however, in Air Force leadership and emphasis from bombers and Strategic Air Command to fighters and Tactical Air Command.[13] Many, chief among them Eliot Cohen, suggest that the jury is still out.[14] As the experience in Kosovo suggests, the debate rages on. Others, such as Robert Pape in his recent book *Bombing to Win: Air Power and Coercion in War,* state flatly, "Strategic Bombing Won't Matter in the Future."[15]

## From External Events to Requirements

Along the way, the urgency of the quest for an air superiority fighter was intensified by external events. The Six-Day War between the Israelis and the Arab world in June 1967 illustrated the need for control of the air. The Israeli preemptive strike successfully destroyed the bulk of enemy air forces on the ground and showed the importance of obtaining and maintaining air superiority from the outset of a war. The Israeli Air Force destroyed roughly 260 of the Egyptians' 340 combat aircraft in the first few hours of the war. It later destroyed large numbers of the Jordanian, Iraqi, and Syrian air forces as well. Israel's enemies lost 368 aircraft. Israel lost 40 aircraft in the war (only 2 in air-to-air combat) and achieved an air combat exchange ratio of 1 to 25. It was a stunning example of the importance of air superiority achieved in both ways.[16]

The next month, the U.S. Air Force received a wake-up call. At the Domodedovo Air Show outside Moscow in July 1967, before the world's press, the Soviets showcased their new generation of combat aircraft. Two aircraft in particular caused a stir, both from the Mikoyan-Gurevich (MiG) design bureau: a swing-wing fighter with the NATO code name Flogger (the MiG-23) and a high-speed, twin-fin fighter called the Foxbat (the MiG-25). A ground-attack version of the MiG-23 appeared slightly later and was designated the MiG-27, or Flogger D in NATO parlance. The MiG-25 Foxbat was clearly superior to the F-4 Phantom II in top speed and altitude and a leap ahead in the race to achieve air superiority. If the Air Force had needed any more incentive to push for its own air superiority fighter, the Domodedovo Air Show supplied it.

The specification, design, development, and procurement of tactical fighter aircraft is a lengthy and complicated process. The F-X project had begun in April 1965 with the concept formulation phase for a multipurpose fighter at Wright Patterson Air Force Base, by the Aeronautical Systems Division under direction of Air Force headquarters. In October 1965 the Air Force asked for full funding of full-scale studies and two months later issued a request for proposals (RFP) for a "Tactical Support Aircraft." That term suggested a lack of focus on air superiority within the Air Force, McConnell's letter notwithstanding. "Tactical support aircraft" did not sound like an air superiority fighter.

Tactical Air Command's first stated requirements for the new plane were released in the Qualitative Operational Requirement. Out of thirteen potential contractors, three were selected for initial funding: Boeing, Lockheed, and North American Rockwell. McDonnell Aircraft was one of the losers at this stage. Grumman Aircraft, though unfunded, opted to remain in the chase for the lucrative contract by funding its own study. The results of the contractor studies became the Concept Formulation Package (CFP), which was not submitted to the DDR&E until June 1967. The CFP was a detailed description of the F-X's purpose, its performance characteristics, and conceptual configurations for avionics and so forth.

There were many problems with and debates about some of the most basic aspects of the proposed plane's design. These included size (both overall dimensions and gross weight), swing-wing versus fixed-wing design, versatility (the plane's ability to perform multiple missions and the relative priority among them), crew size, avionics configuration, lead times for state-of-the-art technologies to be incorporated, and estimated costs. None of the original designs submitted were considered further because of problems with aerodynamic configurations and engine bypass ratios. Additionally, the Navy was proposing a VFAX fleet defense fighter in the same time frame, and the issue of commonality—son of the TFX—reared its head again. There were many bruising battles within the Air Force, with the Department of Defense, and between the department and Capitol Hill, but little happened formally between the summer of 1966 and the autumn of 1967.

## From F-X to F-15

The F-X was to be both the replacement for the F-4 and a follow-on to the F-111. Studies began in 1965 to design the Fighter Experimental. The relationship between its missions—air superiority and ground attack—was not entirely clear, as the difference in the program designation and the RFP suggests. Into all this walked Maj. John Boyd and his energy maneuverability studies. On his arrival at the Pentagon, he started immediately to do trade-off studies focusing mainly on the thrust-to-weight ratio. For nearly all concerned, the swing wing was considered the wave of the future. Everyone, or so it seemed, was thinking in these terms, including Boyd. "Almost an afterthought" is how Jeff Ethell describes Boyd's approach to the fixed-wing option:

He wondered what the trade-offs would look like for a fixed wing. . . . he began to think about the aerodynamic benefits versus the structural penalties in variable sweep wing. As it turned out Boyd started a whole new investigation into fixed wing versus swing wing. All the contractors except Northrop were in favour of the swing wing, but what began to emerge was a structural penalty for swing wings much larger than generally admitted, increasing as the fighter manoeuverability requirements increased.[17]

Eventually Boyd began a series of comparisons of the increased weight of the pivot structure for a swing-wing plane and the associated increased weight, drag, and fuel requirements versus another single wing-position design. The outcomes were dramatic and obvious. The F-111 design concept in the F-X was not only much more expensive, but it also was not as good in many of the critical performance parameters as some other design concepts. The F-X would have to be radically altered. Hundreds of different shapes, sizes, and wing loadings were compared, and thousands of hours of wind tunnel tests were run on them; all combined to prove that a fixed-wing design was the way to go.

Boyd's EM work had shown many shortcomings in existing Air Force aircraft and the need to build maneuverability into the design. The methodology suggested ways to analyze the trade-offs of one performance characteristic against another and its cost in increased weight, additional thrust, wing loadings, fuel requirements, and so on. These trade-off analyses—painstakingly difficult and refined assessments of various performance characteristics and design modifications — were the critical factor in shaping a wish for an air superiority fighter, the F-X, into a reality, the F-15. They represented a mammoth undertaking, comparing each flight characteristic and design configuration against all others in successive pairs and computer runs until a composite picture could be formed of the relevant data and the trade-offs affecting weight, size, and performance of different types under specified conditions. It was classical scientific method in action. All the permutations and combinations of hypotheses were tested. Boyd was relentless in pushing for them and using them to refine the best possible design concept for the F-15.

Designing and building the F-15 was a massive, complex, decade-long project with many major contributors and hundreds of participants in the design process, in both the Air Force and industry. I do not wish to suggest that Boyd was the sole designer of the F-15. Hundreds of people in the Air Force (such as Lt. Col. Larry Welch, later Chief of Staff of the Air Force) and industry (such as McDonnell designer George Graff) were intimately involved in the design of the F-15 and contributed significantly to the final product. Indeed, most of the senior leadership of the Air Force contributed to the project as best they could because it was the major aircraft procurement of their era. More than that, it would be the backbone of the Air Force for the next 40 years. Boyd, however, provided the analytical framework that allowed the F-15 to emerge from the hodgepodge of competing preferences. His studies eliminated the swing wing and reshaped the basic design, and those same studies did much to refine the design process and help make the thousands of choices that resulted in transforming the F-X concept into the F-15 fighter.

Boyd had never designed an airplane before, but as he told Colonel Ricci and Gen. Casey Dempster, "I could fuck up and do better than this." The key was to come up with a rational and objective means (as opposed to personal, political, or professional interests) to assess the myriad aircraft sizes, configurations, avionics packages, and capabilities proposed by all involved. Among those participating in the decisions, some had political clout, some technical expertise, some combat experience. There were few with all three. The trick was to explain the parameters to all in terms they could understand so some logic could be brought to the process.

Another officer involved in the F-15 development process described it this way:

Col. John R. Boyd perfected a novel method of employing computers for parametric trade-off studies to achieve better visibility on optimum design parameters. The trade-off study technique was an invaluable tool in determining impact of or deleting features on the size and weight of the "rubber" conceptual design of the F-X. Those who proposed nice-to-have features or "innovative ideas" for improving weapons system capability could readily see from the trade-off studies how the increased weight would adversely affect wing loading, acceleration, and performance. The trade-off, if these factors were held constant, would be a larger, more complex, and costlier fighter. The parametric study technique was used as a common method by contractors participating in the point design study in presenting the results of their efforts. These studies were very effective in educating the unknowledgeable and in successfully completing the advocacy of the F-X program in Congress and the Pentagon.[18]

So Boyd's methodology helped bring some rationality to the design process. It was a process of analysis, education, and advocacy combined. It was also the test bed for the same sorts of design techniques that would later be used on the F-16.

There were numerous aspects of the development of the F-15 in which Boyd had a direct role. Given space limitations, only a few examples will have to suffice. Realizing that the hardware on the F-4 that got the plane from Mach 1.7 to 2.0 had zero utility in actual combat, Boyd sought to eliminate the variable ramp inlets and associated bellmouth mechanisms on the compressor faces of the engines. They were deadweight and unnecessary complexity. Boyd sought a maximum speed of Mach 2, the Air Force Mach 3.0. The compromise was needlessly high at Mach 2.5. In that most air-to-air combat occurred at subsonic speeds and rarely above Mach 1.5, the costs and design penalties for the higher speed would seem largely unnecessary. Boyd lost on the top speed requirement to the Air Force for the F-15 and the variable ramp inlets. The higher speed requirement caused great difficulty with the engines, however. Cockpit visibility for improved situational awareness also was important, and Boyd demanded a standard as good as or better than that of the F-86. His success on this is greatly appreciated by all who fly the F-15. According to Barry Watts (a retired Air Force officer and industry analyst), "Boyd wanted to go with slats for high-g maneuvering, McDonnell preferred a rolled camber wing, and that's what's on the F-15 to this day. The issue was a trade-off between drag and complexity (although slats had worked perfectly well on the F-86 and are used on the F-16). The added drag of the rolled camber wing is something the F-15 has to haul through the air on every mission, just like the F-4 was foolishly burdened with variable ramps and engine bellmouths."[19] Those are just a few examples of Boyd's contributions, or attempts at them. There were some successes, some failures, but overall, what emerged was a far better product than would have occurred if his methodology had not been applied.

Some of the ideas that improved the F-15 were a result of Boyd's analysis, but others got credit for them. Several observers of the process reiterate that Boyd's competitive personality, dogged fixation, and pugnacious style became his own worst enemy. So some of Boyd's ideas were carried forward successfully by others. He didn't mind, and neither did they. The final product was better for the effort, and that is what counted in the long run.

Everyone even remotely involved had a pet idea, new concept, favorite piece of hardware, or technical gadget to affix to the F-X. Disagreement on the basics was bad enough, but every new notion, however silly or improbable, had to be beaten down or accepted in the long, arduous process of shaping the F-15 conceptually, before any production and the modifications that inevitably follow in that phase. One proponent wanted a trainable gun. Another wanted a helmet sight. New highly maneuverable short-range missiles vied with long-range BVR kill capabilities. Without some actual data provided by Boyd's assessment techniques, the plane would have been reduced to the lowest common denominator of agreements on a wide range of engineering and political pet rocks. In retrospect, it is amazing that the plane turned out to be as good as it is.

## The Difference

What emerged eventually was the F-15. Col. Everest Riccioni, Boyd's boss and ultimately friend and coconspirator on the F-16, assessed Boyd's accomplishments in a long memorandum in 1971. Boyd took on the original F-X concept, a follow-on to the F-111, and systematically analyzed all aspects of the proposal. He found the original proposal for a 62,500-pound variable sweep wing aircraft to be "overweight, under-winged, overly expensive, overly complex, ineffective"[20] and not in the best interests of the Air Force. Criticizing the design assumptions or preferences while saving the concept of the F-X (avoiding throwing the baby out with the bath water) was a neat trick. Boyd proceeded to take on each aspect of the design and do a complex series of trade-off analyses comparing each element to the others to derive the optimum performance for the specified mission of the F-X/F-15.

The Air Staff position on the basic design parameters for the F-X when Boyd was first asked to review it called for an airplane that weighed 62,500 pounds with a thrust-to-weight ratio at takeoff of 0.75, a wing loading of 100 pounds, and a turbofan engine with a bypass ratio of 2.2.[21] Boyd's first cut in his trade-off studies revealed that the more appropriate characteristics were a weight of 40,000 pounds, thrust-to-weight ratio of 0.97, and wing loading of 110 pounds per square foot. Wing loading is the ratio between the surface area of the wing and the load it has to support. Boyd was suspicious of high wing loadings and undertook a series of extensive trade-off analyses regarding wing loading and maneuverability. Doing so required extensive study of drag polars and revealed that an even better solution would be a wing loading of 80 pounds per square foot and an engine bypass ratio of 0.9. At that point it became clear that light wing loadings were competitive with variable sweep wing configurations. Boyd determined that a fixed-wing design with a wing loading of 60–65 pounds per square foot had definite combat advantages over the preferred swing-wing design, and the savings in weight and cost were substantial.[22]

Boyd and his colleagues also anticipated the Navy's move from the fighter attack VFAX concept to the air superiority F-14. Boyd prepared a memo for Gen. L. L. Wilson on this and a briefing on methods for countering the Navy ploy and discouraging commonality (as with the F-4 and supposedly with the F-111). Boyd was also concerned about a declining defense budget and increasing unit costs of the emerging F-15. He used his trade-off studies to show the weight, performance, and cost consequences of several fashionable and expensive but often only marginally effective additions to the F-15. Boyd's consistent, hard-nosed questioning and analysis of nearly every aspect of the F-15 program (concept definition, basic engineering, performance characteristics, unit costs, service rivalry with the Navy, congressional approval for procurement) were largely responsible for the definition of the F-15, its survival, and its outstanding capabilities. No one else had as much to do with the definition of the F-15 as Boyd.

Boyd was critical of the system's assumptions and preferences but supportive of the need for an air superiority fighter. He had to keep saying no to the swing-wing, large F-111 follow-on because it was not capable of performing the mission. Saying so (repeatedly) and having to prove why (repeatedly) took courage and integrity. It made him many enemies. His detailed analyses and trade-off studies using energy maneuverability theory (and the improvements he was making to it along the way) led him to save the concept of a capable multirole fighter while transforming the airplane that nearly everyone had envisioned as the end product. Boyd knew that the supposedly optimum proposed solution for the F-X was a loser on two counts. First, it would be so expensive that Congress might never fund it. Second, even if it were procured, Boyd's EM analyses showed that existing aircraft in the Soviet inventory could defeat it. That was simply unacceptable to all. New solutions were required.

### The F-15 Eagle

By March 1967, the Air Force had clarified its criteria enough to ask contractors to aim for a speed range of Mach 1.5 to 3.0, a large window. It left it to the contractors to make the case for swing or fixed wing, single crew or two. In September 1968 the F-X Concept Development was authorized and an RFP for contract definition offered to the aerospace industry. Eight contractors bid for the contract, but by December 1969 only McDonnell Douglas, Fairchild-Hiller, and

North American remained in the running. By now the F-X had become the F-15. The USAF Development Concept Paper, as Michael J. Getting summarizes it,

defined the overall parameters of the design, and justified it against pressure from the US Navy to take a modified version of their VFAX/F-14 on four counts: it would be a single seat, fixed wing, twin-engined fighter of approximately 40,000 lbs (18,000 kg); there would be no competitive fly-off, as this was not thought desirable; the VFAX was not considered a suitable replacement for the F-4E Phantom, nor could the F-4E be modified to meet the threat; and an air-to-ground capability would be included, but only as an off-shoot of the primary air-to-air role.[23]

In case there was any doubt, it stipulated that the F-15 was to be "optimized for counter air missions." Furthermore, it was to be "superior in air combat to any present or postulated Soviet fighters both in close-in, visual encounters and in stand-off or all weather encounters."

Thus stipulated, work on the F-15 progressed. It had begun in October 1965 with the F-X Study. Four years later, a design was selected in December 1969. The first aircraft was delivered to TAC in November 1974. By today's standards, the time frame of less than a decade looks pretty good. If and when the F-22 (the advanced tactical fighter) flies, it will have taken 30 years from the first plans (1979) to the initial operating capability (projected 2008). Throughout the F-15 development process, Boyd had been analyzing the trade-offs to shape a better plane with better performance and lower cost. Ultimately, he decided his efforts were not good enough. His ideal F-15 was even smaller, more maneuverable, and less expensive. The Air Force wanted what it wanted, the logic of Boyd's analyses be damned, and he was ordered to stop further studies on the F-15. In effect, Lt. Gen. Otto Glasser fired him from the project, but Boyd hung on, knowing that his techniques were necessary to complete the program.

The F-15 Eagle is undoubtedly the world's finest fighter and a superb attack plane as well. Its combination of speed, range, maneuverability, radar, missiles, and gun make it a deadly foe in the air. Its roughly 48,000–58,000 pounds of thrust (depending on the variant of the twin engines) give it record-breaking climb and acceleration. Air Force captains David R. King and Donald S. Massey have summarized the Eagle's record: "The F-15 program has become one of the most successful aircraft development and procurement programs in Air Force history. Although mishaps have claimed a number of F-15s, and two F-15Es were lost to ground fire during operation Desert Storm, the F-15 has triumphed in 96.5 aerial engagements without the loss of a single aircraft."[24] That is an unparalleled record of success.

As a result of the many trade-off analyses and thousands of hours of wind tunnel testing, the plane has outstanding maneuverability. Lt. Col. Jerauld R.

Gentry gives much of the credit for the "fact that the F-15 has much higher maneuvering performance than any previous fighter in the world . . . to John Boyd and his unprecedented tradeoff analyses. He did, however, have some serious reservations about the final F-15 design and equipment decisions, a number of which were made despite the evidence of his tradeoff analyses."[25] After initial engine and stall problems, it has been refined and finely tuned. Its powerful long-range radar can detect targets at 100 miles and, from above, distinguish targets from ground clutter. Its mix of infrared and radar guided missiles as well as a high-speed Gatling gun cannon make it the world's premier fighter. In a tribute of sorts to weight reduction, it now flies with ballast in the nose to compensate for new generations of digital avionics, which are far lighter and take up less space than earlier versions. Its only drawback is its price. The best is expensive. But the United States is lucky to have it, and so are those of our allies who could afford to purchase some.

Boyd knew that whatever the specifications of the first version of the plane, the future modifications would only grow in weight, complexity, and price. He was right. The F-15E Strike Eagle, the last modification of the F-15, has a dry weight of 32,000 pounds with a maximum gross takeoff weight of 81,000 pounds. The price is more on the order of $35 million per plane. What the Air Force really needed, thought Boyd and the Fighter Mafia, was a new lightweight fighter that would be faster, more agile, and, most important, cheaper than the F-15. They also wanted a simpler plane with higher reliability. While they didn't eschew high technology, they wanted to select those technologies carefully.

As Riccioni explained it, "The number of weapons systems that can be employed in battle varies inversely to the square of the level of sophistication."[26] There could be too much of a good thing, and if complex systems don't work, paying for them has produced no real benefits. So it was that the F-15 and the work on it inspired Boyd, Pierre Sprey, and Rich Riccioni to lead the fight for a lightweight fighter. The F-16 was anathema to the leadership of the Air Force, but it was the essence of an air superiority fighter to its supporters. They wanted two to three times as many lightweight fighters as F-15s, so the two fighters could be used in combination in what came to be known as a hi/lo mix. The battles over the lightweight fighter would echo through the halls of the five-sided wind tunnel for years.

# 6.    Designing Fighters: The F-16

All of this is to say that "quality vs. quantity" is a misleading characterization of the U.S. fighter modernization conundrum. The real issue is how much "quality," across what performance spectrum, in what force mix, numerical strength, and sustainability, do we need to give us our desired mission effectiveness for most plausible scenarios at a cost we can afford.

Benjamin Lambeth, "Pitfalls in Force Planning," *International Security*, Fall 1985

**A**s the new F-15 took shape, some of its most ardent supporters grew disenchanted. They saw the F-15 becoming ever more expensive; hence, there would be fewer in the inventory. They saw what they took to be an overreliance on radar and missiles to achieve kills beyond visual range. They saw what had been a slimmed down plane growing fatter again with additional avionics suites and a variety of add-ons. In short, they saw a need for a less expensive, lightweight, highly maneuverable fighter that could be procured in sufficient numbers to use and lose in combat and still retain air superiority. The hard core of LWF advocates—Boyd, Sprey, and Riccioni—led the charge for an alternative.

## Pierre Sprey

Pierre Sprey had been an analyst for Grumman Aircraft before becoming a special assistant to the assistant secretary of Defense for Systems Analysis. He and

Boyd met not long after Boyd arrived at the Pentagon. They were as different as night and day but shared many views as well. Their relationship had an element of symbiosis, as described by James Burton: "To Sprey, the world is black and white. To Boyd, the intuitive, creative genius, on the other hand, the world appears in various shades of gray. Pierre thinks in absolutes; Boyd thinks in relative terms. They are so different, yet so alike—two mavericks who have no patience for bureaucrats or incompetence and who love a good fight with the establishment."[1] They became fast friends and close allies.

Sprey was, if anything, as unusual and rare a collection of talents as Boyd. More eclectic, patrician, and cultured, Sprey was born in Nice, France, and was fluent in French and German. He entered Yale at fifteen and graduated with one of the more interesting double majors one can imagine, French literature and mechanical engineering. He then went to Cornell to get a degree in statistics and operations research. The silver-haired Sprey was a dashing Gallic personality with a penchant for Socratic dialogue, wit, and sarcasm. He was bright, articulate, and exceptionally well read. As one observer described him, "He was as relaxed discussing Goethe and Göring in German as he was in discussing the Maginot Line and Molière's *Le Medecin malgré lui* in French. He would discuss the Golden Section and its influence on the Gent Altarpiece with an art historian or the interquartile deviation and bias of the three point perspective in Van Eyk's work with a fellow statistician."[2] Another unique personality, he and Boyd had an almost magnetic attraction to each other.

Sprey had an encyclopedic memory for facts in military history, a logician's approach to problems, a mathematician's commitment to accuracy, and a healthy dose of skepticism when it came to contractors' claims about technical solutions to complex problems. Sprey's concerns about the F-X (much the same as Boyd's), led to a series of briefings on the nature of tactical air engagements. The plane Sprey and Boyd came up with was radically different from the F-15. It would weigh less than 25,000 pounds, with 35,000 pounds of thrust and exceptional maneuvering performance. They labeled it the F-XX, a backhanded slap at the F-X. Sprey did the initial designs and gave preliminary specifications to two contractors, General Dynamics and Northrop. They confirmed his calculations.

Sprey went public. He did so with malice aforethought and a hint of glee at a conference sponsored by the American Institute for Aeronautics and Astronautics in March 1970 in St. Louis, home of the F-15 contractor McDonnell Douglas. The conference was an opportunity to showcase the F-15 and have aircraft designers sing its praises. Sprey was a keynote speaker. Rather than fulfill his role as cheerleader for the F-15, Sprey told those assembled that they could do better and proceeded to describe his vision for the F-XX. Moreover, he called for at least two contractors to build prototypes that could compete head to head in a fly-off. In suggesting an alternative to the F-15 and a new means by which competitive awards should be made, the speech caused an uproar within the aerospace contractor community.

## Rich Riccioni

The last of the three Musketeers of the Fighter Mafia was Col. Everest E. "Rich" Riccioni, a fighter pilot and aeronautical engineer serving on the Air Staff. In many ways, Riccioni was the most vocal advocate of the lightweight fighter and its most celebrated martyr. He considers himself the godfather of the Fighter Mafia and the one who did much of the hard bureaucratic slogging inside the Pentagon while Boyd pushed their ideas to others outside. He and Boyd argued with each other occasionally about who had the most to do with the LWF, who came up with the idea of super cruise or the advantages of various fighter tactics, but they were fiercely loyal to each other as well. Riccioni nearly got into fights with others in the Air Force over their assessment of Boyd. It was Riccioni who wrote a celebrated memo to get Boyd promoted to colonel, and it was Boyd who worked behind the scenes to get Rich rehabilitated and assigned to Hawaii after his exile to Korea. It was, in short, what good friendship is.

A pleasant yet intense man who still talks with his hands to excess (a characteristic attributed to both his fighter-pilot training and his Italian ancestry), Riccioni is bright, passionate, and dedicated. He has been described in much the same way as Boyd: "a mixture of pugnacious determination and a willingness to examine problems from the other side of orthodoxy."[3] Riccioni and Boyd shared the same interests, had some of the same flying background, and had the same passion for fighter design and tactics. Riccioni is also one of the few fighter pilots other than Boyd to author a manual on jet aircraft tactics. He had flown F-100s too, but in Germany.

Along the way, Riccioni completed all but his dissertation for a Ph.D. in aeronautical engineering at MIT and taught at the U.S. Air Force Academy for five years. There, he had a sabbatical of sorts to look into maneuver and got into Boyd's work. He had met Boyd in 1964 but didn't get to work with him until he was assigned to the Tactical Fighter Requirements Division in the Pentagon in May 1969. In January 1970 Riccioni became chief of Development, Plans, and Analysis, a shop that was to investigate new construction and design technologies. He met Boyd, Sprey, and Chuck Myers and was reinforced in his interest in a small lightweight fighter.

In many ways, Riccioni became the real lightweight fighter advocate, for his version was really stripped down (to 17,000 pounds), and he was exiled for his advocacy in a way that Boyd and Sprey were not. Riccioni and Boyd were not always in agreement on the LWF. There were major differences in their preferences and approaches. Riccioni wanted to soup up the performance, to best an F-15 by 20 percent to 50 percent in speed and maneuverability, at the expense of range if need be. Boyd wanted to keep the performance comparable to the F-15's and keep some legs, with a higher fuel fraction (the ratio of fuel carried to the weight of the airplane) for greater range. Rich later admitted that Boyd had been right and was glad in the long run he had lost the argument. A master at playing the Navy and the Air Force against each other, he may well have saved the day on the F-16. Boyd sold Congress on the F-16, Sprey sold the Secretary of Defense and the secretary's office (OSD), and Riccioni fought the fight within the Air Staff. They made quite a formidable team.

Along the way they had some of the best minds in the Air Force working for them. Ray Leopold, now an executive with Motorola, did a lot of work on budgets and procurement, despite being a Ph.D. in electrical engineering. Chuck Spinney, who was convinced of the inherent corruption in the procurement system, still does mammoth, Boyd-like briefings on the evils of the system as a DOD civilian. Bob Drabant is a methodology genius who generated most of the data on energy maneuverability for Boyd and Riccioni and now works as a civilian at Nellis Air Force Base. They all contributed greatly to the cause. Others too were part of the effort: John "Mike" Loh became the special projects officer for the F-16; the seemingly ever-present and ever-prescient Chuck Myers[4] and a host of other allies, military and civilian, both inside and outside the Pentagon, contributed as the fight for the F-16 became the military reform movement; a network of journalists, defense industry engineers, staffers on Capitol Hill, civilian analysts within DOD, young Turk congressmen and senators from the right and the left—all were enlisted for the cause.

## Harry Hillaker

Harry Hillaker was a General Dynamics engineering hotshot who at 25 had been chief of the Fort Worth Division's preliminary design group. A Michigan-trained aeronautical engineer, Hillaker had been transplanted from Southern California to Fort Worth in 1942 and had been working on designing airplanes ever since. While spending his own time on some design ideas for a small, sleek fighter, he hoped one day to have the opportunity to work on one.

Hillaker met John Boyd at the officer's club bar at Eglin in the summer of 1964. When he entered the club, Hillaker saw several fighter pilots standing at the bar drinking and talking with their hands, as fighter pilots do. He remarked to his host, "That tall guy over there probably thinks he's the world's greatest fighter pilot." His host replied, "He probably is. His name is John Boyd. Would you like to meet him?" Hillaker declined. "No, guys like that don't do a whole lot for me."[5]

As fate would have it though, they did meet and promptly got into an argument about the F-111 and what it could and could not do. Hillaker decided quickly that this was not your typical brash fighter pilot—he knew something about airplanes in a broader and deeper sense than most. Hillaker's reaction was the same as most: Boyd was either a madman or a genius. They shared a passion for flight, for designing fighters that were lean, built for speed, highly maneuverable, and able to outfly anything else in the air. They were drawn to each other because they both asked tough questions of everything and each other. It was the beginning of a deep friendship.

They sought what was to them the holy grail of fighters: small, agile, very high performance fighters. Never mind that the times and the hierarchies of both industry and the Air Force were out to promote bigger, faster, more complex planes, with higher profits and higher technology. What Boyd and Hillaker sought meant smaller budgets for both General Dynamics and the Air Force. It was not a popular set of sentiments to be pushing. It flew in the face of what defense writer and *Wall Street Journal* reporter John Fialka has called the ultimate corruption inside the Pentagon: "There is no low-cost solution to a problem."[6]

Boyd and Hillaker kept in touch and talked with some frequency. After Boyd moved to Washington, they talked more. As the problems with the F-X, then the F-15, increased, Boyd and company became more disenchanted with it, and the contacts with Hillaker increased. Harry would fly in from Fort Worth, sometimes on his own time and at his own expense. He, Boyd, and Sprey would meet at a hotel or home (never an office) and talk, exchange ideas, and crunch numbers. Over several months these sessions grew longer until Hillaker was spending all night in Washington and flying back to Fort Worth the next morning to report for work at General Dynamics. The whole process to design the F-16 would take nearly five years.

Looking back, Hillaker laughs at the combination of naivete, good fortune, and damn-fool luck that eventually led to success. About his own fighter design work he says, "Nobody told me to work on it. I just did. Nobody was stopping me. Under today's standards, I would probably be indicted. I had no budget. The system was such that I could do it. I had that freedom."[7] When he and the Fighter Mafia started holding their all-night sessions after hours, it was merely an extension of each member's passion and individual commitment to a group endeavor. They were outnumbered, outgunned, and essentially outside the system, but they were all totally dedicated. They did what they did because they thought they were right.

It was a combination of skill and luck that led to the adoption of the F-16. All the necessary dominoes for its adoption fell generally at the right place and at the right time. The damned thing had risen from the ashes time and time again when the Air Force thought it had been killed. Some of the setups were so perfect that they boggle the mind. One in particular was a set of briefings from General Dynamics to the Air Force. Hillaker did the presentation. The Air Force officers in attendance were impressed by the ease and skill of his presentation and the deft manner in which he fielded their questions. It was a brilliant performance, particularly for a civilian. He seemed to know so well what they were concerned about and to be able to explain his points to them so convincingly. Boyd asked a few questions, and Hillaker responded brilliantly. He was congratulated afterward on being able to put that damn major in his place and shut him up. Unbeknownst to the other officers, Hillaker and Boyd had stayed up all night rehearsing his presentation and going over the questions he would likely be asked—the same questions that had been supplied to the Air Force brass by Boyd.[8] It was pure Boyd and about as far inside the adversary's OODA loop as you can get.

### Pushing the LWF

Riccioni had been extolling the virtues of the LWF in his Falcon Brief. At a social function before Christmas 1970, Gen. John C. Myer, vice chief of staff of the Air Force, asked Riccioni to expound on his views. Riccioni obliged, stating his concerns about the F-15 and the advantages of a smaller, lighter, faster fighter. Myer was neither impressed nor in agreement. The following Monday, Myer called Riccioni's superior, Lt. Gen. Otto Glasser, and told him he wanted Riccioni gone. Fortunately, the wheels of bureaucracy grind slowly. Riccioni didn't receive orders transferring him halfway around the world to Korea until March, and he didn't depart until September 1971. As long as he remained in the Pentagon, Riccioni pushed the LWF in every way he could.[9]

Almost a year before his deportation, Riccioni had written a memo to his boss, Maj. Gen. Donovan Smith. Smith happened to be unavailable, so Riccioni took it to Smith's boss, Glasser. The memo, citing "a long series of small incidental factors and rumors," outlined why Riccioni thought the Navy was developing a lightweight fighter of its own and its characteristics. He then stated:

> 3. This effort is fed by the desire of these elements of the Navy to have a hedge in case the Congress denies them their $13m stand-off weapon, the F-14A/B. This is very good thinking, which analysis the Air Force was encouraged to do some year and a half ago.

4. This state of the Navy, and results of the study could have a serious impact on the F-15 program. If the F-14 fails to get the production go-ahead from lack of funds in a cutback era, a $2M–$3M fighter proposal would seriously threaten the F-15's chances for survival. Even the International Freedom Fighter would see perturbation.

5. Lt. Col. John Boyd and I are quietly pushing an informational probe deeper to get more information and more substantial, precise information.[10]

It was a masterpiece of manipulation. Riccioni planted the seeds for their project by suggesting that it was not just worthy of consideration but almost mandatory because the U.S. Navy was doing it in a way that threatened Air Force programs. He raised the red flag of congressional action to change funding and suggested that he and Boyd be permitted, surreptitiously, to find out more. Glasser scratched a note to Riccioni on the bottom that said, "Stay on this. I've long urged an a/c of this type—We could have scooped all with it—Run with this."[11] This was a license to steal, a con man's dream: permission to do what you wanted to do by the party you were conning.

And run with it Riccioni did. He shopped his masterful briefings around the Air Staff and elsewhere. In one, he focused on two threats, internal and external, and ended with a telling slide: "Unless the U.S. Air Force thoroughly studies high performance austere fighters and is prepared to consider them as a necessary complement to other air superiority aircraft, the U.S. Air Force may be: A. Outgunned by the Navy (again) and/or B. Outfought by the Russians."[12] It was a stroke of genius. Neither the need for air superiority nor even air-to-air combat with the Soviets might spur the Air Force to action, but by God, they would not be snookered again by the Navy! In a way, the Air Force owes the existence of the F-16 to the Navy.

As these factors intersected and accumulated with the growing mountain of data regarding the LWF, the Air Force leadership panicked. Orthodoxy became rampant. As James Fallows explained it, "Within the Air Force, loyalty to the F-15 became what profession of faith in the Blessed Virgin is within the Church: a prerequisite act of belief for all who seek membership."[13] The Air Force didn't want to be left holding an empty bag without an air superiority fighter. Capitalizing on that argument, Riccioni and Boyd put together a proposal entitled "Study to Validate the Integration of Advanced Energy Maneuverability Theory with Tradeoff Analysis." The cost was $149,000 (a pittance in the DOD budget), and General Dynamics and Northrop were the contractors for the February 1971 study. Despite the innocuous title, the project's real aim was to test preliminary design and analysis of three different lightweight fighter configurations.

The problem was that no one thought the Air Force could get *two* fighters approved, and the F-15 was an approved program. You were either for it or against it; there was no middle ground. Any new program would siphon money and effort away from the F-15. The idea and the very discussion of an LWF had to be promoted carefully and quietly or the whole thing would blow up. James Burton described the campaign:

A serious student of guerrilla warfare would do well to study the operations of the Fighter Mafia. Quietly, secretly, it worked the hallways, back doors and alleys of the Pentagon and the aircraft industry. Its members probed the establishment everywhere and looked for any signs of support for their theme of building a better fighter than the F-15 at half the cost. Slowly but surely, they established a network of sympathetic key officials within the Air Force and the Office of the Secretary of Defense that would be instrumental when it came time to strike in the open.[14]

It was a military campaign, just not a typical one that most officers wage.

## How Good Things Happen

The continued success of the Fighter Mafia's efforts seemed to defy explanation. It was aided by a series of fortuitous concerns, which the Fighter Mafia took advantage of and promoted for its own purposes. First, there was increasing concern in Congress and the public at large about the growing cost of weapons systems. The F-14 and the F-15 were the most visible, high-dollar examples. Second, there was concern about how the DOD procured weapons. After the scandals surrounding the F-111 and the C-5, sentiment was strong for a return to prototyping and procurement decisions made only after prototypes had been built, tested, compared, and selected for the best combination of value and price. Critics charged that "the entire DOD-contractor weapons system acquisition process was out of control."[15] A presidential blue-ribbon report released in July 1970 substantiated complaints and made several suggestions for improving weapons acquisition.

Third, interest was growing abroad in a replacement for the F-5, the small, capable, but dated export fighter that so many nations had bought. The need for a new, capable, less expensive fighter for U.S. allies and friends reinforced the Nixon Doctrine announced in Guam in 1969, calling on America's allies to do more in providing for their own defense but promising to assist in providing the necessary hardware. Secretary of Defense Melvin Laird requested congressional approval of funding for the international fighter aircraft program to advance a capable, inexpensive, and simple-to-maintain fighter for the export market. Some $58 million was authorized for its development in fiscal years 1970 and 1971.[16]

In June 1970 John Foster, head of DDR&E, suggested that sharing research and development expenses with allies might be a way to cope with declining defense budgets and that sharing technical expertise could promote programs and systems of benefit to all concerned at lower cost. Finally, all the contractors that were not involved in the F-14 or F-15 contracts saw this as their salvation and were interested in promoting the combined notion of a lightweight fighter for the U.S. Air Force and an export fighter for allies. Aerospace defense firms live off the next big U.S. government buy. They use the export business and upgrades to sustain them between major equipment purchases. The chance to do both in one massive buy sounded to them like winning a jackpot. The Fighter Mafia took full advantage of the possibility.

### Specifications and Politics

Boyd, Sprey, and Riccioni pushed for fairly strong but general technical specifications to allow the manufacturers in the prototyping competition to figure out how best to implement them. Rather than detailed specifications, the contractor guidance contained simple directives, such as visibility should be not less than that achieved in the F-86 Saber Jet. Riccioni believed

these ultra-austere, high performance fighter designs should weigh less than 20,000 pounds (his goal was about 17,000 pounds) and have only the avionics and armament required for a visual day fighter (no radar or other systems not essential for the mission). He also stated no requirement for a maneuvering capability above Mach 1.6. Six combat tasks or maneuvers were stipulated at a 225-mile radius and at 30,000 feet altitude: an acceleration from Mach 0.9 to Mach 1.5, three complete turns at Mach 0.8, and two complete turns at Mach 1.2.[17]

That type of thinking led to the equally important requirement that contractors follow a task-oriented design and mission rules that were combat relevant. It was no longer merely a specification of how high, how far, or how fast a plane could go. As a result of Boyd's EM work and trade-off studies, Sprey's concern for demonstrated useful capabilities, and Riccioni's passion for a truly hot lightweight fighter, the contractors had to make iterative, Boyd-like trade-off calculations for parameters such as lift, drag, acceleration, fuel capacity, combat radius, and so forth.

The quest for a stripped-down, austere fighter was accompanied by a similar management approach to its specification and selection. The Statement of

Work for the F-16, written by Boyd and Sprey, was the contractual document outlining what the government sought from the contractors. It was, like the desired plane itself, small and simple. It was only 25 pages long. Such statements usually run into the hundreds and thousands of pages. Even more dramatic was the requirement that the contractors limit their proposal responses to 50 pages. That was a real revolution. As Jim Burton comments, "Doing this today inside the system would take ten years, cost billions and result in contractual documents 25 feet high. I invite anyone who doubts this to examine the B1-B and B-2 bomber programs as well as a host of others."[18] To advocates of the LWF, the limit was sheer genius. To its detractors, it proved just how crazy these people really were.

A factor in the background that made the F-16 possible was the dissatisfaction with McNamara's Total Package Procurement program. In this approach, design teams and systems analysts created mountains of paperwork and computer-generated analyses of hypothetical airplanes as a way to cut initial contractor costs and assess the performance characteristics of the airplanes they wished to build. Unfortunately, many of these paper airplanes bore little resemblance to the real ones that emerged. Contractors' promises turned into cost overruns, delays, compromises, specification changes, and less-than-promised performance. David Packard (the deputy secretary of Defense) in particular and to some degree Secretary of Defense Laird (a former congressman) and later Secretary of Defense James Schlesinger all supported a return to prototyping and the "fly before you buy" procurement approach.

Packard spelled out his views on the process in a memorandum dated 16 February 1971, annotating the following comments to a memorandum he had received from John Foster in DDR&E.

It is important that each program have these features:
1. . . . Only price should be firm. All specifications should be open.
2. At least two projects should be authorized for each class of plane.
3. A plan for fly-off testing will be required.
4. It must be made clear that there is no commitment to go ahead with a further program.
5. At the same time, we will lose benefit of this approach if after a fly-off, we go back to some other competition for full development and production.

In other words, the fly-off testing is the source selection if we decide to go ahead.[19]

Allan Simon, the assistant director for air warfare, then designed the Fighter Attack Aircraft Prototype Study to assess the validity of prototyping and to propose guidelines should it be pursued. The Simon Study, as it was known, dovetailed nicely with the Packard guidelines.

## Time Out for an Overseas Tour

Before getting too deeply involved in Boyd's fight to preserve the F-16 and to reform various aspects of the military, we need to take an excursion, as did Boyd, tracing his overseas tour during the war in Southeast Asia. He had not had an overseas tour since his first years in the Air Force in Korea nearly 20 years earlier. It was time. Boyd received the orders for his tour in 1972 and spent thirteen months, from April 1972 through April 1973, in Thailand at a secret Air Force base involved in intelligence gathering and the monitoring of sophisticated sensors for the war in Vietnam. The base (Nakom Phanom, known as NKP) was the headquarters of an operation known as Igloo White, among others, and a large group called Task Force Alpha. It exposed Boyd to the political demands of the local Thais, the top-secret nature of the Air Force work, and the hassles of coordinating a disparate group of people and missions in a remote location. It had many general officers who visited or ran tenant programs on the supersensitive base.

Boyd seemed to thrive in the environment. It was a change of pace. Though he wasn't flying, he was at least in a war theater for the first time in 20 years. Not that the work was easy. The business of the base was deadly serious. It was the center of several disparate operations, but all with one purpose, to keep track of North Vietnamese infiltration routes along the Ho Chi Minh Trail through Laos and Cambodia into Vietnam. It had begun, on the recommendation of several scientists to Secretary of Defense McNamara, with the formation of the Defense Communications Planning Group (later the Defense Special Projects Group) in 1966. Its purpose was to conduct research into the development of unattended ground sensors for the detection and surveillance of guerrilla forces and activities. The idea was to sense the presence of NVA or Viet Cong trucks, bicycles, or personnel along the trail by olfactory ("people sniffing") devices, microphones, motion sensors, magnetic and seismic readouts, and the like. By the time Boyd arrived at NKP, somewhere between $2 billion and $4 billion, according to various estimates, had been invested in the program, and it was in full swing.

The program operation for aerial attack of sites identified by the sensors was known as Igloo White. The massive effort to position sensing devices all along the Ho Chi Minh Trail to monitor truck traffic and troop movements toward South Vietnam was a major but little known aspect of the Vietnam War. Since the trail meandered through Laos and Cambodia (as well as Vietnam) for many miles, it took a lot of well-disguised sensors of all kinds to monitor the traffic. The electronic signals then had to be monitored and the information assessed and disseminated to plan air strikes on bodies of troops and convoys of equipment that were moving along the trail. NKP was the heart of the operation.

This was the origin of the electronic battlefield that has evolved into the image of the digital battlefield of the future.[20] Boyd was not particularly enamored with much of the high-technology effort and thought the success rate not worth the investment. The sensors were passive and indiscriminate and in many cases could tell little about the number of enemy in the area. They did not discriminate between civilians and military, good guys or bad. They could be detected and used by the enemy to their advantage by directing strikes elsewhere, for instance, using bomb blasts to clear jungle areas for new trails. Still, NKP was home for thirteen months, and Boyd had to cope with a myriad of problems, sublime and ridiculous.

### The Process to Develop an F-16

As Boyd prepared to leave for Southeast Asia, prospects heated up for the F-16. The Fighter Mafia, now much diminished but well down the road to success, would have to carry on without him for more than a year. DOD made $200 million available to test the prototyping concept. The Air Force, rather than see the money go to another service, submitted two requirements. Both were selected. One was a medium short takeoff and landing transport intended to replace the C-130 Hercules, a plane still being built (not just flown) over a quarter of a century later, and the other was a lightweight fighter. General Dynamics got $38 million to develop and fly two prototypes of the YF-16. The Y (development) designation was substituted for the usual X (experimental) to emphasize the combination of off-the-shelf and experimental technologies. Northrop got $39 million for two prototypes of the rival YF-17. In addition, Pratt and Whitney got funding to develop a single-engine configuration of the F-100 engine, and General Electric got funds for a new, smaller YF-101 engine.

It had been a dozen years since Chuck Myers had begun pushing for a small air superiority fighter. It had been six years since Boyd had begun work on the F-X. It had been three years since Riccioni had entered the fray, two since Sprey had promoted the F-XX publicly, and nearly a year since Riccioni had been exiled to Korea for his heresy. They had won a modicum of success, but the fight was not over. Most in the Air Force thought this was the best way to deal with the Fighter Mafia: let them win a battle but scuttle the project later and insure that they lost the war. The other funding let at the same time (to Boeing and McDonnell Douglas for jet transports) died a quiet death, and many predicted the same for the LWF.

General Dynamics and Northrop were chosen to develop and flight-test hardware, and the contract was let for two prototypes on 13 April 1972. These were technology demonstration programs with the option of development into a service aircraft. The average flyaway cost at the time was $3 million per plane for an assumed production run of 100 a year for three years. The contractor was given general guidance and allowed to decide how best to meet the combat specifications. In the midst of the development process, certain verities of the Fighter Mafia were reinforced by the Yom Kippur War of October 1973. Israel lost nearly 40 percent of its Air Force in a matter of weeks, underscoring the need for small, easy-to-maintain, cheap, and hence plentiful fighters. The General Dynamics plane was the YF-16, a single-engine, single-tail plane powered by the Pratt and Whitney F-100 turbofan engine. Northrop's YF-17 was a twin-engine, twin-tail design based on Northrop's P-530 Cobra design and powered by two General Electric YF-101 "leaky turbojet" engines.

The YF-16 had several novel features. To begin with, it was a beautiful plane to look at, as much sculpture as aeronautic engineering. It had strakes and a blended wing where the wing and fuselage flowed into each other. Its short, stubby wings had leading- and trailing-edge flaps for variable wing camber and fly-by-wire control. (The latter means that the plane is inherently unstable if left to a pilot alone; it can be flown only by the simultaneous interactions of computers and control surfaces throughout the plane.) The seat was canted at 30 degrees to allow the pilot to pull more g's more easily than if it were upright. Although these elements were novel, they were not high-risk technologies in terms of either production or maintenance. The engine proved troublesome but provided cost savings, as it was the same one utilized in the F-15. The whole plane was a pleasing blend of simplicity and sophistication. General Dynamics engineers did trade-off analyses on 78 different variables and 1,272 hours of wind tunnel tests before determining the plane's ultimate shape and configuration.[21] All was not lost for Northrop and the YF-17, however, as the Navy rejected a naval version of the F-16 and instead developed the F-18 from the YF-17 design. That saga, with its complicated lineage, politics, and procurement process, is well told by Jim Stevenson in his book *The Pentagon Paradox: The Development of the F-18 Hornet*.

## The F-16 Decision

The F-16 looked good in the competition and had exceeded the expectations of most with its performance and cost projections, but it was still essentially an unwanted stepchild to the senior leadership. Demonstrated competence and logic would need some assistance from old-fashioned guile and cunning if the project was to proceed. The F-16 was headed for an ambush, according to Jim Burton: "Boyd received a tip from one of the moles in his information network. The senior leaders' game plan was to let Boyd proceed up the Air Staff and get a positive endorsement on each level until he got to the top, where the three star generals would shoot him down in flames and disapprove the proposal. This would give the outward appearance that his proposal had received an honest and serious consideration but simply did not make the final cut, so to speak."[22] It was more guerrilla politics, Pentagon style. In retrospect, it was terribly important for Boyd's appreciation of perceptions, deception, ambiguity, and what he ultimately called "the strategic game of isolation and interaction." The battle to win approval for the F-16 was a laboratory demonstration of the insights presented in his later briefing.

As the appointed day for the showdown approached, the senior Air Force brass girded their loins for the fight. Many Air Force three-stars were in the room to receive what they thought would be the last briefing from Boyd regarding the F-16. They had worked hard for nearly three years to marshal their support throughout the Air Force and to insure that the F-16 would not continue to threaten the F-15 by siphoning money from its procurement. Meanwhile, Boyd and Sprey had gone over the generals' heads. Sprey had already persuaded Secretary of Defense James Schlesinger to give the go-ahead for the F-16. That had only just occurred, and there had been no leaks. What the Air Force saw as the final battle in the contest to procure the F-16 had been made irrelevant. Boyd began the briefing with a statement: "Gentlemen, I am authorized by the Secretary of Defense to inform you that this briefing is for information only. The decision has been made to procure the F-16."[23]

The room exploded. That fucking Boyd had struck again. They had been outmaneuvered. However difficult it is at times, a hierarchical system does work, and the decision had been made at the top. Air Force Secretary John McLucas announced the YF-16 selection on 13 January 1975. It had significantly better performance—acceleration, endurance, and turning capability—than the YF-17.

A deal was struck that made the decision palatable. Schlesinger and the new chief of staff of the Air Force, Gen. David C. Jones, managed to reach a hard-won agreement after some tough negotiations and compromises on the part of each. Jones, like his predecessor Gen. George Brown and the bulk of the Air Force, was reluctant to accept a low-cost F-16 in place of the costlier, state-of-the-art F-15. Schlesinger knew, however, that Jones and the service also wanted to see the Air Force expand to 26 tactical fighter wings (each with 72 aircraft) from the presently authorized level of 22. As Schlesinger later explained it, General Jones "did some shrewd bargaining along the lines of the golden handshake. He said in effect: The price, sir, is four additional tactical air wings. It was the introduction of the F-16 (eventual winner of the competition)—at roughly half the cost of the F-15—that permitted the expansion to 26 wings."[24] There were, unfortunately, other parts of the deal too. The Air Force was supposed to adhere to a ceiling in manpower as well, but when Schlesinger was fired, it began annual increases in personnel.

The development process was not over either. The Air Force would have to buy the little sucker, but the plane didn't have to stay the way it was when it was approved. Most decisions in Washington are never final. They can always be amended, modified, revisited, and occasionally ignored. The F-16 approval was no exception. The Air Force added some codicils to the agreement that allowed significant modifications of the YF-16. Gen. Alton Slay, head of the Air Force's Configuration Control Committee, dubbed the Configuration Add-on Committee by the Fighter Mafia, exacted his revenge on behalf of the Air Force. The F-16 was not going to challenge the F-15, and it would become a multirole airplane. Making it so caused all sorts of changes.

In the process of "full-scale engineering development," over two tons of avionics were added to the plane, the fuselage was lengthened, and much of the design philosophy that had created the F-16 was vitiated in the process. All this took place in the development stage. Boyd and company knew full well that over the course of the aircraft's life, it would be modified and would only grow in weight. That was why the initial performance characteristics were so important. The rule of thumb in the Air Force is that a plane will gain a pound of weight a day for the life of the aircraft. Given a 30-year life span for the F-16, Boyd could expect five tons of modifications and additions to be made to the original model.

There is no doubt that the F-16 as procured in its various blocks and models can do more than the original design, but it cannot accomplish its intended purpose as well as when first developed. It is heavier, slower, and harder to maintain than it could have been. In part to serve the Air Force's needs and in part to meet the demands of allies, it has been developed into a multirole plane with a ground-attack capability, not an unrivaled air superiority fighter. Each new block constructed has grown in weight, complexity, and cost. Secretary Schlesinger had vowed the F-16 would never carry nuclear weapons and made an agreement with General Jones to that effect. One week after Schlesinger left office, the Air Force ordered the F-16 modified to carry nuclear weapons.

In the end, the Air Force brass won and molded the plane that they wanted the F-16 to become. Originally projected to cost only $3 million, the F-16 as modified and upgraded quickly climbed to $6 million and then to $12 million a copy. In the process, it could do more types of tasks and became better at certain tasks. That cannot be denied. However degraded the F-16 is from its original vision and version, it is still a very good airplane. The F-16 has a canopy without a bow frame and with a 360-degree field of view, carries both gun (20 mm cannon) and missiles, can perform in the ground-attack role, is agile and has a reasonable combat radius, and is considered "the best close combat fighter in the world today."[25] It is also cheaper than its predecessor, something that will not likely ever happen again. Still, as Jim Fallows laments, "it is so much less than it might have been."[26]

## The Implications and Current Realities

Without Boyd, there might well have been no F-15. Nearly all are agreed that it would not be as good as it is without his considerable efforts. If it had been better, as he and others had desired, there would have been no F-16. Dennis Smith pointed that out in 1985: "Put another way, had the Air Force in 1968 decided on a more austere, higher performance F-15, there would almost certainly be no F-16 today and, perhaps, no military reform movement."[27] Without a grudging willingness of the system to explore specialized, less expensive aircraft (the A-10 and the F-16), we would not have the inventory of fighters that we have today. Without Boyd and the Fighter Mafia, there would have been no F-16. Harry Hillaker, the engineer who really designed the plane, states simply, "No F-16 would be flying today were it not for his tenacious efforts."[28] Without the F-16, the U.S. Air Force would have more than 2,000 fewer fighters in its inventory (there are now nearly twice as many F-16s as F-15s). Given the no-fly zones established in northern and southern Iraq and in Bosnia, it is doubtful the Air Force could perform its assigned duties without them.

There really is a correlation between quantity and quality. No one would want to go to war with inferior equipment. Quality is important. No one would want to go to war with insufficient quantities of major weapons systems either. Numbers count too. What is at stake is the relative mix, something the Air Force came to call the hi/lo mix in its fighter force. Of the total number of fighters produced, F-16s represented 54 percent of the tactical aircraft, the F-15, 27 percent (see table 1). One finds it hard to imagine the U.S. Air Force without the F-16.

As for foreign sales, only the Japanese, the Saudis, and the Israelis have been able to afford F-15s, and they have purchased 22, 74, and 149, respectively,

**Table 1. U.S. Air Force Fighter Production**

| Aircraft Type | No. Produced |
| --- | --- |
| F-15 (all variants) | 1,100 |
| F-16 (all variants) | 2,206 |
| A-10 | 713 |
| F-117 | 59 |
| Total | 4,078 |

*Source:* "USAF Almanac 2000: The Air Force in Facts and Figures," *Air Force Magazine* 83, no. 4 (May 2000), pp. 137–141.

**Table 2. Foreign Purchasers or Coproducers of F-16s**

| Country | No. F-16s |
| --- | --- |
| Bahrain | 22 |
| Belgium | 160 |
| Denmark | 70 |
| Egypt | 220 |
| Greece | 80 |
| Indonesia | 12 |
| Israel | 210 |
| Korea, South | 160 |
| The Netherlands | 213 |
| Norway | 74 |
| Pakistan | 68 |
| Portugal | 20 |
| Singapore | 38 |
| Taiwan | 150 |
| Thailand | 36 |
| Turkey | 240 |
| Venezuela | 24 |
| Total | 1,797 |

*Source: Jane's All the World's Aircraft 2000–2001* (Alexandria, Va.: Jane's Information Group, 2000), p. 707.

for a total of 245 F-15 foreign sales. Over seven times that number of the cheaper, easier-to-maintain F-16s have been bought by nearly a score of friends and allies (table 2). Many are still being built abroad under joint venture or co-production agreements.

The United States has purchased 2,206 F-16s. Foreign sales bring the total purchased up to 4,003, almost three times the F-15's production total of 1,345. The foreign sales of the F-16 have been chronicled elsewhere.[29] Egypt and Greece are purchasing more F-16s, and the Chileans and the United Arab Emirates will likely procure the upgraded F-16 rather than its European rivals. Their purchases have recently pushed the F-16 total to well over 4,000, nearly half of them purchased and in many cases coproduced by foreign countries.

The foreign sales would not have happened if the plane were not part of the Air Force's front-line inventory. The Northrop F-20 Tigershark never made it as a replacement for the F-5 because it was not adopted by the Air Force. The Air Force wouldn't have adopted the F-16 if it hadn't been rammed down its organizational throat by the Fighter Mafia and the decisions made by David Packard and Secretary of Defense Schlesinger. Packard's concern was not air superiority as much as establishing a new procurement system to replace the fiascoes of the McNamara era. Schlesinger had budgetary, organizational, and international concerns in mind. The serendipitous intersection of all those concerns with the zeal, dedication, and dogged persistence of the Fighter Mafia made the Fighting Falcon a reality. The little plane that nobody outside the Fighter Mafia wanted, that had limited range, that was too unsophisticated to hold its own, that would cost less than its predecessor, and that would be the mainstay of the Air Force became a reality. As Harry Hillaker concluded, "The F-16 was a Camelot. There is no way today I or anybody else can ever start something similar."[30]

# 7. The Military Reform Movement

Clearly the people across this broad spectrum are not going to agree on everything. But as a result of their efforts, there is at least a chance that John Boyd and his friends have started something—a realization that defense is too important to continue to be a shuttle-cock in a private game between the systems analysts and the members of the Army-Navy Club, that it is time to call a halt to our Hatfield-McCoy defense policy feuds of the last 15 years and get busy, together, to find a better way.

R. James Woolsey, former undersecretary of the Navy
"A New Kind of Reformer," *Washington Post,* 13 March 1981

Boyd returned to Washington in April 1973. His family was glad to have him home from Thailand. The last American combat troops had left South Vietnam in January of that year, and the South Vietnamese were left to fend for themselves, the result of the Vietnamization of the war, a euphemism for American withdrawal. Congress had cut off any further funding for U.S. military forces. The debacle in Southeast Asia was entering its final phase but wouldn't end for another two years, when Saigon fell in April 1975. Boyd had enjoyed his tour abroad. There had been a new environment to figure out and a new set of challenges that he loved. Because of the secret nature of the work, much of which remains classified to this day, he was not able to talk much about it. Back home, he entered into the fray of the military reform movement with a renewed vigor.

It had become clear to those who sought to change the way in which the nation conducted the business of defense that something more than forays against individual weapons systems, policy initiatives, or funding decisions would be in order. In the wake of Vietnam, a group of loosely affiliated defense analysts, journalists and reporters, legislators, and academicians became increasingly vocal and active in taking on the DOD. A spate of articles appeared in the press and journals calling for various reforms in the American military. The military itself, embarrassed about its performance in Vietnam, filled with pot-smoking, drug-using enlisted troops with racial animosities, was debating how to clean up its own act. The reserve components had problems in that their ranks were largely filled with those who joined to escape the draft and service in Vietnam. All in all, the 1970s was not a good time for the American military. Military reform was, therefore, in the air, if not a focused reality.

The saga of the controversies surrounding nonperforming weapons systems has been told and retold many times.[1] Many of these media exposés reflect overheated rhetoric, but public findings on problems in force structure planning and weapons acquisition are a matter of record. One of the more succinct statements of the problem comes from the President's Blue Ribbon Commission on Defense Management in 1986, also known as the Packard Commission, for its chairman, David Packard. In many ways, the commission vindicated the previous decade's efforts at military reform:

Today, there is no rational system whereby the Executive Branch and the Congress reach coherent and enduring agreement on national military strategy, the forces to carry it out, and the funding that should be provided—in light of the overall economy and competing claims on national resources. The absence of such a system contributes substantially to the instability and uncertainty that plague our defense program. These cause imbalance in our military forces and capabilities, and increase the costs of procuring military equipment.[2]

If the problems were so self-evident, why weren't they easily remedied?

In essence, the United States has a defense committee of 535 members of Congress far more concerned about federal jobs and money in their districts than with the nation's defense. The more seniority a member has, the bigger the benefits. Even when there are supposed victories and defense spending is cut, it turns out to cost more in the long run. Hedrick Smith summed it up:

Inevitably, a Pentagon budget is a negotiated treaty to satisfy all these constituencies, like a politically balanced ticket in Los Angeles or Chicago. The list of "priority" weapons is terribly long because each weapon has its own constituency. So when Congress asks Weinberger for guidance on where to cut, his inclination is to resist rather than alienating some constituency. Congress is forced to make an overall cut and then have the services do what is least effective for national strategy: cut programs across the board from everyone, so that market shares are not disturbed. Hard choices are not made. Nothing is killed. Programs are stretched out. Costs rise because of inefficiency. The taxpayer gets less bang for the buck.[3]

To the public, the real evils of the Pentagon were seen through the seemingly endless stories of ineptitude, high-priced spare parts, graft, and corruption that filled the press, particularly in the 1980s when the Reagan defense budget threw money at DOD faster than it could absorb it.

This laxity in defense spending and accountability was obvious and of long standing. Why did it continue? The reformers thought they knew. "The generals ordered weapons built, and lieutenant colonels felt compelled to deliver weapons, *not* bad news. The optimistic reports kept the generals locked into programs, such as Divad, for the incentives of the defense game are to build, spend, and appropriate, *not* to oppose, question, or delay."[4] Boyd understood that while all this was true, piecemeal attacks and marginal successes were only tactical victories of little significance: "That's the strategy in the Pentagon. Don't interrupt the money flow."[5] Unless there was some fundamental transformation in the thinking about defense, the process would never change. As long as the process remained as it was, the nation would be saddled with an inefficient, perhaps ineffective, military establishment to carry out our national security strategy.

### True Reform: Changing Thinking about Defense

At a meeting in the summer of 1992 to create an oral history of the congressional Military Reform Caucus, Dave Evans made an important comment:

I think it goes far beyond simply, as Congressman [G. William] Whitehurst indicated in his memoirs, the implied agenda or the need went far beyond his perception of a process to develop a meaningful alternative to the conventional pattern of weapons acquisition in the Pentagon. I think it was far more than that. We were really looking at nothing less than a way of changing our way of thinking about defense issues. . . . I think there was clearly an effort to go beyond the notion of being cheap hawks, of producing more with less money.[6]

Boyd and his associates (principally Ray Leopold, with additional help from Chuck Spinney) tried to do so—change the thinking and the planning process—inside the system before Boyd retired. A paper they drafted had five goals.

1. To provide the decision makers with an understanding of the planning process
2. To identify the crucial steps in the planning process

3. To explain how current planning is not fiscally pragmatic
4. To show the progress we have made toward producing planning options
5. To show what remains to be done and what support is required.[7]

The document, a mere 8 pages in length, had 140 pages of appendices on five subjects: "Planning's Evolving Approach," "Budget Analysis," "Soviet Weapons Potential," "Combat Tasks," and "Matching Hardware Options to Combat Tasks." It followed Gen. Glenn Kent's "strategy to tasks" approach. It is a model of lucid thinking, cogent analysis, and important recommendations. In the maw of the system, however, it disappeared.

The paper sought to improve Air Force planning so decision makers can "make choices that increase force effectiveness within available resources." Though concerned with the future, it makes the point that planning "is actually concerned with the future consequences of current decisions." The effort was occasioned by concern over the Air Force budget and the realization that the Air Force's pursuit of its wish lists was mortgaging its future. To acquire everything it wanted and sought in the FY79 budget would require resources from then through FY83. If that wasn't an incentive for more realistic planning, what was?

The Fighter Mafia did not intend to reform the American military. They wanted to build the best air-to-air fighter for the least amount of money so the Air Force would have enough of them if ever called on in combat against the forces of the Warsaw Pact. Along the way, the Fighter Mafia's interests evolved into something that would eventually be known as the military reform movement.

The dedication and zeal with which the antagonists supported competing views was more akin to religious fervor than a rational difference of opinion. The reformers inside the Pentagon referred to their growing criticism of military design and procurement of modern weaponry and their efforts to improve it as "doing the Lord's work." In labeling it thus, they presumed the inherent righteousness of their cause, recognized that there would be martyrs to it (like Riccioni), and that they would be persecuted, right or not, by the powers that be. Their faith in their crusade would be sorely tested. Ultimately, the heresy that they represented to the orthodoxy of the military services and the defense establishment was something that could not, and would not, last. In the short run, however, Boyd and his circle of conspirators had some remarkable successes.

Retirement from the Air Force on 1 September 1975 gave Boyd the time to do even more and freed him from the shackles of the military hierarchy. It was hardly retirement at all, as Boyd continued to work in the Pentagon and put in ten to twelve hours per day, sometimes six days a week, but he did so on his terms. He wanted to work as an unpaid consultant. He was told he could not. He had to be on a pay status to gain routine access to the building. His terms were one day's pay each two weeks, the least he could get to satisfy that condition. Money is corrupting, you know.

Boyd became a special consultant in the Office of the Secretary of Defense, but he migrated back to the TAC Air Shop and the band of recruits he had formed (Chuck Spinney, Ray Leopold, Barry Watts, Jim Burton), and he kept in touch with others (Pierre Sprey, Tom Christie, Chuck Myers, Rich Riccioni). He also began to widen his circle of contacts and to include media and political contacts who were essential for the sort of guerrilla campaigns they would be fighting for the next decade on a variety of fronts.

The military reform movement was never formally founded or chartered. Indeed, even those who were identified as major participants had a hard time agreeing on when it could be said to have started and why, although all agreed on the key persons involved and the centrality of John Boyd in the effort. Essentially, it spanned the decade from 1976 to 1986. Boyd the person, known for his campaign for the F-16 on the Hill, and Boyd's ideas in the initial "Patterns of Conflict" briefing were the glue that held the movement together and gave it shape and substance. In 1981, Michael R. Gordon described Boyd's role this way:

So far, it [the military reform movement] has leaned heavily on the work of such thinkers as retired Air Force Col. John Boyd, whose four hour briefing on the "Patterns of Conflict" draws on the writing of Chinese philosopher Sun Tzu (400 B.C.) and stresses flexible command structures and rapid maneuvers to disorient the enemy. Boyd, who presents his case with the intensity of a revivalist, has briefed several Members of Congress, including Gingrich, as well as congressional staffers, Pentagon reporters and . . . military officials.[8]

The movement's origins lie in the work of the Fighter Mafia and the battle to get the F-16 approved, but its issues branched in many directions with profound military and economic impact over the next decade.

## The Context

The period from Jimmy Carter's presidency to Ronald Reagan's second term was one of intense soul-searching and turmoil within the U.S. defense establishment. A host of issues gripped the government and the nation. The Vietnam War had ended with the fall of Saigon in April 1975. There was confusion about national security strategy, national military strategy, the transition from conscription to an all-volunteer force, militarily relevant technologies, arms control, budget battles for defense versus other needs, fights among the services on individual weapons systems and just why the war had been lost. After being lied to about Vietnam, the American public was increasingly skeptical of its government's claims. In part, it was this uncertainty and confusion that gave rise to the opportunity for a military reform movement. These issues were both the saving grace that created the interest and the damning sin that doomed it to failure.

The American military had to reinvent itself after military defeat and steel itself for challenges at both ends of the conflict spectrum. ICBM inventories and capabilities, the vaunted window of vulnerability, and discussions of nuclear winter vied with revolution in Iran, wars in Afghanistan and El Salvador, and rescue missions on the *Mayaguez* (a success) and at Desert One (a failure). A series of issues seized the spotlight in the public debate in foreign policy and national security affairs. Detente gave way to both arms control and preparations for strategic nuclear war. The seemingly omnipresent but ill-applied rhetoric and policies regarding human rights under Carter gave way to Reagan's rhetoric about the Soviet Union as the "evil Empire" and "the focus of evil in the modern world."[9] Groups as disparate as the Council for a Livable World and the Catholic Bishops on the one hand argued with Paul Nitze's Committee on the Present Danger and the National Conservative Political Action Committee on the other. The CIA's unprecedented Team B was assembled to create a more dangerous profile of the Soviet enemy, while Greenpeace made headlines with its antinuclear activism.

A whole set of rather complex issues seized the headlines over the next decade. Debates over new weapons systems clashed with arms control initiatives such as the Strategic Arms Limitation Treaty process, and a new-found emphasis on ballistic missile defense and the Strategic Defense Initiative (labeled Star Wars by its detractors) all vied for attention and resolution. So too did the Nuclear Freeze Campaign and efforts at congressional procurement reform. Given growing weapons system costs and press reports of obscene payments for spare parts, there emerged a public debate on defense the likes of which hadn't been seen since the 1930s.

In the middle of this context stood Boyd and the Fighter Mafia. They had a much narrower range of concerns than those suggested above, but a broader vision about the ultimate solutions. They raised questions about affordability, readiness, performance, and sortie generation of the weapons most likely to be deployed and employed in large numbers in conventional engagements—chiefly tanks, mechanized infantry vehicles, and airplanes. Although not disdaining high-technology capabilities, they wished to be selective in adopting them and were concerned about becoming overly sophisticated in weaponry, command and control, and tactics on the battlefield. Like Carl von Clausewitz in 1832, they were concerned about the effect of fog, friction, chance, and luck in war.

Like Sun Tzu in China around 400 B.C., they were increasingly concerned that war, when it came, should be short in duration, quick in tempo, low in casualties, and strategic in consequence. They were concerned, at base, about what Chuck Spinney would later call "the plans/reality mismatch." They disliked what they considered to be "gold-plated" weaponry and state-of-the-art technology promising to achieve near-perfect performance in new multirole capabilities.

## The Debate between Technologists and Reformers

The debate has been variously characterized as one between proponents of quantity versus quality or of low-tech versus high-tech solutions. There is some truth in each, but as with most shorthand descriptions, they are distortions of reality. Perhaps the best short explanation of the schools of thought is found in Serge Herzog's *Defense Reform and Technology: Tactical Aircraft:*

Succinctly stated, reformers hold the following positions: (1) overemphasis on high technology has driven the cost of modern weapons out of control; (2) high technology has introduced a level of complexity that seriously hampers force readiness; (3) high technology is pushed in areas often irrelevant to success in combat and may even endanger its user; (4) the added increment in performance resulting from high technology rarely justifies the cost involved; and (5) high technology stretches acquisition and maturation, causing critical delays in technology integration and frequently unexpected technical problems.[10]

In opposition were those characterized as the technologists, also referred to as the planners or the establishment. They were seen and saw themselves as defenders of orthodoxy and keepers of the true religion of the faithful against the heretics. They were vocal critics of the reformers' efforts and held the following views: "(1) technology acts as a force multiplier; (2) technology provides force flexibility; (3) technology has the potential to improve cost and equipment reliability and maintainability; and (4) technology is indispensable given the alternatives."[11] The issues were—and still are—complex and not easily summarized, but these characterizations are generally correct, if limited.

The issues were essentially those raised by Boyd and Sprey regarding the lightweight fighter, expanded into a general suspicion of technology for technology's sake. Walter Kross summarized Boyd and Sprey's position:

Both men see only one way for the United States to maintain reasonable numerical parity with the air forces of the Soviet Union and its allies—keep fighter costs down and performance up to superior standards. . . . More specifically, Sprey and Boyd had three goals: Omit all subsystems not absolutely essential to the mission, resist the desire for advanced technology engines, eliminate requirements for complex avionics, high top speeds, and excessive ranges. These men have been pressing for these changes in the character of USAF TACAIR fighters since the late 1960s. In the early 1980s, when readiness became a concern, important people started to listen.[12]

Despite the antitechnology tone to some of the reformer rhetoric, neither Boyd nor Sprey were the neo-Luddites that some of their critics have suggested. They were skeptical of contractor claims and military technologists who promised great performance for only marginally greater cost. They believed in what Jim Stevenson has called the Pentagon paradox: "Benefits are inversely proportional to the promise."[13] Stevenson wrote an entire book about it using the evolution of tactical aviation in general and the development of the F-18 Hornet in particular as the case study. The reformers countered the technologists with their own sometimes overstated or overgeneralized convictions. These included arguments that the promise of technology is always greater than what is delivered (not true) and that the cost of a weapons system increases by at least the pi factor (3.14) from first estimate to final billing (closer to the mark). More particularly, they worried about an adversary with a large quantity of technologically less advanced systems and the problems these might present. As Vietnam demonstrated then and discussion of asymmetric warfare demonstrates now, those are relevant concerns.

On the other hand, not all who opposed Boyd and the reformers were either personally or professionally devoid of honor, intelligence, or a concern for America's defense. Not all those opposed to the reformers' preferences were necessarily the embodiment of evil they were sometimes portrayed to be. A military cannot dispense with technological advances as a way of achieving superiority, particularly in a democracy such as ours. As an economically powerful democratic political culture, Americans prefer firepower rather than manpower and quality rather than quantity. The two sides in the military reform debate differed less in their ends and far more in how to accomplish them. Both sides thought themselves true patriots, and they were.

As important as the supposed characteristics of the weapons system itself are the budgetary environment in which we acquire these systems and the strategic environment in which we employ them. Boyd and Sprey never developed a system in isolation or without concern for these two issues. In one of his more graphic illustrations of their concerns, Sprey created a chart that showed sorties per day per million dollars. It combined the initial cost of tactical aircraft along with their maintenance and reliability record to derive the number of planes that could fly on a given day for a given cost, in this case $1 million. The figures

**Table 3. U.S. Fighter Sortie Cost**

| Aircraft | Sorties per Day per $1 Million |
|---|---|
| F-86 | 2.1 |
| F-5 | 1.25 |
| F-4 | 0.12 |
| F-15 | 0.05 |
| F-14 | 0.028 |

*Source:* Pierre Sprey, reprinted in James Fallows, *National Defense* (New York: Vintage Books, 1982), p. 100.

were adjusted for inflation in 1978 dollars. The results, shown in table 3, reveal a steep decline from the F-86 (2.1 sorties per day per $1 million) to the F-14 (0.028). Sprey plotted these on a graph, showed that current rates were one eightieth of what they had been 35 years earlier, and called the resulting curve "The Curve of Unilateral Disarmament."[14]

Of course, sorties per $1 million is a fabricated indicator that may or may not have any bearing whatsoever on combat capability. It does, however, show the increasing cost of high-technology weaponry. It is, unfortunately, symptomatic of the debates between the two groups that their zeal to score debating points sometimes obscured the seriousness of the issues under review. The hyperbole and name-calling reached extremes at times, and misrepresentations of each other's views were rampant.[15] The passions were just as hot as the rhetoric. Cries of "foul" and "cheap shot" echoed from each side, with reason.

## The Widening Web of Conspirators

The reformers were both helped and hindered by their wide array of sympathizers, who had disparate reasons for supporting reform. In the context of the times, the Military Reform Caucus on the Hill provided a way for liberal and conservative alike to be publicly concerned with defense reform and yet not break faith with party or conviction, be they dove, hawk, chicken hawk, or cheap hawk. There was something for everybody. How could a congressman not be against fraud, waste, and abuse? Why shouldn't congressmen be concerned about how tax dollars are spent? Who would argue against improved efficiency and effectiveness in the military?

Regardless of motivation or sympathy, from the mid-1970s to the mid-1980s, they all shared some portion of a common goal—to change the way the DOD did business. But they differed sharply on what should be done. Such a disparate group (it included Pentagon insiders, both civilian and military, journalists, academics, and members of Congress) would rarely, if ever, achieve unanimity.

They had vastly different priorities, approaches, and agendas, which turned out to be the fatal flaw in the group. Size, disparate agendas, factionalism, and disinterest took their toll.[16] As long as there was good news coverage for folks back home, an issue of personal or political interest, or a chance to score points against the DOD and the executive branch, fine; but few in Congress were genuinely committed or interested over time.

Yet Boyd and the reformers understood a central reality of national security. It flowed from Boyd's affinity for trade-off analyses and his propensity for trade-off thinking. What does X mean in terms of Y? If I have only so much money, Z, how much of X or Y, or combination of the two, should I buy? The reality is that despite the intellectual progression that would have budgets flow from strategy and military capabilities determined by objectives, they are seldom developed in that manner. Far more likely is that a budget will drive strategy and that threats will determine which capabilities are deemed necessary. That being so, the central questions of defense are "How much is enough?" and "To do what?" Boyd was always concerned about trade-offs and cost because cost has both immediate and long-term consequences.

Beyond that, those considerations were the last that one should worry about. Boyd's trinity held people first, ideas second, and things third. Often, the military has as its first priority the things, the high-tech weaponry. Ideas are second, and people, in that they are trained to be interchangeable parts, a tertiary consideration. That is not meant to seem as heartless as it sounds but merely to point out that we often seem to value the capabilities of our technology more than the people who use it. Those who serve in the military are expendable for the nation's purposes. That sense of unlimited liability, laying down one's life for his or her country, is what separates being in the military from being a civilian. Boyd was convinced that one's mind was the best weapon, and hence, well-trained and well-educated people, who think well and quickly, were the most important asset, followed by ideas, in turn followed by the equipment they had at their disposal.

## Congress, the Media, and Reform

Several different groups and many different issues came to be involved in the military reform movement.[17] Congressional members of the Military Reform Caucus, formed in early 1981, initially consisted of a couple of dozen bipartisan members of the House and Senate and was chaired by Senator Gary Hart (Democrat from Colorado) and by Representative William G. Whitehurst (Republican, Virginia). Members hailed from across the nation and represented the entire political spectrum and the array of concerns about American national security. By 1983 the caucus had a letterhead and 57 members listed. By 1985 more than 100 members had signed on. Eventually, more than 130 members of Congress claimed membership in the rather loose and amorphous organization. Still, a group with over a quarter of the Congress is hardly a lightweight in the political arena.

Its original executive committee included Representatives Norman D. Dicks (D, Washington) and Newt Gingrich (R, Georgia, later Speaker of the House), and Senators Sam Nunn (D, Georgia, chair of the Senate Armed Services Committee), Gary Hart (D, Colorado, former presidential candidate), and William S. Cohen (R, Maine, who became President Clinton's token Republican in the Cabinet as Secretary of Defense). Representative Richard Cheney (R, Wyoming, Secretary of Defense under George Bush) was also a member. Those who were particularly active included a retired Air Force officer turned Republican congressman from Oregon, Denny Smith; Senator Charles Grassley (R, Iowa); and Senator Nancy Kassebaum (R, Kansas). They could hardly be described as liberal, antimilitary pacifists. Congress's entry into the fray was heralded by a series of articles, written by the politically odd combination of Gary Hart and Newt Gingrich, that criticized defense policy and publicly stated the case for reform.[18]

Equally important was a coterie of sympathetic journalists that Boyd and company had cultivated over the years. They knew they could get information from Boyd and that he would give them advance warning on how situations were likely to play out. Boyd knew he could count on them for publicity when he needed it and could thus go outside the system (military and political) to get things public. Jim Fallows received much of his information for his seminal article, entitled "The Muscle-Bound Super Power" in *Atlantic Monthly* (October 1979), from Boyd and company. It launched the public portion of the military reform movement. A major step in the critical debate (and in Fallows's career) was the publication a year later of his best-selling book *National Defense*, which expanded on the same themes raised in the article and publicized Boyd and the Fighter Mafia's views to the outside world.[19]

Meanwhile, both the use of the term and its implications grew. " 'Military Reform,' however, is more than a press fancy," wrote Theodore J. Crackel in 1983. "West Point has hosted a three-day conference on the subject; and in Washington, members of Congress have formed a joint House/Senate caucus dedicated to it. Meanwhile, there have been a host of books dealing both generally and specifically with the subject. 'Military Reform' may prove one of the most powerful sets of ideas of our time."[20] It became a staple for the press and the public. John Fialka at the *Wall Street Journal*, Michael Getler at the *Washington Post*, Walter Isaacson and Hugh Sidey at *Time*, and Michael Gordon at the *Na-

*tional Journal* in the early 1980s all wrote stories chronicling the reform movement's clout, trials, issues, and positions. Their coverage gave a dimension to the debate that was hard for opponents to ignore or to combat successfully. Even some of the military's own publications (*Air University Review* and the *Marine Corps Gazette* in particular) published the reformers' views and devoted large sections to the debates that they began.

Inside the Pentagon, Boyd kept briefing his constantly evolving "Patterns of Conflict," and he, Sprey, and others kept looking for allies and converts. In time, they ended up with a diverse group composed of some Air Force officers, some Marines interested in military history and strategy, some young Navy officers, people at the U.S. Army's Training and Doctrine Command, consultants at Beltway-bandit think tanks, and the occasional academic, all of whom became familiar with the sort of thinking that Boyd and others were doing. Slowly, a following emerged. Added to them were others trying to take on the system; people like Tom Amlie and Ernest Fitzgerald originally made charges from inside the system, while Dina Rasor and Andrew Cockburn fought with insider information as they published books and articles from outside.[21]

Equally important, if not more so, were members of personal staff and committee staff on Capitol Hill who provided access to others throughout the government and the press corps. Catalysts of the process, they played a particularly important role in spreading the ideas to people who could in turn make a difference. Among the staff members who helped spread the word of the Fighter Mafia and reformers inside the Pentagon were Bob Weed and Mike Burns, who worked for Representative Newt Gingrich; Bill Lind, who worked first for Senator Robert Taft Jr. of Ohio and, after he lost his reelection bid, for Senator Gary Hart of Colorado; Charlie Murphy, who worked for Representative Jack Edwards; Dave Evans, who worked for Representative Bill Whitehurst; and Winslow Wheeler, who held a variety of positions on the Hill and later at the Government Accounting Office.

Since it was taxpayer money at issue, nearly any member of Congress, regardless of committee assignment, could initiate another story printed in the press about various outrages that should be investigated. This would generate more heat and eventually fire as another member decided to have his committee or subcommittee hold hearings on the matter. That would then generate a committee report or legislation to change some aspect of the way DOD was doing business. It worked like a charm for years. Though it caused a great deal of embarrassment at times and publicized some of the more egregious examples of waste, inefficiency, and greed, it did not alter a fundamentally flawed procurement system. Business as usual prevailed.

There were a few successes, some salient failures—a mixed bag. That was all that could be expected from the ad hoc alliance of political forces involved. When they won, they won big. When they lost, as they ultimately did, they were overwhelmed by a system entrenched in its established habits of pork, politics, profits, and promotions. No doubt, Gary Hart's ill-fated dalliance and his abortive presidential campaign hurt the movement, but it did have some success, nonetheless. Strangely, the realm of individual weapons systems and military tactics was where the reformers had their greatest impact. Actions taken to cancel the Division Air Defense gun (DIVAD), to improve the Ticonderoga class of cruisers and the Bradley Fighting Vehicle, and the general promotion of maneuver warfare could all be judged successes. An overall reform of the budget process, the procurement system, or contracting practices, however, proved beyond their reach. There is only the occasional rebuke, such as the cancellation of the A-12 by Secretary of Defense Dick Cheney, an early member of the caucus on military reform.[22] The military services rarely cancel any of their own programs. That usually takes action by the Secretary of Defense or a cutoff of funds by Congress. Over the last thirty years, similar recommendations made by numerous blue-ribbon panels and presidential commissions to reform the procurement system have been largely ignored and routinely ineffectual. The reformers fared no better.

## Paranoia, Reprisals, and Legacies

Much of the military reform movement went well beyond Boyd directly, but he seemed always there, in the background, the éminence grise of the movement. His counsel, advice, and contacts on the Hill and in the press were on call. One of the more salient battles fought by the reformers was over the issue of weapons testing and their desire for accurate, unbiased testing of new military hardware with proper oversight by someone other than the service procuring the item. It was hardly an unreasonable request and one for which there are countless rules and regulations, but the politics of the process were vicious. Though some might find it melodramatic, Jim Burton has described the day-to-day environment in the Pentagon; as he says, even Machiavelli would be a rank amateur in some of the contests waged there.

Coalitions form and dissolve overnight between the strangest of bedfellows. Dire enemies momentarily join forces to battle someone else, then resume their old fight as if nothing had happened. The only way to get a decision to stand is to "shoot the losers"—line up everyone who opposes the decision and shoot them down. Otherwise, they begin to undermine the decision before the ink is dry on the paper. Quite often, the real debate begins only after a major decision has been made. Time and again, I have listened to senior officials express total frustration when issues they thought were settled suddenly reappeared.[23]

Burton says he took Boyd's advice in coping with it: "Jim, you may not win, but you can't give the bastards a free ride. Make them work for it."

Burton was military assistant to three secretaries of the Air Force from June 1979 through June 1982. In that position, he did all he could to follow Boyd's teachings and make sure bad news was delivered as well as good and to keep the system honest. The word got out that he was not a team player, and he and his old associates (Boyd, Sprey, Spinney) had to be careful about being seen with each other, leaving phone messages for Burton, or what could be said on the telephone. They devised a system of aliases to address each other. Sprey became Mr. Grau. Boyd became Mr. Arbuthnott. Burton asked Boyd where he had gotten that name; Boyd replied that it had just come to him. Months later, Burton was rereading Anthony Cave Brown's book on allied intelligence in World War II, *Bodyguard of Lies*. The title is from a Churchill quotation, "In war, truth is so important it must be protected by a bodyguard of lies." As Burton read he encountered a picture (across from page 276) of the London Controlling Section, "the secret organization formed by Churchill to plan the stratagems that would leave Hitler 'puzzled as well as beaten.'"[24] One of the nine members in the photo was a Commander James Arbuthnott (RN). Boyd's mind and its habit of forming appropriate connections had scored again.

Fearing their telephones were tapped and that at certain times those assigned to their offices might keep track of conversations, the reformers resorted to meeting in front of the flags in the A ring of the Pentagon's second floor (where the NATO displays and flags were prominently placed). Occasionally, they would meet in the parking lot of the Pentagon so as not to be overheard. All this subterfuge was for good reason, as Burton would later find out. Boyd's daughter, Mary, recounts the experience of calling home from school one day and being connected instead to the Pentagon switchboard. Boyd figured his home phone was being tapped, but someone who wanted him to know had intentionally bungled the job.

The group's concerns were anathema to the Reagan administration and to the defense buildup under way. The charges and countercharges, politics and leaks, personal and political leverage applied, only grew in intensity. Perhaps the high-water mark of the military reform movement came in the spring of 1983, when *Time* magazine wanted to do a cover story on Boyd and the movement. Boyd and others met regularly with a reporting team and the magazine's editorial board at the Washington Bureau offices. Boyd knew that a great many people were risking far more than he was. He was retired and living off his military pension. Others were dependent on their jobs for their families' well-being. He couldn't see them sacrificed in the process.

Chief among them was Franklin C. "Chuck" Spinney, a young analyst in the TAC Air shop, former Air Force captain, and protégé of Boyd. Spinney had been systematically assessing the Pentagon's weapons procurement practices in general, those of the Air Force in particular. His briefings would become almost as famous as Boyd's, and by virtue of longevity as well as his Internet-assisted network, he has become an even bigger pain in the ass than Boyd. When *Time* approached Boyd to be the subject of that 1983 cover story, he demurred. Why not appeal to the public with a David and Goliath story that will both inform them and tug at their heartstrings a bit? Why not put 37-year-old Chuck Spinney on the cover and leave the old warhorse Boyd in the background? The editorial board agreed, and thus was born the Chuck Spinney cover of *Time* on 7 March 1983.[25] It was the cheapest and most important life insurance policy Boyd could arrange for his most loyal disciple. DOD could never afford to take the heat for firing Spinney in the future. The fallout would be too great.

That article was a national public indictment of the Defense Department and the way it did its business. In the middle of Ronald Reagan's first term as president, it questioned the entire Reagan approach to defense, its definition of the threat and understanding of the strategic environment, its national security strategy and weapons procurement programs—everything about the Republican defense buildup. It had sidebars on the ridiculous extent of mil specs (military specifications) for products that DOD bought, profiles of Spinney and of Bob Dilger (who had designed the ammunition for the GAU-8 on the A-10), and on gold-plated weapons (the B-1, the Bradley Fighting Vehicle, the F-18, and the Sparrow missile). There was also a picture of a Republican senator who was listed as a reform leader and prominently featured in the article: Senator William Cohen, later Secretary of Defense. How times change.

Boyd and the military reform movement provided nearly all the information. It was one of the reformers' most impressive coups in the public relations war. It led to much more publicity, but the victory was only temporary. The system carried on much the way it had before, despite the occasional pinpricks of disclosure and embarrassment over some of its practices. Senators Hart and Nunn have retired from the Senate. Chuck Spinney still works in the Pentagon. Although a few reformers continue to take on the system, most of the group have moved on to other jobs and different issues. Many of the debates are still the same, with little progress being made over the last two decades. The embers of reform may glow, but the fires have been quenched.

## An Assessment

The bottom line on the defense reform movement is hard to establish. It is a mixed bag of people, issues, successes, and failures. Is American national security better off for the experience or worse? The answer would probably depend more on one's bias and conviction than a rational assessment. There are many who see failure, and they may well be right.[26]

The many critics and criticisms of the military reform movement are not totally without merit, but the movement was broad and its members (formal and informal) numerous. The movement's causes and subcauses reflected a diverse set of opinions about weapons systems, commentaries on doctrine, and readings or misreadings of military history by amateur and professional alike. I do not seek to label the reformers right and their opponents wrong on all issues. Many of the critiques of the larger effort at military reform have some validity; so too do some of the claims of the reformers. Both had their zealots and excessive rhetoric. A case-by-case analysis of claim and counterclaim is beyond the scope of this summary. Suffice it to say both sides overreached at times.

Reformers think of William Perry (the former director of Defense Research and Engineering, described as a man who never met a technology he didn't like) as Secretary of Defense and know that the last fifteen years have reversed whatever modest gains they may have made. Technologists can point to the B-2, work on the airborne laser, JSTARS, and a host of studies on the future (*Spacecast 2020, New World Vistas, Joint Vision 2010, Air Force 2025*) and know that American eggs rest squarely in the technological basket. There are still some, both in uniform and out, who ask questions reminiscent of the reformers. Just how much value is an F-22 against an asymmetric threat represented by a mujahideen and a goat? Can the Apache helicopter or the B-1B ever be used effectively in sustained combat? Has the technology of deception surpassed the technology of timely verification?

Perhaps more important than some subjective test of success or failure is a recognition that what was important about the military reform movement was that it occurred and tried to keep the system honest. Such a movement (it was not an organization, a committee, or a lobby) would be difficult to institutionalize and sustain. Many of the systems the reformers railed against are now the backbone of American military might, but many perform better or cost less than they would have without reformer questions and publicity. The A-10 ground attack plane, a major success for the reformers and spectacularly effective in the Gulf War, has been relegated to the reserves and mostly mothballed. Even the successes are short-lived. It is also clear that the scrutiny the reformers provided is a necessary antidote for the less efficient and effective business-as-usual doldrums with which all large organizations must contend. The problem is, there are no John Boyds around to give a new reform movement life and orchestrate its success. We do have Boyd's thought, and that is a good place to begin. The Department of Defense, in its civilian and military guises, needs to reexamine the fit, or lack of it, among all the components of the puzzle. These include the environment, budgetary support in the coming years, national security strategy, national military strategy, and our training, organization, and equipment to accomplish the entire range of military missions.

Although there are many loyal, dedicated, exceptionally well-trained officers, enlisted personnel, and civilians in the Department of Defense, from time to time it is healthy, even necessary, to challenge the way things are done, who is in control, and how decisions are made (or not made) in "providing for the common defense." The decade of the 1980s was one of those times. So too is the first decade of the twenty-first century. To applaud some of the work of the military reform movement is in no way meant to demean the contributions of the men and women who have served their country as part of the all-volunteer forces during that period. It is meant to question the politics in the process of decision-making on national defense.

Whatever the success or failure of individual programs and weapons systems, all pales in comparison with the systemic problems in defense planning, budgeting, and procurement. All three systems are broken, a fact that most senior general officers will readily admit in private, but they cannot agree on how to fix them in public. At least there is more awareness, and there have been some changes in thinking about the problems encountered. Whether they last or have any real impact depends as much on the simultaneous appearance of a coterie of mavericks in the military, the Office of the Secretary of Defense, the Hill, and the executive branch as on any injunctions to pursue efficiency and effectiveness. To change the system in any lasting and meaningful way would require a string of John Boyds, all strategically positioned at the right place for a decade or more. Even then, true reform would be doubtful and not likely to happen. The system endures.

# 8.                    Patterns of Conflict

The significance of Boyd's theory is that these principles, based on the records of combat over more than two millennia, lead to a demand for a military establishment that is very different from the one the United States has created.

James Fallows, *National Defense*, 1981

**D**uring the first year of his retirement (in September 1975), Boyd did a lot of reading and thinking. His investigations led him to write, almost exactly a year after his retirement, the only piece he ever wrote in prose outside the Air Force. A sixteen-page essay entitled simply "Destruction and Creation," it is his sacred text. On one level it is deceptively simple. To create, we have to destroy. If humans aren't willing to break the bonds of convention and destroy the old definitions, perceptions, and ways of doing things, then we are not likely to create a truly novel breakthrough, concept, product, or methodology to produce change. But the work is much more profound than that.

He finished an early draft of the basic concepts in March 1976 but then took nearly six months to refine his thoughts. "Destruction and Creation" is the culmination of a quest to find scientific, mathematical, and logical verification for principles Boyd knew intuitively to be true. Thus tested and refined, it became the basis for most of his thought thereafter. It took a year to refine and condense his thoughts to the final sixteen pages. The difficulty of that experience probably deterred him from writing prose. Though it could have been the subject of a long book, Boyd never succumbed to entreaties to expand "Destruction and Creation."

Where to place it in the large body of "A Discourse" troubled Boyd for years. For him, as the basis of his thought, it came first. In "Destruction and Creation" Boyd explains the importance of his scientific trinity of Gödel, Heisenberg, and the second law of thermodynamics. The abstractions and their implications, discussed in some detail, were for him absolutely essential to his cosmology. Yet, starting with "Destruction and Creation" turned off most audiences, so he left it at the end of "A Discourse" for nearly ten years. Even there, it seemed out of place and noticeably different in tone and style from the other components.

The second law of thermodynamics states that all observed natural processes generate entropy. As Boyd explained it, "entropy is a concept that represents the potential for doing work, the capacity for taking action or the degree of confusion and disorder associated with any physical or information activity. High entropy implies a low potential for doing work, a low capacity for taking action or a high degree of confusion and disorder. Low entropy implies just the opposite."[1] The tendency is for entropy to increase in a system that is closed or cannot communicate with external systems or environments. Over time, entropy increases, energy dissipates, efficiency decreases, and confusion and disorder increase. Thus the character or nature of a system, its consistency, does not remain constant and is unpredictable.

Werner Heisenberg (1901–1976) was a German physicist, a founder of quantum theory, and a Nobel Prize winner (1932) for his work in nuclear physics and quantum theory. Noted too for his work in matrix mechanics, he is perhaps best known for his uncertainty or indeterminacy principle. It states essentially that it is impossible to determine both the position and momentum of subatomic particles with high accuracy. That is, uncertainty, rather than certainty, lies at the base of our physical universe and theoretical understanding of it. The effect of this principle is to change the laws of physics to relative statements instead of absolute certainties. We can have a proximate understanding based on measurement, but not an absolute one.

Kurt Gödel (1906–1978) was a Czech-American mathematician and logician whose most important contribution was made in 1931, though it was not fully appreciated until much later. He demonstrated proof of a theorem stating that the various branches of mathematics are based in part on propositions that are not provable within mathematics itself, though they can be proved by logic external to mathematics. That is, it is impossible to embrace mathematics within a single system of logic. Gödel proved that any consistent system is incomplete. There are statements of concepts that are true within the system that cannot be deduced from postulates within the system. In Boyd's words, "Gödel's proof indirectly shows that in order to determine the consistency of any new system we must construct or uncover another system beyond it. Over and over this cycle must be repeated to determine the consistency of more and more elaborate systems."[2] Thus, there is always something beyond the system — no explanation is self-contained.

Boyd's "Destruction and Creation" essay is based on the synthesis of those three insights. It is cosmic in its sweep and fundamental in its insight. It is an elegant yet simple proof of how we learn and why one must be able to destroy before one can create. Boyd proved to himself that logic, mathematics, and physics all proffered explanations of the same basic notion. Taken together these three notions support the idea that any inward-oriented and continued effort to improve the match-up of a concept with observed reality will only increase the degree of mismatch. Boyd saw Gödel, Heisenberg, and the second law as keys to how to think, how to compete successfully, and how to adapt and survive.

Boyd thought abstractly and assumed others were equally capable. Many are not. There are no concrete examples in his essay to help explain it to others. That was not his purpose. "Destruction and Creation" is more a conversation with himself than it is an essay for others. His purpose was to seek rigorous scientific corroboration for his intuitive insights developed over the years and to prove to himself that they were logically sound, not some harebrained set of insights known only to him without real weight or substance.

"Destruction and Creation" represents the didactic approach Boyd took toward analysis and synthesis. He looked at things in terms of their opposites, both ends of the continuum, and trade-offs between the extremes. Black-white, on-off, up-down, slow-fast, and countless other pairings dot his thinking routinely. Boyd could not deal with only half a concept. He had to explore its opposite, an alternative, and, more important, the relationship between the two. Examining the gray area between came naturally. It was his way of thinking. This led him with greater frequency than most to challenge the so-called conventional wisdom and to assess the opposite interpretation. Why is a variable sweep wing better than a fixed wing of the right size and shape? Shouldn't we be as concerned about the high probability but lower risk of threats posed by guerrilla war as we are about the low probability but very high risks of nuclear war? What are the trade-offs between quantity and quality? To Boyd, such questions came naturally.

## Close Air Support and Military History

Boyd would devote the next 20 years to exploring the implications of these simply stated ideas in a variety of ways. "A Discourse on Winning and Losing" is the result. It started out as "Patterns of Conflict" and grew from a presentation of one and a half hours to thirteen hours plus. It was a discourse, a conversation, refined over and over again through nineteen different versions, and it was never quite right. It was always tentative. The fruits of the effort contained in "A Discourse" are valuable insights into ancient problems. How one thinks about such things is critical. The realization that coping with uncertainty, imprecision, and mismatches is a fundamental part of reality is a good place to begin. "Destruction and Creation" defines the initial terms of reference for the continuing inquiry.

What exposed Boyd to the need to study war in its historical context was the experience he had with Pierre Sprey while working on the plans for the A-10 Thunderbolt II (or Warthog), the Air Force's close air support attack plane. The A-10 is not even painted like an Air Force plane; it wears the mottled green, brown, and black of Army camouflage. In that sense, it looks more like a tank, not a jet aircraft. It is slow, ugly, and somewhat awkward. Its primary mission in life is to kill tanks. It is armored and rugged in order to survive heavy ground fire at low level in a lethal battlefield environment. Developed in the early 1970s, it was the first product of competitive fly-offs, selected in January 1973, two years before the F-16.

The A-10 was a pet project of Pierre Sprey's, although Sprey maintains that Boyd's trade-off analyses, energy maneuverability theory, and views on warfare in general were as influential in its development as Sprey's expertise on ground attack.[3] Slow and not very maneuverable, it was the product of careful research on how best to kill tanks and support ground troops. The A-10 has a titanium-armored area to protect the pilot and a high loiter time to provide on-call fire support with laser-guided bombs and Maverick missiles. It also has its own gun, the GAU-8, a seven-barrel, rotary, 30-mm cannon using spent uranium cores for armor penetration.[4]

Back to Boyd and how the A-10 caused him to study military history. The reformers managed to get access to the experts in close air support and armor operations, the Germans of World War II. As a part of the contract for the ammunition developed for the GAU-8 gun, several former Nazi officers were brought clandestinely from Germany in the early 1970s to CIA safe houses on Maryland's eastern shore. Boyd, Sprey, and others interviewed Stuka pilots and German armor commanders. They wanted to know the time a pilot required to find, target, and kill a tank from the air without being shot down and other tactical information that would prove useful in designing the A-10 and its gun, armor, and ordnance. Encouraged by the badgering of Pierre Sprey, Boyd began to investigate German military tactics and strategy in World War II.

Not only did the roots and causes of World War II lie in World War I, so too did many of the weapons, tactics, and strategies that evolved in the interwar period. That led him back to World War I and from there to the technological advances of the nineteenth century. From there, he had to go back to Carl von Clausewitz and Baron de Jomini and the great era of Napoleonic warfare on which they were based. Similarly, he read backward chronologically through early modern Europe and the Middle Ages. He made side trips into the campaigns of the Mongols, Byzantines, and Ottomans. He read the theorists and military histories of the Romans and Carthaginians, the Greeks, and the Persians, and eventually through ancient warfare in the Middle East all the way to Sun Tzu in China nearly 2,500 years ago. Studying military history in this manner made him focus on what had remained the same rather than on what had changed, which is what tends to emerge if one reads history forward. Going backward gave him a sense of the continuity as well as the significant changes that had occurred, but clearly emphasized the continuity. After a year and a half of study, the beginnings of the "Patterns of Conflict" briefing emerged. This is still the core and largest component of his magnum opus. Originally a little over an hour long, the presentation gradually grew to nearly six hours. Only the most serious listeners possessed the interest and stamina to sit through it.

## Patterns of Conflict: An Overview

Reversing Boyd's course of study, "Patterns of Conflict" proceeds in a generally chronological fashion and focuses on the evolution of war fighting. It is long, 193 vu-graphs to be exact, including sources. Wide-ranging and complex, it combines an immense amount of historical data, insightful interpretations, and provocative questions. It is a discourse about the events, people, issues, social forces, political motivations, and technologies of the past and how they affect the process of winning and losing. Even the Army War College at Carlisle Barracks, Pennsylvania, was impressed. The college's commandant, Maj. Gen. Jack N. Merritt, admitted, "It's a real tour de force. He really is one of the most innovative and original guys I've ever had anything to do with, and he created a lot of excitement up here among strategists and historians."[5] Hardly a ready-reference document, it nonetheless became the touchstone of the military reform movement and the means by which the philosophy of the movement was spread.

Boyd stated his mission: to make manifest the nature of moral, mental, and physical conflict; to discern a pattern for successful operations; to help generalize tactics and strategy; to find a basis for grand strategy. The intent was to unveil the character of conflict, survival, and conquest. Hardly either simple or modest in goal, Boyd plunged ahead nonetheless. The essence, for Boyd, was human perception, not weapons or the circumstances. "Machines don't fight wars. Terrain doesn't fight wars. Humans fight wars. You must get into the minds of humans. That's where the battles are won."[6] He dealt with both ends of the scale—from minute details calculated to multiple decimal places to the grand sweep of human history—with equal interest and zeal, but it was the big questions that were the important ones and the most interesting.

He began with what he knew best: air-to-air combat, along with the generalization that what was needed was a fighter that can lose energy and gain energy more quickly while outturning the enemy. In other words, a fighter must be able to pick and choose engagement opportunities, yet have fast transient characteristics that can be used to force an overshoot by an attacker. One must change speed, direction, or altitude faster than an adversary can, to vary the tempo of the engagement and thereby gain an advantage. Expanding these notions, the idea of fast transients (changing quickly from one direction, maneuver, speed, or altitude to another) suggests that to win, one should operate at a faster tempo or rhythm than one's adversaries.

Boyd would come to describe that as getting inside the adversary's observation-orientation-decision-action time cycle, or OODA loop. Why? Such activity will make us appear ambiguous (unpredictable), thereby generating confusion and disorder among our adversaries. This will cause our adversaries to be unable to generate mental images that agree with the menacing and faster transient rhythm or patterns they are competing against. Boyd sees successful application of this approach in the German blitzkrieg against France in 1940, the engagements between the F-86 and the MiG-15 in Korea in 1951–1953, and in the Israeli raid on Entebbe in 1976. Such is the emphasis on the OODA loop, aerial combat, and the importance of energy maneuverability that the first version of "Patterns of Conflict" was actually entitled "Asymmetric Fast Transients."

Boyd sought to develop a new conception of action to exploit operations and weapons to inhibit an adversary's capacity to adapt. This simultaneously compressed time and stretched out time to generate a favorable mismatch, impairing the adversary's ability to shape or adapt to change. The goal was to collapse the adversary's system into confusion and disorder by causing him to over- or underreact to activity that appeared simultaneously menacing and ambiguous, chaotic, or misleading. This is exactly what was achieved in the opening hours of the air campaign in the Gulf War. Saddam Hussein's forces had their eyes (radar), ears and mouth (communications), and hence their brains (command and control) greatly impaired, so they could not respond effectively to coalition attacks.

Boyd's recipe for generating confusion and disorder in air-to-air and air-to-ground operations combined quick, clear scanning sensors with a suppressed or distorted signature of one's own forces. Quick shoot fire control systems and high-speed weapons enhance the effect. This recipe was improved by planes with supercruise speed; rapid energy gain and loss capability, high turn rates, and low turn radii; high pitch, roll, and yaw rates; and enhanced ease of control. These characteristics placed in the hands of well-trained pilots with precision-guided munitions would be hard to defeat. Admitting such and valuing the technology that could provide these characteristics gives the lie to the criticism that Boyd was antitechnology.

Next, Boyd turned from the specifics of air-to-air combat to the more general. What follows in the briefing is a series of abstractions and historical snapshots to illustrate his points. The goal of human beings, said Boyd, is not merely to survive but also to survive on our own terms. Thus there emerges a rather Hobbesian view of life that involves conflict, survival, and conquest. It conjures up a Darwinian view of existence ruled by natural selection and survival of the fittest. Boyd's review of the literature on these approaches led him to the following impressions. It is advantageous to possess a variety of responses that can be applied rapidly to gain sustenance, avoid danger, and diminish an adversary's capacity for independent action. Organisms must cooperate or, better yet, harmonize their activities in their endeavors to survive in an organic synthesis. To shape and adapt to change, one cannot be passive; indeed, one must take the initiative. The combination of variety, rapidity, harmony, and initiative—particularly their interaction—seems to be the key that permits one to shape and adapt to an ever-changing environment. These qualities aid in getting inside an adversary's OODA loop. With these insights in mind, Boyd began his historical review of conflict, theorists, and practitioners of the art of war.

### The Ancient World

Boyd began with Sun Tzu and *The Art of War*, around 400 b.c.[7] As Boyd summarized Sun Tzu, his main themes could be reduced to the following: One needs a certain harmony of ends and means if one wishes to succeed. Deception is critical to defeating the enemy, as is swiftness of action. A certain flow is essential, along with fluidity of action and the need for modulating dispersion and concentration artfully. Last, surprise and shock are significant factors in attaining victory. The combination of these themes or traits explains the way one should attempt to win with the least cost and the greatest benefit. Guile, movement, training, and quickness are seen as essential to success.

Boyd also characterized Sun Tzu's strategy. First, one should probe the enemy's organization and disposition of forces to unmask his strengths, weaknesses, patterns of movement, and intentions. Next, using these, one should endeavor to shape the enemy's perception to manipulate his plans and actions. The most successful strategy is to attack the enemy's plans or strategy; second, his alliances; third, his army. Attack his cities only if there is no other alternative, for that is the most costly and least efficient strategy. The key to successful attack is the skillful use of cheng and ch'i maneuvers. Cheng and ch'i are fundamental concepts to both Sun Tzu and Boyd. They are abstractions that are difficult to explain in the fullness of their meaning. Basically, they involve deceptive tactics. The enemy is confronted and fixed by cheng (orthodox) forces and then defeated by the application of ch'i (unorthodox) forces.[8] Cheng and ch'i are the yin and yang of tactics and strategy, but should be applied together to achieve the desired effect. One wants to identify, nurture, and exploit mismatches and hurl strength against weakness. The ultimate test of success for Sun Tzu was to subdue the enemy without having to fight him. At all costs, one should avoid a protracted war.

As Boyd reviewed ancient warfare, the strategies and successes of such commanders as Alexander, Hannibal, Belisarius, Genghis Khan, and Tamerlane, he saw a certain consistency with the ideas of Sun Tzu, and some exceptions. To Boyd, it appeared that Western commanders were more concerned with winning the battle. Eastern commanders, on the other hand, were closer to Sun Tzu in attempting to shatter the adversary prior to the battle. In any event, there was a strong reliance on cheng and ch'i maneuver schemes, which were used to expose an adversary's vulnerabilities and weaknesses (a la cheng) for exploitation and decisive stroke (via ch'i).

Boyd then examined in detail what he called the tactical themes from about 300 B.C. to A.D. 1400. These were characterized by the use of light troops equipped with bows, javelins, light swords, and so on, who performed reconnaissance, screening, and swirling hit-and-run actions. Their tactics were used to unmask enemy dispositions and activities, cloud one's own dispositions, and confuse enemy operations. Heavy troops equipped with lances, bows, and swords and protected by armor and shields would charge and smash either thinned out and scattered troops or disordered but massed enemy formations generated by interaction with light troops. Or they would menace enemy formations to hold them in rigid arrays, thereby making them vulnerable to the missiles of swirling light troops. Light and heavy troops in appropriate combination pursued, enveloped, and mopped up isolated remnants of enemy host.

The basic idea he took from this was the combination of maneuver by light troops and thrust by heavy troops to confuse, break up, and smash enemy formations. Boyd saw these patterns played out time and time again in the Battle of Marathon (490 B.C.), the Battle of Leuctra (371 B.C.), the Battle of Arbela (331 B.C.), and the Battle of Cannae (216 B.C.), among others. In every case, the victor emphasized an unequal distribution of forces to gain a local advantage and decisive leverage to collapse adversary resistance, a tactical mismatch that became a strategic one. What about other factors, wondered Boyd. What of doubt, fear, anxiety? How could you frighten people into submission?

Boyd next focused on Genghis Khan and the Mongols. He found the key asymmetries in their victories to be based on superior mobility, communication, intelligence, and leadership. They were able to employ widely separated strategic maneuvers, with appropriate stratagems, baited retreats, hard-hitting tactical thrusts, and swirling envelopments, to uncover and exploit adversary vulnerabilities. The Mongols used multiple avenues of advance, strategically and tactically, to intimidate their adversaries and confuse them. They seemed to come from all quarters of the compass. In conjunction with the clever, calculated use of propaganda and terror, they played on the adversary's doubts, fears, and superstitions, undermining his resolve and destroying his will to resist. If a city would not surrender, it would be taken, sacked, and all inside killed. They would then build a pyramid of the skulls of their victims to serve as a warning to others who might resist.

These tactics proved very effective in the creation, preservation, and expansion of the Mongol empire. The Mongols, though frequently outnumbered, managed to maneuver in widely scattered arrays without being defeated in detail. Why? How? The combination of superior mobility, communications, intelligence, and leadership with propaganda and terror allowed them to operate inside their adversary's OODA loop. They appeared to be coming out of nowhere, yet to be everywhere. They not only created vulnerabilities and weaknesses, said Boyd, but also played on moral factors that drained away resolve, produced panic, and brought about collapse. These may have been as important as the military maneuvers in defeating their enemies.

## The Napoleonic Synthesis

Boyd then jumped to the eighteenth-century theoreticians, Saxe, Bourcet, Guibert, and Du Tail. The themes he uncovered in their works included the importance of a plan with several branches, a concern for the mobility and fluidity of forces as well as for cohesion, and the careful orchestration of dispersion and concentration. Napoleon was deeply influenced by the ideas of these men, and he set about to exploit them. In his early campaigns as a general, he successfully combined variety, rapidity, and harmony to achieve ambiguity, deception, and rapid, easy movement to surprise and defeat fractions of superior forces. Boyd also saw a tragic flaw in his later campaigns as emperor. Napoleon began to exchange variety and rapidity for the rigid uniformity of massed direct artillery fire, dense infantry columns, and heavy cavalry going against regions of strong resistance. Those preferences resulted in ever-higher casualties and crippling manpower costs that could not be borne forever.

At the same time (the eighteenth and early nineteenth century) there were other trends under way. American colonists, Spanish guerrillas, and Russian irregulars all devised their own tactics against the more formal set-piece approaches of drill and movement used by the British and the French. They exploited variety and rapidity and the environmental advantages they could wrest from terrain, weather, and darkness with considerable success. The destruction of General Braddock's forces in North America, the Peninsular campaign against Napoleon, and the long French retreat from Moscow are all examples. Perhaps the best example of a more modern guerrilla campaign is that of Gen. Paul Emil von Lettow-Vorbeck, commander of forces in German East Africa from 1914 to 1918. He tied down a British force ten to twenty times the size of his own and, though greatly outnumbered, carried out effective offensive operations for four years without major defeat until the war's end. What we have come to call asymmetric warfare seemed to be the norm in many cases. What was conventional for one side was guerrilla warfare for its opponent, a reality highlighted by U.S. involvement in Vietnam.

Boyd assessed Napoleon's art of war and its strategic themes. Napoleon sought to use a unified or single line of operations as the basis for mutual support between separated adjacent and follow-on units. He would then menace and try to seize his adversary's communications to isolate the opposing forces from outside support or reinforcement. He would force them to fight under unfavorable circumstances by using a fraction of his force to divert the adversary's attention with feints, demonstrations, and pinning maneuvers. Napoleon would then exploit "exterior maneuvers" against exposed flanks or "interior maneuvers" through a weak front to place the bulk of his forces in the adversary's flank or rear. He set up supporting bases of operation, alternative lines of communication, and kept some safe and open as a basis to maintain freedom of maneuver. The purpose of this choreography of the dance of battle was simple: it was designed to destroy the enemy's army.

Napoleon utilized both a strategy of envelopment and a strategy of central position. Boyd discerned, as did David Chandler and others, a major distinction between the earlier and later tactics and strategies employed by Napoleon. Chandler characterized Napoleon's early tactics:

The action was opened by a cloud of sharpshooters, some mounted, some on foot, who were sent forward to carry out a general rather than a minutely regulated mission; they proceeded to harass the enemy, escaping from his superior numbers by their mobility, from the effect of his cannon by their dispersal. They were constantly relieved to ensure that the fire did not slacken, and they also received considerable reinforcement to increase their overall effect. . . . Once the chink in the foe's armour had been revealed, . . . the horse artillery would gallop up and open fire with canister at close range. The attacking force would meantime be moving up in the indicated direction, the infantry advancing in column, the cavalry in regiments or squadrons, ready to make its presence felt anywhere or everywhere as required. Then, when the hail of enemy bullets and canon balls began to slacken . . . the soldiers would begin to run forward, those in front ranks crossing their bayonets, as the drums beat the charge; the sky would ring a thousand battle cries constantly repeated: "En avant, Vive la Republique!"[9]

Napoleon's later tactics are described as:

At the outset, a heavy bombardment would be loosed against the enemy formations, causing fearful losses if they failed to seek shelter, and generally lowering their power of resistance. Under cover of this fire, swarms of *voltigeurs* would advance to within musketry range and add a disconcerting "nuisance" element by sniping at officers and the like. This preliminary phase would be followed by a series of heavy cavalry and infantry attacks. The secret of these was careful timing and coordination. The first cavalry charges were designed to defeat the hostile cavalry and compel the enemy infantry to form squares, thereby reduce fire in any one direction and enable the columns to get to close grips before the enemy could resume his linear formation. The infantry (deployed or not) and accompanying horse artillery would then blaze a gap in the enemy formation and finally the cavalry would sweep forward, again, to exploit the breakthrough.[10]

Why is there such a difference in the manner in which Napoleon fought?

In his early tactics, Napoleon was able to capitalize on the operation of his forces, without apparent design, in a fluid, adaptable manner to uncover, expand, and exploit the adversary vulnerabilities and weaknesses. Later tactics emphasized massed firepower and stereotyped formations working formally together to smash adversary strength. Napoleon exploited ambiguity, deception, and mobility at the strategic level but increasingly emphasized formal battering-ram methods in his tactics. There he deemphasized loose, irregular methods (e.g., skirmishers) at the tactics level via a return to and increasingly heavy-handed application of the 1791 Drill Regulations.

Why, wonders Boyd, did he do this? His answer is that Napoleon emphasized the conduct of war from the top down. He created and exploited strategic success to procure grand tactical and tactical success. To support his concept, he set up a highly centralized command and control system, which, when coupled with essentially unvarying tactical recipes, resulted in strength smashing into strength by increasingly unimaginative, formalized, and predictable actions at lower levels. The results were strategic maneuvers that were ambiguous and deceiving prior to tactical concentration; after concentration, the maneuvers became stereotyped and obvious. This meant that tactical maneuvers could not easily procure victory because of their obvious, predictable nature. According to Boyd, the essence of the later Napoleonic campaigns can thus be characterized as strategic fog followed by stereotyped and ruinous tactical assaults.

### Theories of War: Clausewitz and Jomini

Having assessed one of the major practitioners of war in the modern era, Boyd turned his attention to two of the nineteenth century's greatest theorists of war, Carl von Clausewitz and Antoine de Jomini.[11] Clausewitz sees war as an act of policy, to use violence to impose one's will on another. In the conduct of war, uncertainty of information acts as an impediment to vigorous activity, as does friction (the interaction of many factors beyond our ability to control).

Boyd saw the principles of Clausewitz's strategy, as described in his 1832 work *On War,* as focused on the center of gravity and decisive battle. One should exhaust the enemy by influencing him to increase his expenditure of effort and seek out those centers of gravity on which all power and movement depend and, if possible, trace them back to a single center. One should then compress all effort, against those centers, into the fewest possible actions and subordinate all minor or secondary actions as much as possible. Last, one should move with the utmost speed and seek the major battle (with superiority of numbers and conditions) that will promise a decisive victory. The aim of all this, according to Clausewitz, is to "render the enemy powerless" generally through "the destruction of his armed forces."

Boyd had two fundamental critiques of Clausewitz. First, Boyd thought he overemphasized the concept of the decisive battle. In doing so, he underestimated the importance of strategic maneuver. Clausewitz emphasized methods and routine at the tactical level, which for Boyd was a sin and likely to be a mortal one in battle, for it makes one predictable. Boyd understood that Clausewitz was trying to overcome, or reduce, friction and uncertainty. But he failed utterly, according to Boyd, to address the idea of magnifying the adversary's friction and uncertainty. Second, Clausewitz sought to exhaust the adversary by influencing him to increase his expenditure of effort. Again, he failed to develop the notion of trying to paralyze the adversary by denying him the opportunity to expend effort. An army can be worn down and defeated by a refusal to give battle as well as by engagement in a decisive battle. Napoleon found this out in his invasion of Russia, where Clausewitz himself was a participant and observer for the Russians.

Clausewitz stated, "A center of gravity is always found where the mass is concentrated most densely."[12] He then argued that this is where the blows must be aimed and where the decision should be reached. Why, wondered Boyd, need this be so? If one could defeat an adversary by opposing weakness with strength, why would one choose instead to oppose strength with strength? One might still gain victory, but at a much higher cost. Clausewitz, according to Boyd, failed to develop the idea of many noncooperative centers of gravity. By striking at those vulnerable yet critical connections and activities that permit a larger system's center of gravity to exist, one could paralyze an adversary by denying him the opportunity to operate in a directed fashion at less cost. The result of Clausewitz's recommended operations is a bloodbath via well-regulated, stereotypical attrition, an expensive way to win.

Clausewitz was not the only student and theorist of Napoleonic warfare. Baron Antoine Henri de Jomini, also a prolific writer on early nineteenth-century warfare, was far more widely known at the time than Clausewitz. Jomini, too, thought he had discerned the secret of success.

The narratives of Frederick the Great commenced to initiate me in the secret which had caused him to gain the miraculous victory of Leuthen. I perceived that this secret consisted in the very simple maneuver of carrying the bulk of his forces upon a single wing of the hostile army. . . . I found again, afterwards, the same cause in the first success of Napoleon in Italy, which gave me the idea that by applying, through strategy, to the whole chess-table of a war this same principle which Frederick had applied to battles, we should have the key to all the science of war.[13]

Of course, it would prove not to be so easy.

Boyd's critique of Jomini is that he is preoccupied with the form of operations, spatial arrangement of bases, formal orders of battle, and tactical formations. Besides making one predictable, such forms are exceedingly difficult to do well and to adjust in the heat of battle. Jomini, according to Boyd, lacks appreciation for the use of loose, irregular swarms of guerrillas and skirmishers to mask one's own dispositions, activities, and intentions as well as to confuse, disrupt, delay, degrade, and disorder enemy operations. The result, once again, is a formulaic approach to war and stereotyped operations rather than the creative adaptation Boyd would prefer.

Boyd found the insights from Napoleon, Clausewitz, and Jomini an accurate description of war in the nineteenth century.[14] They all understood it, and misunderstood it, in essentially the same ways. The major flaw, according to

Boyd, was that they did not generally appreciate the importance of loose, irregular tactical arrangements and multiple activities to achieve a strategic purpose. Napoleon, Clausewitz, and Jomini viewed war and its conduct as top-down arrangements. Although they understood the need to adapt and change one's plans, adaptability at the top and in strategic planning was often impaired by the regularity and rigidity in tactical operations at the bottom. In most cases the results were contests in the attrition of tremendous quantities of blood and treasure. There had to be a better way to fight and win wars. Did technology hold some promise?

## Technology, Ideology, Society, and War

There are other important variables to be considered in the evolution of war in the last century. Industrialization, the advance in technology, and the social and economic transformations caused in turn are all-important elements. The major influences of technology on the conduct of land war in the nineteenth century include the railroad and the telegraph, quick-fire artillery, the machine gun and repeating rifle, smokeless powder, barbed wire, and trenches. The last can hardly be called a technological development per se, but their frequent use as the lethality of the battlefield increased is a noteworthy transformation nonetheless. The collective effect of these developments was a move toward massed firepower by large-scale armies supported by rail logistics. There was an increased emphasis on a holding defense and flanking or wide-turning maneuvers into the adversary's rear areas to gain a decision. Large stereotyped infantry formations supported by artillery barrages continued to use frontal assaults against regions of strong resistance. The result was huge armies massing deadly fires on the battlefield, which were in turn supported by a massive and complicated logistics structure. Collectively, they suppressed ambiguity, deception, mobility, and surprise.

Warfare had been transformed, and not necessarily for the better. Technology was being misapplied as a crude club that generated massive casualties throughout the century. War became a contest of industrial might and manpower, with the side that could inflict, but also absorb, the greatest amount of attrition the victor. The major wars of the latter half of the nineteenth century shared many of the same features, despite vastly different locations and conditions. The American Civil War (1861–1865), the Austro-Prussian War (1866), the Franco-Prussian War (1870), the Russo-Japanese War (1904–1905), and ultimately World War I, and even the irregular Boer War of 1899–1902, all exhibited varying degrees of mass formations, high lethality, and ponderous movement and logistics dependency. The evolution of tactics simply did not keep pace with the increased lethality of weaponry developed by nineteenth-century technology. Why, asked Boyd, were the commanders unable to evolve better tactics to avoid over half a century of debilitating casualties?

Here Boyd took a more expansive view and looked at the linkages between technology and society. The answer lay in the social and economic transformations that were fueling political change and military conflict throughout the nineteenth century. Boyd examined the effect of nineteenth-century capitalism on insurrection and revolution with a Marxian flavor. Much of the turmoil unleashed in the century stems from the opposing tendencies within capitalism itself. The interaction of competition, technology, specialization (the division of labor), concentration of production in large-scale enterprises, and the taking and plowing back of profits into this interaction produced opposing tendencies and periodic crises. More workers were competing for jobs in fewer but larger firms that favored the use of more machines and less labor. The result of these trends was that many low-paid wage earners hated the system that permitted others to live in luxury while they lived a life of toil under harsh factory discipline. Witnessing these unfolding circumstances, disillusioned intellectuals, bankrupt owners, and others took the side of the workers as an enlightened vanguard to mold a powerful opposition.

According to Marx, Engels, and their followers, the only way out was by revolution, creating a dictatorship of the proletariat (workers) to smash the capitalistic system and replace it with one that did not oppress the masses. Discontent and misery of the masses and vacillation by authorities who were unable to come to grips with the existing instability generated a crisis. The vanguard that offered leadership provided a way out and had the support of the masses. The crisis represented the height of confusion and disorder due to many opposing tendencies (centers of gravity) that magnify friction, paralyzing efforts by the authorities to dominate such turmoil.

In this sense, crises were periods of vulnerability and weakness that begged to be exploited. The vanguards represented disciplined moral, mental, and physical bodies focused to shape and guide the masses as well as to participate in action to exploit and expand confusion and disorder. These shook society's will to respond in a directed way. As Boyd explained it, crises and vanguards are the golden keys that permit us to penetrate to the core of insurrection and revolution and, as we shall see later, modern guerrilla warfare. The upshot was that the creation of crises and vanguards via nineteenth-century capitalism made evident the foundations on which to conduct insurrection and revolution in order to destroy a society from within. On the other hand, it was not yet clear how these notions changed or fit into the exploitation of technology and the conduct of war against societies from within as well as from without. The social, economic, and political context of war and warfare was as important to Boyd as the conflict itself. There are moral as well as physical dimensions.

## World War I and the Emergence of Infiltration and Guerrilla Tactics

Boyd's investigation of World War I had three stages: Plans and Execution, Stagnation, and Finale. Large-scale but simple plans and axes of advance (the Schlieffen Plan and Plan 17) characterized the opening gambits. Maintaining the evenness of advance was crucial to protect the flanks and provide artillery support as the armies made headway against each other. Reserves were thrown in whenever the attack was held up to maintain the direction and momentum of the advance. Any regions or points of strong resistance were attacked with more forces to overwhelm them. They were not bypassed.

The defense was organized in depth with successive belts of fortified terrain and defense lines. Massed artillery and machine gun fire was utilized and designed to arrest and pin down the attacker. Counterattacks were utilized wherever possible to win back lost ground and slow the offensive's advance. The result of all this was a general stagnation and enormous attrition of men and equipment. The advances were made generally as expected along predictable lines of hardened resistance largely because of a dependence on rail lines for logistics and the enormous consumption rates of supplies and ammunition. The choice of tactics sought to reduce strong points by massed firepower and infantry attacks.

Boyd was less interested in the important, emerging role of the new technologies (the submarine, the airplane, and the tank) than in the basic nature of the struggle itself. He wanted to understand the dynamics of the ground struggle and the tactical innovations and strategic concepts relating to how forces were employed. Capt. Andre Laffargue, General Hutier, and General Ludendorff all arrive at the notion of infiltration tactics as a potential way out of the dilemmas they then faced.[15] Boyd was intrigued with these.

Infiltration tactics were characterized by brief but intense artillery bombardment that included gas and smoke shells to disrupt and suppress enemy defenses and obscure the assault. Then groups of "Stosstruppen" (small teams or squads equipped with light machine guns and flame throwers) thrust forward close behind the rolling artillery barrage with no effort to maintain a uniform rate of advance or to keep formations aligned. Instead, they created many tiny, irregular swarms, spaced in breadth and echeloned in depth to seep or flow into any gaps or weaknesses that would allow them to drive deep into the adversary's rear areas. "Kampfgruppen" (small battle groups consisting of infantry, machine gunners, mortar teams, artillery observers, and field engineers) followed up to collapse exposed flanks and mop up isolated centers of resistance from flank and rear. Reserves and stronger follow-on echelons moved through newly created breaches to maintain momentum and exploit success, and they attacked the flanks and rear to widen penetration and consolidate gains against counterattack.

Several key points must be emphasized. Fire at all levels by artillery, mortars, and machine guns was exploited to hold the adversary's attention and pin him down. Such fire, together with gas and smoke (as well as fog and mist), was designed to capture the adversary's attention, force heads down, and dramatically obscure view, thereby cloaking the infiltrators' movements. The dispersed and irregular character of moving swarms permitted the infiltrators to blend against the irregular and changing terrain features as they pushed forward. Taken together, these factors (captured attention, obscured view, and indistinct character of the advance) denied the adversary the opportunity to gain an accurate picture of what was happening, or in this sense, "taking place." The infiltration teams suddenly appeared to loom out of nowhere to blow through, around, and behind the disoriented defenders.

The essence of these tactics was to cloud or distort the signature of the attacking forces. They sought to improve mobility and avoid enemy fire while focusing the effort on penetrating, shattering, enveloping, and mopping up disconnected and isolated troops and debris of the adversary's forces. The intent was to exploit tactical dispersion in a focused way to gain grand tactical success on the larger battlefield. The implication was exactly the opposite of the lessons of the preceding centuries of European warfare. Rather than large formations abiding by the principle of concentration, small units were exploiting tactical dispersion in a focused way that could have strategic impact. By penetrating the adversary, they created many noncooperative, isolated centers of gravity as a basis to magnify friction, paralyze effort, and bring about collapse. Until the rise of infiltration tactics and the use of tanks by the Allies in the latter part of World War I, there was stalemate. Neither the nineteenth-century nor the twentieth-century commanders were able to evolve effective tactical penetration maneuvers that could affect the massive increase in weapons lethality developed during the same period. Why? According to Boyd, the aristocratic tradition, the top-down command and control system, the slavish adherence to the principle of concentration, and the drill regulation mind-set all combined to reveal an obsession for control.

Infiltration tactics enjoyed immediate success at lower levels coupled with ultimate failure at the corps and army level. Why? In the case of the Germans, General Ludendorff violated his own concept by continuing to use strategic reserves to reinforce against hardened resistance. Hence, at the strategic level, he seduced himself into supporting failure, not success. He allowed the adversary to determine his rate of advance and create an inability to exploit initial successes. Exhaustion of combat teams leading the assault ensued. Logistics were too inflexible to support a rapid, fluid penetration and deeper exploitation of initial breakthroughs. Communications were too immobile to allow command to identify quickly and reinforce successful advances. Eventually, "elastic zone defenses," which were developed by the Germans but practiced well by Pétain, turned the tide. They emphasized artillery and flank attacks against penetrating forces when they stretched beyond their own artillery support.

T. E. Lawrence and Paul von Lettow-Vorbeck suggested guerrilla tactics rather than infiltration as a potential solution.[16] The purpose of guerrilla tactics was to gain support of the population. One did so by "arranging the minds" of friend, foe, and neutral alike. Getting inside their minds and creating one's preferred perceptions were critical to successful guerrilla warfare. As Lawrence suggested, one must "be an idea or thing invulnerable, without front or back, drifting about like a gas." Utilizing this inconspicuousness and fluidity of action, one must execute an attack in depth. As Lawrence described them, one's tactics should be those of "tip and run, not pushes but strokes" with the "use of the smallest force in the quickest time and the farthest place." This would lead one to fight a war by avoiding direct or prolonged contact and instead presenting a threat seemingly everywhere. Lawrence was able to succeed at this because he utilized a mobility and fluidity of action against the backdrop of vast desert. His constant, fluid movement maximized surprise and did not give the enemy a predictable target. Thus, his forces were a constant thorn in the side of the adversary governments. Lawrence summed up his strategy: "In a real sense, maximum disorder was our equilibrium."[17]

Thus, Boyd found much of what has proven to be successful in twentieth-century warfare to have old roots. It rested on a willingness to experiment and create new syntheses of strategies, tactics, and technologies appropriate to the environment one was in, the adversary one faced, and his choice of strategies, tactics, and technologies. Boyd defied traditional Western teachings and the emphasis in the curricula of most of the nation's war colleges. He identified serious flaws in both Napoleon's conduct of war and Clausewitz's assessment of war. Instead, he gathered more useful insights from Sun Tzu and the Mongols on the one hand and Marx, Engels, and Lenin on the other. In the middle of the Cold War, battling against the godless hordes of Soviet Russia and Communist China, this amounted to serious intellectual heresy.

# 9.    From Patterns of Conflict to Maneuver Warfare

The Boyd Theory defines what is meant by the word "maneuver" in the term "maneuver warfare." Maneuver means Boyd Cycling the enemy, being consistently faster through however many OODA loops it takes until the enemy loses his cohesion—until he can no longer fight as an effective, organized force.

William S. Lind, *Maneuver Warfare Handbook*

True to form, Boyd looked at the period between the world wars and focused less on the integration of technological advances (the airplane, radio, tank, and motorized infantry) than on the evolution of strategy and tactics. Boyd mused that Ludendorff's infiltration tactics seemed similar to Lawrence's guerrilla tactics. Both stressed clouded or distorted signatures, mobility, and cohesion of small units as the basis to insert an amorphous yet focused effort into or through an adversary's weakness. Boyd then turned to examine what happened to these concepts in the interwar period, linking them back to the social movements and ideologies that had emerged in the nineteenth century as well. He looked at Soviet, German, and Chinese contributions to develop a tantalizing notion of where his analysis and synthesis might be headed. He then examined each in detail.

Soviet revolutionary strategy under Lenin and Stalin exploited the Marxian ideas of crises and vanguards arising from contradictions within capitalism. The result was a scheme that emphasized moral and psychological factors as the basis to destroy a regime from within. Though Marx may have been a poor economist, he was an excellent sociologist. The concept of alienation is central to many of the political and social dilemmas of the twentieth century. Creating alienation, exploiting it, and increasing it was a time-honored technique for expanding Communism.

In the German interwar case, Boyd found the infiltration tactics of 1918 were mated with the technological advances that had occurred largely through the application of the internal combustion engine, aircraft, and radios to warfare. These led to many advances, most notably the tank, motorized artillery, tactical aircraft, motor transport, and better communication, and their integration through the work of J. F. C. Fuller, Heinz Guderian, and Charles DeGaulle.[1] This synthesis resulted in the concept that came to be known as blitzkrieg ("lightning war").[2] Blitzkrieg tactics generated a breakthrough by piercing a region with multiple thrusts using armor, motorized infantry, and follow-on forces supported by tactical aircraft to achieve rapid advances and greater disorientation in the adversary's disintegrating forces.

Boyd then took a brief look at Mao Tse Tung before returning to him later in some detail. Mao, said Boyd, was able to synthesize Sun Tzu, classic guerrilla strategy and tactics, and Napoleonic mobile operations under an umbrella of Soviet revolutionary ideas to create a powerful way of waging modern guerrilla warfare. The result was an integrated, overall political, economic, social, and military framework for a different kind of total war. It combined elements of guerrilla, conventional, and revolutionary warfare into a potent type of conflict with enormous implications. Note, too, that it was not technology dependent. It was the thinking and the orchestration of factors (the synthesis, not the technology) that gave it power.

Boyd returned to each of these examples in detail, beginning with the Soviet revolutionary strategy of Lenin and Stalin. They sought to employ agitation and propaganda to exploit opposing tendencies and internal tensions. The object was to bring about a crisis as well as to convince the masses that there was a way out. This was accomplished when the vanguard was first able to fan discontent and the misery of the working class and to focus it into hatred toward the existing system, which in turn caused indecision among the authorities, who could not come to grips with the existing instability. Third, the vanguard must "confuse other elements in society so that they don't know exactly what is happening or where the movement is going."[3] Last, it must convince the proletariat class that they have a function, "promoting revolution in order to secure the promised ideal society."

These combined to concentrate "the main forces of the revolution at the enemy's most vulnerable spot at the decisive moment, *when the revolution has already become ripe,* when the offensive is going full steam ahead, when the insurrection is knocking at the door, and when bringing the reserves up to the vanguard is the decisive condition of success" (emphasis is Boyd's). To quote Lenin paraphrasing Marx and Engels:

> Never play with insurrection, but, when beginning it, firmly realize that you must go to the end.
>
> Concentrate a great superiority of forces at the decisive point, at the decisive moment, otherwise the enemy, who has the advantage of better preparation and organization, will destroy the insurgents.
>
> Once the insurrection has begun, you must act with the greatest determination, and by all means, without fail, take the offensive. "The defensive is the death of an armed uprising."
>
> You must try to take the enemy by surprise and seize the moment when his forces are scattered.
>
> You must strive for the daily successes, even if small (one might say hourly, if it is the case of one town), and at all costs retain the "moral ascendancy."

Timing is critical. One has to select "the moment for the decisive blow, the moment for starting the insurrection, so timed as to coincide with the moment when the crisis has reached its climax, when the vanguard is prepared to fight to the end, the reserves are prepared to support the vanguard and maximum consternation reigns in the ranks of the enemy." According to Lenin, the decisive moment arrives when the following conditions are met:

> All the class forces hostile to us have been sufficiently entangled, are sufficiently at loggerheads, have sufficiently weakened themselves in a struggle which is beyond their strength;
>
> All the vacillating, wavering, unstable, intermediate elements—the petty bourgeoisie, the petty bourgeois democrats as distinct from the bourgeoisie—have sufficiently exposed themselves in the eyes of the people, have sufficiently disgraced themselves through their practical bankruptcy;
>
> Among the proletariat a mass sentiment in favor of supporting the most determined, supremely bold, revolutionary action against the bourgeoisie has arisen and has begun to grow vigorously. Then revolution is indeed ripe. Then, indeed, if we have correctly gauged all the conditions indicated above . . . and if we have chosen the moment towards that goal, our victory is assured.

At that moment, one must maneuver "the reserves with a view to effecting a proper retreat when the enemy is strong, . . . when, with the given relation of forces, retreat becomes the only way to escape a blow against the *vanguard* and retain the *vanguard's* reserves. The object of this strategy is to gain time, to disrupt the enemy, and to accumulate forces to assume the offensive" (emphasis is Boyd's). The goal of all this activity was to destroy capitalism as well as its offspring imperialism and replace it with a dictatorship of the proletariat.

## Blitzkrieg and Guerrilla Strategies

Boyd was fascinated by the many similarities between blitzkrieg and guerrilla strategies. I have quoted at length from his briefings in this regard as it is here that the essence of his ideas on maneuver warfare is found. These represent the central insights as to why maneuver warfare was so important and demonstrate the logic by which he eventually won many in the Marine Corps and the Army over to his convictions. In what follows I have attempted to turn his slides into prose describing his concepts, paraphrasing as necessary to make it readable, but relying to the greatest extent possible on his words as well as his ideas to give some sense of the dialogue Boyd held with himself and his audience.

The essence of both blitzkrieg and guerrilla strategies is a combination of infiltration and isolation. First, one infiltrates a nation or regime at all levels to soften and shatter the moral fiber of the political, economic, and social structure. Simultaneously, via diplomatic and psychological means, one strips away potential allies and thereby isolates the intended victims for the forthcoming blows. To carry out this program using blitz and guerrilla approaches, one needs to

> probe and test the adversary and any allies that may rally to his side, to unmask strengths, weaknesses, maneuvers, and intentions;
>
> exploit critical differences of opinion, internal contradictions, frictions, obsessions, etc., to foment mistrust, sow discord, and shape both the adversary's and allies' perception of the world. This in turn will
>
> create an atmosphere of mental confusion, contradiction of feeling, indecisiveness, and panic;
>
> manipulate or undermine the adversary's plans and actions;
>
> make it difficult, if not impossible, for allies to aid the adversary during his time of trial.

When combined with external political, economic, and military pressures to weaken the foe to minimize his resistance against military blows that will follow, the purpose of all this activity is to force capitulation.

Boyd offered a detailed explanation of how and why blitzkrieg works.

Intelligence (signal, photo, agent, etc.), reconnaissance (air and ground), and patrol actions probe and test the adversary before and during operations to uncover as well as shape the changing patterns of strengths, weaknesses, moves, and intentions.

Adversary patterns and associated changes are weighed against the friendly situation to expose attractive or appropriate alternatives that exploit adversary vulnerabilities and weaknesses, hence help shape the mission commitment and influence command intent.

Mission assigned. The schwerpunkt (focus of the main effort) is established before and shifted during combat operations to bypass adversary strength and strike at weakness. The nebenpunkt (other related or supporting effort) is employed to tie up or drain away adversary attention and strength elsewhere.[4]

Special seizure or disruption teams infiltrate (by air or other means) the enemy rear areas where, with agents already in place, they seize bridges and road crossings, sever communications, incapacitate or blow up power stations and fuel dumps, as well as sow confusion and disorder via false messages and fake orders.

Indirect and direct aerial firepower efforts together with sudden, brief preliminary artillery fires are focused in appropriate areas to impede or channel adversary movement, disrupt communications, suppress forward defensive fires, obscure the advance, and divert attention.

Armored reconnaissance or storm trooper teams leading armored columns advance rapidly from the least expected regions and infiltrate the adversary front to find paths of least resistance.

Armored assault teams of tanks, infantry, antitank guns, and combat engineers as well as other specialists, together with close artillery and air support, quickly open breaches (via frontal and flank fire and movement combinations) into the adversary rear along paths of least resistance uncovered by armored reconnaissance or storm troopers.

When breakthrough occurs, relatively independent mobile armored teams led by armored recce with air support (recce, fire, and lift) blow through to penetrate at high speed deep into the adversary interior. The object is to cut lines of communication, disrupt movement, paralyze command, and envelop adversary forces and resources.

Motorized or foot infantry farther back supported by artillery and armor pour in to collapse isolated pockets of resistance, widen breaches, and secure the encirclement of captured terrain against counterattack.

The purpose of the attack was to conquer a region in the quickest possible time. One does this by gaining initial surprise and exploiting the fast tempo and fluidity of action of armored teams with air support. In this way one could repeatedly penetrate, splinter, envelop, and roll up disconnected remnants of the adversary to confuse, disorder, and shatter his will or capacity to resist. Blitzkrieg generated many noncooperative centers of gravity as well as undermining or seizing those that the adversary depended on to prevent a response to magnify friction. This paralyzed the adversary by denying him the opportunity to act in a directed, unified way. One diminished his will and capacity to resist not by destruction but by disruption. This disruption is caused by severing the neural networks of intelligent response, by impeding command and control, by denying an accurate picture of what is happening so as to make reaction more difficult, if not impossible. In a complex, ever-changing environment such as battle, asked Boyd, how do those who utilize blitzkrieg sustain this rapid pace while adapting to changing circumstances without losing cohesion themselves or the coherency of their overall effort?

## German Operational Philosophy

Answering this question requires a solid understanding of the "blitz operational philosophy," as Boyd called it. Each level, from platoon to theater commander, has its own OODA loop. As the number of events to consider increases, the longer it takes to observe, orient, decide, and act. This suggests that faster tempo or rhythm at lower levels should work within the slower rhythm but larger pattern at higher levels so that the overall system does not lose its cohesion and coherency. Harmonizing these disparate rhythms is accomplished by giving the lower-level commanders wide freedom to shape and direct their own activities within the larger pattern of the commander's intent.

Doing so requires a high level of implicit trust, based on a thorough knowledge of the commander's intent. If this is clearly understood, one trusts subordinates to exercise their best tactical judgment on the scene as quickly as possible to take advantage of opportunities. The mission concept must be completely understood throughout the organization. This is what fixes responsibility and shapes a commitment, not real-time command and control. Centralized control means a slower, more rigid plan of action. Decentralized execution allows all units to focus on the schwerpunkt but with differing paces, patterns, and means for achieving the success of the operation.

According to Gen. Gunther Blumentritt, such a scheme presupposed a common outlook. It was based on "a body of professional officers who have received exactly the same training."[5] Furthermore, it presupposes "a very great measure of freedom of action and freedom in the manner of executing orders and which primarily calls for independent daring, initiative and sense of responsibility." That is, there must exist a common outlook of all officers at lower ranks in order for superiors to permit them the freedom of action while maintaining overall coherency. This is the bridge between subordinate initiative and superior intent. How did the German concept of mission and schwerpunkt give shape to this scheme?

The German concept of mission can be thought of as an implicit agreement between superior and subordinate. The subordinate agrees to make his actions serve his superior's intent in terms of what is to be accomplished, while the superior agrees to give his subordinate wide freedom to exercise his imagination and initiative in terms of how that intent is to be realized. Both superior and subordinate should understand their actions within the wider context of why they are doing what they seek to accomplish. As a part of this concept, the subordinate is given the right to question the feasibility of the mission in terms of either the intelligence about it or the resources to accomplish it.

The concept of schwerpunkt constitutes the axis, a harmonizing agent that is used to help shape commitment and carry out intent at all levels from theater to platoon. Schwerpunkt is a focusing agent that naturally produces an unequal distribution of effort, generating superiority in some sectors by thinning out others. It is also a medium to realize superior intent without impeding subordinate initiatives. It is the unifying concept. It provides a way to shape, focus, and direct effort rapidly and to harmonize support activities with combat operations.

The German operational philosophy in World War II was based on a common outlook that permitted freedom of action through the concepts of mission and schwerpunkt. It emphasized implicit over explicit communication. The secret of the success of the German command and control system lay in what was unstated or not communicated. It relayed higher-level intent, diminished friction, and reduced time, and did so with greatly increased quickness and security. As a result, the Germans were better able to operate inside their adversaries' OODA loops. As stated by General Blumentritt, "The entire operational and tactical leadership method hinged upon . . . *rapid*, concise assessment of situations, . . . *quick* decisions and *quick* execution, on the principle: each minute ahead of the enemy is an advantage."

Boyd then traced the development of the blitzkrieg by reaching back to the use of flying columns (the Mongols) and the concept of envelopment (from Cannae and Leuctra). He then added infiltration tactics (Ludendorff), the advent of the internal combustion engine in World War I, and the use of the tank attack and motorized vehicles (J. F. C. Fuller), to arrive at the synthesis created by Guderian that leads to blitzkrieg. Seen in this light, blitzkrieg seems a natural evolution of capabilities that could have stunning, rapid results, as indeed they did in the first two years of World War II.

Blitzkrieg used multiple thrusts and bundles of multiple thrusts to succeed. Their purpose was to present many fast-breaking, simultaneous, and sequential actions to generate confusion and disorder. Doing so stretched out the time required for the adversary to respond in a directed manner. It created opportunities to splinter the organism (the adversary's forces) and envelop disconnected remnants, thereby dismembering the adversary at the tactical, grand tactical, and strategic levels. Fast-paced multiplicity (variety and rapidity) along with initiative and harmony is the key to success. The battle is unpredictable because the breakthroughs to be exploited are not predetermined but unfold in the battle itself. It demands confidence and trust in lower-echelon subordinates to take advantage of opportunities as they see fit.

For Boyd, the essence of blitzkrieg was the employment of a nebenpunkt and schwerpunkt maneuver philosophy that could generate ambiguity, realize deception, exploit superior mobility, and focus violence to accomplish several instrumental goals. "*Create* and *exploit opportunities* to disrupt his system for communication, command, and support, as well as undermine or seize those connections or centers that he depends upon. [Doing so shakes] his will or capacity to decisively commit his back-up echelons, operational reserves, and strategic reserves, causing him to be unable to adapt to rapidly changing circumstances thereby convincing him to give up."[6] The strategy is to infiltrate and penetrate the adversary's positions and system to generate many moral, mental, and physical noncooperative centers of gravity. One then undermines or seizes those centers of gravity on which the adversary depends, thereby magnifying friction, producing paralysis, and ultimately causing collapse.

Boyd then listed the successes and failures of blitzkrieg beginning with World War II (see table 4). The characteristics of successful blitzkrieg attacks were mission concept, schwerpunkt, flexible command, low-level initiative, deception, fast tempo, superior mobility, slim essential logistics, rapidity, variety, and harmony of purpose. Failures occurred when these elements were lacking, the weight of enemy forces was too great, or supply of resources was insufficient to accomplish the mission.

## Modern Guerrilla Campaigns

Boyd then turned his attention to modern guerrilla campaigns. The essential actions, as he saw them, are:

> Capitalize on discontent and mistrust by corruption (real or imagined), exploitation, oppression, incompetence, and unwanted presence of ex-

**Table 4. Blitzkrieg, World War II to 1973**

| Successful Region Invaded, Date | Unsuccessful Region Invaded, Date |
|---|---|
| Poland, 1939 | |
| France, 1940 | |
| Balkans, 1941 | |
| Russia, 1941 | |
| North Africa, 1941–1942 | |
| | Russia, Winter 1941–1942 |
| | North Africa, 1942 |
| Russia, Summer 1942 | |
| | Russia, Fall-Winter 1942–1943 |
| Russia, Feb.–March 1943 | |
| | Russia, Summer 1943 |
| Advance through France, 1944 | |
| Manchuria, 1944 | |
| | Ardennes, Winter 1944–1945 |
| Middle East, 1967 | |
| Czechoslovakia, 1968 | |
| Middle East, 1973 | |

*Source:* John R. Boyd, "Patterns of Conflict" (part of the August 1987 version of the larger unpublished briefing "A Discourse on Winning and Losing"), p. 89.

isting regime to evolve a common cause or unifying theme as a basis to organize and maintain mass popular support through a militant political program.

Set up administrative and military organization, sanctuary, and communications network under the control of the guerrilla political leadership without arousing the regime's intelligence and security apparatus. Build up a shadow government, with "parallel hierarchies" in localities and regions that can be made ripe for insurrection or revolution by infiltrating cadres (vanguards) who can not only subvert existing authority but also convert leaders and people to the guerrilla cause and organizational way.

Exploit subversion of government and conversion of people to the guerrilla cause to create an alien atmosphere of security and intelligence to blind the regime to guerrilla plans, operations, and organization yet make visible the regime's strengths, weaknesses, moves, and intentions.

Shape propaganda, foment civil disorder (such as rallies, demonstrations, strikes, and riots), use selected terrorism, perform sabotage, and exploit resulting misinformation to expand mistrust and sow discord, thereby magnifying the appearance of corruption, incompetence, etc., and the inability of the regime to govern.

Employ tiny cohesive bands for surprise hit-and-run raids against lines of communications to gain arms and supplies as well as to disrupt government communication, coordination, and movement. Retreat and melt into the environment when faced by superior police and armed forces.

Disperse or scatter tiny guerrilla bands to arouse the people (and gain recruits) as well as to harass, wear out, and spread out government forces, while larger bands, or mobile formations, concentrate to wipe out dispersed, isolated, and relatively weak fractions by sudden ambush or sneak attack.

Play on the grievances and obsessions of people (via propaganda, reeducation, and selected successes) as well as encourage government to take indiscriminate harsh reprisal measures against them, connecting the government with an expanding climate of mistrust, discord, and moral disintegration. Simultaneously, show by contrast that guerrillas exhibit moral authority, offer competence, and provide desired benefits, in order to erode government influence, gain more recruits, multiply base areas, and increase political infrastructure, hence expanding guerrilla influence or control over the population and the countryside.

Demonstrate disintegration of the regime by striking in cheng-ch'i fashion, with small bands and ever larger mobile formations, to split up, envelop, and annihilate fractions of major enemy forces.

The purpose of all these actions was to defeat the existing regime politically by showing that it had neither the moral right nor the demonstrated ability to govern.

The essence, then, of a modern guerrilla campaign is to capitalize on corruption, injustice, and incompetence (or their appearance) to generate an atmosphere of mistrust and discord and to sever the moral bonds that bind people to the existing regime. Simultaneously, one needs to share the existing burdens with the people and work with them to root out and punish corruption, remove injustice, and eliminate grievances, forming moral bonds between the people and guerrillas to bind them to guerrilla philosophy and ideals. The intent of all this is to shape and exploit crises in the environment that permit the guerrilla vanguards or cadres to pump up their resolve, attract the uncommitted, and drain away adversary resolve, building a foundation to replace the existing regime with a guerrilla regime.

Guerrillas, Boyd said, by being able to penetrate the very essence of their adversary's moral, mental, and physical being, generate many noncooperative or isolated centers of gravity. They then subvert or seize those centers of gravity that the adversary regime must depend on, thereby magnifying friction, producing paralysis, and bringing about collapse. They shape or influence the moral, mental, and physical atmosphere so that potential adversaries, as well as the uncommitted, are drawn toward the guerrilla philosophy and are empathetic toward guerrilla success.

Guerrilla vanguards play on a regime's internal frictions and obsessions by sowing discord. They also stimulate discontent with the regime and the regime's mistrust of the people. They thereby paralyze the regime's ability to come to grips with crises, which further fans the atmosphere of mistrust and discord, which feeds the crises in a repetitious cycle that eventually spins out of control. Guerrilla vanguards help people cope with the turmoil thus created, which demonstrates their ability to deal with the surging crises and shapes the belief that only they offer a way out of the existing unpleasant circumstances. Insurrection or revolution becomes ripe when the people see themselves as exploited and oppressed for the undeserved enrichment of an elite few. Thus, guerrilla success depends on the support of a large portion of the people.

Guerrillas must be able to blend into the emotional, cultural, and intellectual environment of the people until they become one with them. The thoughts and feelings of the general public must become the thoughts and feelings of the guerrillas. The people's aspirations must be the guerrillas' aspirations, the people's goals must become the guerrillas' goals. If successful, the guerrillas and the people become indistinguishable from each other, and the government, the regime in power, becomes isolated from both. The keys to guerrilla success are:

> The ability to demonstrate continuously government weakness, to erode government influence, and to cause the government to alienate itself from the people.

> The support (both psychological and physical) of the people for intelligence, recruits, shelter, transportation, refuge, food, money, and medical aid.

> Access to safe sanctuaries or base areas and mobile bases that can be shifted from place to place, away from enemy forces, where guerrillas can rest, recuperate, repair materiel, etc., as well as indoctrinate, train, and equip recruits.

> The use of stealth, fast tempo, fluidity of action, coupled with cohesion of guerrilla bands, as a basis for *dispersion* (to arouse people, to avoid adversary strength, and to force government to thin out, or disperse, its strength), *concentration* (to hit and wipe out isolated fractions), and *shifting of effort* (to gain and keep the initiative and force the government to react to surprises in unexpected areas and activities).

**Table 5. Guerrilla Results over the Last 200 Years**

| Successful Region, Date | Unsuccessful Region, Date |
| --- | --- |
| American Colonies, 1775–1781 | |
| Spain, 1808–1814 | |
| Russia, 1812 | |
| | Philippines, 1899–1902 |
| | South Africa, 1900–1902 |
| German East Africa, 1914–1918 | |
| Arabia, 1916–1918 | |
| China, 1927–1949 | |
| Russia, 1941–1945 | |
| Yugoslavia, 1941–1945 | |
| | Greece, 1944–1949 |
| Indochina, 1945–1954 | |
| | Philippines,* 1946–1954 |
| | Malaya,* 1948–1960 |
| Algeria, 1954–1962 | |
| Cuba, 1956–1959 | |
| South Vietnam, 1958–1975 | |

*Source:* John R. Boyd, "Patterns of Conflict" (part of the August 1987 version of the larger unpublished briefing "A Discourse on Winning and Losing"), p. 97.

* The regime exercised particular care not to inflict casualties and to protect the civilian population.

It would seem that guerrilla strategy and tactics have been very successful, regardless of time period and technology, culture or geography. Boyd's examples of guerrilla results are listed in table 5. Why was the track record over 200 years and across most continents so good?

## Blitz-Guerrilla Themes

True to his calling and self-appointed mission as the "Great Synthesizer," Boyd sought what could be learned by combining these two themes. There are several essential points of guerrilla and blitz themes. The first characteristic of the two is to avoid battles. In this he echoed Sun Tzu's notion that the acme of skill is to subdue the enemy without fighting him. Instead of fighting a pitched battle of attrition, pitting strength against strength, one should penetrate the adversary to subvert, disrupt, or seize those connections, centers, and activities that provide cohesion (psychological and moral bonds, communications, command and control, and supply centers). The second lesson is to shape the adversary's perceptions and the pace of his reactions to events. One exploits ambiguity and deception, so the adversary doesn't really know what is going on and utilizes superior mobility and sudden violence to control the pace of events. This generates surprise and shock that are constantly repeated. Finally, one shatters the enemy's forces and commitment through subversion, surprise, shock, disruption, and the seizure of forces, people, territory, or other assets. All this is accomplished not necessarily by destroying the adversary's military assets but rather by making it impossible for him to utilize them effectively. By generating confusion, disorder, panic, and chaos, one paralyzes the enemy, who eventually collapses. Again, the emphasis is on disruption, not destruction. Such destruction as occurs is incidental to the real aim to deny the adversary the ability to perceive accurately what is happening and to react effectively. Boyd sought to dictate the mind-space-time framework of the conflict.

Blitz and guerrilla strategies succeed by being able to operate in a directed yet more indistinct, more irregular, and quicker manner than their adversaries. They concentrate and disperse more inconspicuously and more quickly without losing internal harmony. They use this as a basis to penetrate the moral, mental, and physical being of their adversaries to bring about their collapse. The underlying idea, said Boyd, is that such amorphous, lethal, and unpredictable activity by blitz and guerrillas makes them appear awesome and unstoppable. This produces uncertainty, doubt, mistrust, confusion, disorder, fear, panic, and, ultimately, collapse. Such notions were implied by Sun Tzu around 400 B.C. and more recently by J. F. C. Fuller observing the impact of Ludendorff's infiltration tactics in 1918.

What would a successful counterblitz or counterguerrilla strategy look like? If one could break down the cohesion of effort, slow down the fast tempo, then it could probably be defeated. A counterblitz strategy for Boyd would consist of the following elements. One would emphasize intelligence and reconnaissance (air and ground) and set up a screen of forward outposts and patrols to report on adversary activity and to warn of any impending or actual incursions. One should deploy, disperse, and frequently redeploy and redisperse reconnaissance and mobile antitank, infantry, and armor teams together with artillery so that they can shift local efforts against adversary thrusts. Armored teams should be placed as a mobile reserve in echelon behind recce, antitank, armor, and artillery so that they can check local breakthroughs or push off for a blitz counterstroke.

The action that unfolds would be characterized by the use of air assets and fast-moving mobile armored reconnaissance teams to determine direction and strength of enemy thrusts. They would also continuously harass by repeated delaying actions and hit-and-run attacks. Hitting adversary thrusts and resupply efforts with ambuscades and with repeated sudden, sharp flank and rear counterthrusts will channel as well as drain away momentum and break up cohesion of the blitz. Then, while the adversary is moving forward, one must rapidly concentrate swift armored combat forces, held in reserve to this point, and use these with air support to drive a counterstroke, shallow or deep, to swing behind and roll up the blitz offensive in detail.

The idea is to smash the blitz by turning its own techniques against itself. The inconspicuous, stealthy use of fast tempo, fluidity of action, and cohesion of the counterblitz combat teams is the key. They form, redirect, then halt the enemy's advance. This places the adversary on the defensive, not the offensive, halts his advance, and at least locally destroys the adversary's capacity to resist. In this military ju jitsu, one uses the adversary's own momentum and offensive intent to one's defensive advantage. One employs his own techniques of fast pace, infiltration, penetration, and flanking movements to defeat him. The key is rapid OODA loop cycles to permit one to respond quickly to the unfolding tactical circumstances.

The main features, then, of blitz and counterblitz strategy and tactics are similar, if not identical. Both must emphasize (as listed by Boyd):

Intelligence and recce action

Infiltration, penetration, and isolation

Ambiguity, deception, speed, and violence to generate surprise and shock

A mission-schwerpunkt philosophy

Acceptance of gaps and related risks in support of the mission-schwerpunkt philosophy

Echelon in depth for both the offense and defense

Reserves reconstituted and accumulated at all levels to support or generate success

A posture that includes positions, alternative positions, dummy positions, and roving positions to mask maneuvers and intentions.

The artful mix of these factors and their timely utilization will determine the success or failure of blitz and counterblitz attacks. Doing so effectively depends on skill, trust, and freedom of action of the subunit commanders, who must respond quickly and effectively to each new twist and turn in the course of the battle. This can be explained and even practiced to some degree, but it is art as well as science, intuition as well as thought, reflex as well as an order, that will make the difference.

## Guerrilla and Counterguerrilla Campaigns

Boyd then reviewed the key points of guerrilla and counterguerrilla campaigns. Guerrilla vanguards need a cause and the support of the people, which depends on the regime's unwillingness or inability to come to grips with crimes of its own making. Put more simply, crises and vanguards represent the marriage of instability and initiative that creates and expands the guerrilla effort. At this point, the thought occurred to Boyd that to dry up a guerrilla upsurge, one should strike at those root causes of illegitimate inequalities and discontent that generate and exacerbate the crises and provide a favorable climate in which vanguards operate. If the cause of the discontent no longer exists, mobilizing the populace to overthrow the regime to redress their grievances cannot occur.

How should a regime pursue a counterguerrilla campaign? Boyd laid out an array of tools:

> Undermine the guerrillas' cause and destroy their cohesion by demonstrating integrity and competence of government to represent and serve the needs of the people rather than exploit and impoverish them for the benefit of a greedy elite. (If you cannot realize such a political program, Boyd noted, you might consider changing sides now to avoid the rush later!)

> Take political initiative to root out and visibly punish corruption. Select new leaders with recognized competence as well as popular appeal. Ensure that they deliver justice, eliminate major grievances, and connect the government with its grass roots.

> Infiltrate the guerrilla movement as well as employ the population for intelligence about guerrilla plans, operations, and organization.

> Seal off guerrilla regions from the outside world by diplomatic, psychological, and various other activities that strip away potential allies as well as by disrupting or straddling communications that connect these regions with the outside world.

> Deploy administrative talent, police, and counterguerrilla teams into affected localities and regions to inhibit guerrilla communication, coordination, and movement, minimize guerrilla contact with the local inhabitants, isolate their ruling cadres, and destroy their infrastructure.

> Exploit the presence of these teams to build up local government as well as recruit militia for local and regional security to protect people from the persuasion and coercion efforts of the guerrilla cadres and their fighting units.

> Use special teams in a complementary effort to penetrate guerrilla-controlled regions. Employ the guerrillas' own tactics of reconnaissance, infiltration, surprise hit-and-run, and sudden ambush to keep roving bands off balance, make base areas untenable, and disrupt communications with the outside world.

Expand these complementary security and penetration efforts into the affected regions to undermine, collapse, and replace guerrilla influence with government influence and control.

Visibly link these efforts with local political, economic, and social reform to connect central government with the hopes and needs of the people, thereby gaining their support and confirming government legitimacy.

The purpose of all this activity is to break the guerrillas' moral, mental, and physical hold over the population, to destroy their cohesion, and bring about their collapse via political initiative that demonstrates moral legitimacy and the vitality of the government.

Relentless military operations should emphasize stealth, fast tempo, fluidity of action, and cohesion of the overall effort to defeat the guerrilla forces. The single most important factor is support of the people. Legitimacy is critical. Without it, the guerrillas have neither a vast hidden intelligence network nor an invisible security apparatus that permits them to see into adversary operations yet blind the adversary to their own operations. Therefore, the side that wins the struggle for the hearts and minds of the people will ultimately win. We had the right goals but the wrong strategy in Vietnam.

## Toward Maneuver Warfare

Two concepts underlie Boyd's analysis and synthesis of warfare. They are time and movement, or, more precisely, speed and maneuver. If one moves and constantly presents an opponent with a changing situation and does so quickly, one has a tremendous advantage. If one cannot do this, according to Boyd, the chances for success in almost any kind of combat are seriously degraded. That insight became one of the primary contributions of the reformers to the American military. Shifting the U.S. armed forces toward a philosophy of maneuver warfare was the most important and lasting contribution of Boyd and the reformers. There are many heroes in this tale, and many different versions of it have been recounted, but many of the major players in the drama (from those on Capitol Hill such as staffer Bill Lind and former senator Gary Hart to those in the Marine Corps such as the retired vice president of Marine Corps University Col. Mike Wyly and former commandant Al Gray, and Army officers such as Maj. Gen. Huba Wass de Czege and others more grudgingly) will admit that it was the constant drumbeat of Boyd's briefings and ideas that slowly drew the U.S. military into step with maneuver warfare.

Just what is maneuver warfare, and how does one go about fighting it? There are many views on the subject.[7] Boyd came to understand and emphasize the essential characteristics of maneuver warfare through his notion of the OODA loop, his focus on the adversary's perception, and the need for initiative and trust. His focus on what he called the mind-time-space dimension of an adversary rather than a quantitative comparison of force levels lies at the base of his understanding of maneuver warfare. Perhaps the best way to explain it is to juxtapose maneuver warfare with the preferred American way of war, attrition warfare. The following characterization is overly simplistic, but it does highlight the differences between the two schools of thought on how best to fight war and the nature of the different styles of warfare. It also serves to show the degree of change that Boyd and his colleagues in the military reform movement were trying to inculcate in the American military. That they had even partial success in a decade of effort is rather remarkable.

Table 6 compares features of attrition warfare and maneuver warfare. While not opposites, they represent alternative approaches to the fighting and winning of wars. These competing notions of conflict suggest different approaches to organizing, training, and equipping different styles of militaries and would lead to totally different strategies, technologies, doctrines, and organizations. Boyd and company represented a huge threat to the American military. They questioned its very existence as presently constituted. Moving it from attrition to maneuver was an awesome task.

Maneuver war theory is a way of thinking about how to contend with an adversary. It is not a checklist approach, a Jominian science of war so much beloved by the American military. Rather it is Clausewitzian in approach, about war as art and, therefore, nonlinear. It begins with the importance of the commander's intent, the vision of what is to be done vis-à-vis the enemy. This must be shared with principal subordinate commanders and cascade through all levels of command so that all pieces of the units involved know their role in the larger vision and understand their mission. It operates through what is called reconnaissance-pull; that is, forward elements of the force find or create gaps for large units to follow. It is strength against weakness, not strength against strength. Force should flow like water traveling the path of least resistance. The aim is to infiltrate and penetrate the enemy's forces with multiple thrusts. A driving principle is the concept of surfaces and gaps; one wants to create gaps to flow through and thus flow around surfaces rather than crash against them.

The implicit contract in maneuver warfare is mission-type orders and *auftragstaktik*. The subordinate agrees to take near-term actions in keeping with the commander's intent. The superior agrees to allow his subordinate the freedom of judgment to determine exactly how that should be accomplished. He is thus empowered to both recognize and take advantage of opportunities that he may encounter. The purpose is to harmonize, as Boyd would say, the action and

**Table 6. Comparison of Attrition Warfare and Maneuver Warfare**

|  | Attrition Warfare | Maneuver Warfare |
|---|---|---|
| Focus | Battle: fielded forces, force ratios and loss ratios; quantity | Enemy's cohesion: mental, moral, physical stability; quality |
| Emphasis | Military capability, planning: overwhelm by superiority, mass | Trust, innovation, speed: win by OODA loop dislocation |
| Nature | Hierarchy | Network |
| Style | Integrative, centralized, competitive, prescriptive, standardized | Decentralized, distributed, collaborative, adaptive, unique |
| Means | Destruction of adversary forces and war-waging ability | Creation of perception that adversary cannot win |
| End | Destruction of adversary | Creation of new paradigm |
| Examples | Napoleon, Grant, D-Day, United States in Vietnam | Hannibal, blitzkrieg in 1940, Viet Cong–NVA against United States |
| Requirements | Massive firepower, technology, industrial might, centralized control | Trust, professionalism, individual leadership |
| Risks | Asymmetric threats, collateral damage, duration, sustainment, casualties | Depends on individual initiative, high morale, accurate assessments, creative responses, difficult to infuse |
| Characteristics | War is Jominian, a science quantifiable, systematic | War is Clausewitzian, an art qualitative, nonlinear |

*Source:* This formulation is mine but was suggested by an article by Com. Joseph A. Gattuso, Jr., U.S. Navy, "Warfare Theory," *Naval War College Review* 49, no. 4 (Autumn 1996), pp. 112–123.

initiatives of subordinate commanders with the superior's intent. This demands decentralization of tactical operations within the framework of a centralized strategic vision. It provides a bottom-up, outside-in, real-world response in real time to transformations on the battlefield and thereby creates operational fluidity. To take advantage of a weakness discovered in this manner, one must have a large and ready reserve to commit to exploit the main effort. One does all this with combined arms and a combination of mass and maneuver, firepower and movement, so that in taking up a defense against one, the enemy becomes vulnerable to another form of assault. It is an operational OODA loop cycle that adjusts to its own rhythm and tempo. It displays Boyd's critical concepts of variety, rapidity, harmony, and initiative.

## Instilling Maneuver Warfare in the United States

The people, books and articles, host of discussions and conferences (including one at West Point in 1982 where Boyd was a featured speaker), and other activities of those that championed maneuver warfare did bear fruit. The Army's earlier edition of its Field Manual 100-5: Operations (1976), which promoted something called active defense, was not well received. It was soon followed by another version in 1982. According to Alvin and Heidi Toffler, this version was largely the brainchild of Brig. Gen. Don Morelli and Maj. Gen. Donn Starry.[8] It was in development for several years and sought to replace the Army emphasis on firepower and attrition with a more fluid doctrine based on maneuver and deception. It eventually became what was called AirLand Battle. Morelli and Starry, then the Army's Training and Doctrine Command, and finally Army chief of staff General Sullivan all claimed credit at one point or another along the way for the basic notions of AirLand Battle. There were even claims that the Army had developed the OODA loop (attributed to Army tankers) and the basic notions of maneuver warfare that Boyd had been briefing since the mid-1970s. Jim Burton refutes many of those claims in his book *The Pentagon Wars* and gives his version of the role Boyd and company had in infusing maneuver warfare theory into the Army and the Marine Corps.[9] There is little doubt that Boyd's hundreds of "Patterns of Conflict" briefings around the Pentagon and throughout the U.S. military had prepared the ground for a different approach to war fighting for the American military.

Although Boyd railed against one of the core concepts in the 1982 manual that promulgated the doctrine known as AirLand Battle, it was a mighty improvement over the previous version, known as Active Defense. The concepts the Army embraced (in part because of Boyd's proselytizing) included agility, innovation, depth, and synchronization. Save for the latter (Boyd argued, "You synchronize watches, not people"), it was a move toward maneuver warfare in a big way. Just how one was to display innovative agility in depth while remaining synchronized was a little more difficult to understand. Second, the Marine Corps adopted maneuver warfare in its Fleet Marine Force Manual (FMFM-1: Warfighting) document of March 1989. What had started out as Friday-night discussions at Bill Lind's townhouse in Alexandria and was leavened with Wednesday-night meetings at the officer's club at Fort Myers (which continue to this day among Boyd followers) became a movement. More formal aspects included lectures at tactics courses and war colleges and briefings on "Patterns of Conflict" shopped around town endlessly to anyone who was interested. All created a torrent of interest. Suddenly, hundreds of people—politicians, journalists, military officers, scholars—became interested in this thing called maneuver warfare, the concept of an OODA loop or Boyd cycle, and continuing discussions of what it all meant for the American military. The expansion of "Patterns of Conflict" into "A Discourse on Winning and Losing" would prove even more successful and continue the dialogue.

# 10.

# A Discourse on
# Winning and Losing

If this work presents a coherent world view, it is in large part because I was fortunate
enough to hear Colonel John Boyd deliver a brilliant series of lectures, "A Discourse on
Winning and Losing." In a world of analysts, he is that rare breed—a synthesist. I had long
hoped to write a book explaining the power of a "systems" approach to solving America's
problems, and Colonel Boyd gave me an orientation, a paradigm for integrating information from several fields.

Joseph J. Romm, *The Once and Future Superpower:
How to Restore America's Economic, Energy, and Environmental Security*

**B**oyd began work on two new briefings after finishing the last version of
"Patterns of Conflict" in December 1986. "A Discourse on Winning
and Losing" was created with the addition of two new briefings, entitled "An
Organic Design for Command and Control," completed in May 1987, and "The
Strategic Game of ? and ?," completed in June of the same year. He developed
the thoughts on the command and control system in concert with the strategic
insights and vice versa. Boyd's desire for connections and harmony were at
work again. The version of "A Discourse" that has been most widely disseminated is dated August 1987. The final major part of "A Discourse" was "The
Conceptual Spiral," added in July and August 1992. Boyd presented the whole
thing as one briefing, but it is really a collection of these different briefings.

## The Strategic Game

One of the most fundamental of Boyd's briefings, "The Strategic Game" was not developed until almost a decade after the first version of "Patterns of Conflict." Both an explanation and demonstration of how one goes through the OODA loop process, it serves as the link between "Destruction and Creation" (1976) and "The Conceptual Spiral" (1992) in Boyd's intellectual odyssey. It is the best example of how Boyd's mind wrestled with abstract concepts and their concrete implications.

"The Strategic Game of ? and ?" begins by asking a series of questions: What lies under the question marks? What is strategy? What is the aim or purpose of strategy? What is the central theme and what are the key ideas that underlie strategy? How do we play this theme and activate these ideas?[1] His approach was somewhat oblique, however, for he began in a rather unorthodox but very effective manner with what he called a thought experiment.

Imagine that you are on a ski slope skiing down a mountain. Retain that image. Now imagine that you are in sunny Florida riding in an outboard motor boat. Retain that image. How else might you move about on a nice spring day? On land, riding a bicycle would be nice. Retain that image too. Now imagine that you are a parent taking your son to a department store and you notice that the toy tractors with rubber caterpillar treads fascinate him. Retain this image too. What could you fashion from these disparate images? Selecting parts of these items and images, what can we create from them? Pull the skis off the ski slope, the outboard motor from the motorboat, the handlebars off the bicycle, and the rubber treads off the toy tractor. Discard the rest of the images. What do you have? A snowmobile!

Boyd presented his allusion to the components for building snowmobiles as an illustration of synthesis. "Snowmobile" was one of Boyd's favorite shorthand terms. He classified people into two types, those who could build snowmobiles and those who couldn't. The former would be winners in this complex, unknown world in which we had to exist. The latter would fail to adapt and would inevitably lose. Boyd then surveyed a variety of disciplines, repeating his views on how we set about to survive and prosper and what that requires. How do we do this? Boyd answers with an array of quotations from newspapers, books, and speeches. Only a few are reproduced here to reveal the eclectic nature of his mind at work and the snowmobiles he built routinely in his thought.[2]

Boyce Rensberger, "Nerve Cells Redo Wiring . . . ," *Washington Post*

Dale Purvis and Robert D. Hadley . . . have discovered that a neuron's fibers can change significantly in a few days or weeks, presumably in response to changing demands on the nervous system. . . . research has shown neurons continuously rewire their own circuitry, sprouting new fibers that reach out to make contact with new groups of other neurons and withdrawing old fibers from previous contacts. . . . This rewiring process may account for how the brain improves one's abilities such as becoming proficient in a sport or learning to play a musical instrument. Some scientists have suggested that the brain may use this method to store facts. . . . The research was on adult mice, but since all mammalian nervous systems appear to behave in similar ways, the researchers assume that the findings also apply to human beings.

Richard M. Restak, "The Soul of the Machine" (review of *Neuronal Man,* by Jean-Pierre Changeux), *Washington Post Book World*

Changeux suggests that the complexity of the human brain is dependent on the vast number of synapses (connection) between brain cells. . . . these synaptic connections are established or fall by the wayside according to how frequently they're used. Those synapses which are in frequent use tend to endure ("are stabilized") while others are eliminated. . . . In other words, . . . interactions with the environment [exert] tremendous influence on the way the human brain works and how it has evolved.

Ilya Prigogene and Isabelle Stenger, *Order Out of Chaos*[3]

Equilibrium thermodynamics provides a satisfactory explanation for a vast number of physicochemical phenomena. Yet it may be asked whether the concept of equilibrium structures encompasses the different structures we encounter in nature. Obviously the answer is no.

Equilibrium structures can be seen as the results of statistical compensation for the activity of microscopic elements (molecules, atoms). By definition they are inert at the global level. . . . Once they have been formed they may be isolated and maintained indefinitely without further interaction with their environment. When we examine a biological cell or a city, however, the situation is quite different: not only are these systems open, but also they exist only because they are open. They feed on the flux of matter and energy coming to them from the outside world. We can isolate a crystal, but cities and cells die when cut off from their environment. They form an integral part of the world from which they can draw sustenance, and they cannot be separated from the fluxes that they incessantly transform.

Alexander Atkinson, *Social Order and the General Theory of Strategy*[4]

Moral fibre is "the great dam that denies the flood of social relations their natural route of decline towards violence and anarchy." . . . In this sense, "a moral order at the center of social life literally saves society from itself."

Strategists must grasp this fact that social order is, at once, a moral order. . . . If the moral order on which rests a fabric of social and power relations is compromised, then the fabric (of social order) it upholds goes with it.

In other words, "the one great hurdle in the strategic combination (moral and social

order) is the moral order. If this remains untouched the formation of new social relations and social ranking in status and power either never gets off the ground or faces
the perennial spectre of backsliding towards the moral attraction of established social
and power relations."

The strategic imperative, then, becomes one of trying "to achieve relative security
of social resources by subverting and reweaving those of the opponent into the fabric
of one's own order."

Boyd, "Destruction and Creation"

According to Gödel's Incompleteness Theorems, Heisenberg's Uncertainty Principle,
and the Second Law of Thermodynamics one cannot determine the character or nature
of a system within itself. Moreover, attempts to do so lead to confusion and disorder.

Dimitry Mikheyev, "A Model of Soviet Mentality" (a speech)

Interaction between the individual and his environment starts with his perception of
himself as a separate entity and the environment as everything outside of self. He
learns his physical limits and desires, and how to fulfill them through interaction with
the physical and social environment. . . . I maintain that the way the individual per-
ceives the environment is crucial for his orientation and interaction with it.

Man's orientation will involve perceptions of self as both a physical and a psychological entity, as well as an understanding of the environment and of the possibilities
for achieving his goals. (Fromm, 1947) Society, meanwhile, has goals of its own—
preservation of its physical integrity and spiritual identity. Pursuing these goals involves mobilizing and organizing its inner resources and interaction with the outside
environment of other societies and nations. . . . An individual becomes a member of
the society when he learns to act within its limits in a way that is beneficial to it.

Boyd then added a few more items before asking what this mélange of insights
and ingredients means.

Old Fable: But sir, the emperor is naked, he has no clothes.

Sun Tzu: Know your enemy and know yourself; in one hundred battles
you will never be in peril.

Seize that which your adversary holds dear or values most highly; then
he will conform to your desires.

Jomini: The great art, then, of properly directing lines of operations, is so
to establish them in reference to the bases and to the marches of the army
as to seize the communications of the enemy without imperiling one's
own, and is the most important and most difficult problem in strategy.

Leadership: The art of inspiring people to cooperate and to take action enthusiastically toward the achievement of uncommon goals.

So what are we to make of all of these seemingly random insights? How do they help us to understand strategy? To Boyd, it was quite clear and relatively simple.

> Physical as well as electrical and chemical connections in the brain are shaped by interacting with the environment. Point: Without these interactions we do not have the mental wherewithal to deal or cope with that environment.

> Gödel's Incompleteness Theorems, Heisenberg's Uncertainty Principle, and the Second Law of Thermodynamics, all taken together, show that we cannot determine the character or nature of a system within itself. Moreover, attempts to do so lead to confusion and disorder—mental as well as physical. Point: We need an external environment, or outside world, to define ourselves and maintain organic integrity, otherwise we experience dissolution and disintegration—i.e., we come unglued.

> Moral fiber or moral order is the glue that holds society together and makes social direction and interaction possible. Point: Without this glue social order pulls apart toward anarchy and chaos, leaving no possibility for social direction and interaction.

> Living systems are open systems; closed systems are nonliving systems. Point: If we don't communicate with the outside world—to gain information for knowledge and understanding as well as matter and energy for sustenance—we die out to become a nondiscerning and uninteresting part of that world.

Interaction permits vitality and growth; isolation leads to decay and disintegration. Thus, the theme that is associated with all the pieces of "A Discourse on Winning and Losing" to date is one of interaction and isolation. "An Organic Design for Command and Control" emphasizes interaction, "Patterns of Conflict" emphasizes isolation, and "Destruction and Creation" is balanced between interaction and isolation. Ultimately one is involved in a game in which one must be able to diminish an adversary's ability to communicate or interact with his environment while sustaining or improving one's own ability to do so.

Just how does one go about doing this? Boyd focused on three planes: moral, mental, and physical. The physical one represents the world of matter, energy, and information we are all a part of, the world we live in and feed on. The mental plane represents the emotional, intellectual activity generated to adjust to, or cope with, that physical world. The moral represents the cultural codes of conduct or standards of behavior that constrain, as well as sustain and focus, one's emotional and intellectual responses.

Physical isolation occurs when one fails to gain support in the form of matter, energy, or information from others outside oneself. Mental isolation occurs when one fails to discern, perceive, or make sense out of what is happening. Moral isolation occurs when one fails to abide by codes of conduct or standards of behavior in a manner deemed acceptable or essential by others. Looked at from the opposite perspective, physical interaction occurs when one freely exchanges matter, energy, or information with others. Mental interaction occurs when one generates images or impressions that match the events or happenings that unfold. Moral interaction occurs when one lives by the codes of conduct or standards of behavior that one professes and others expect us to uphold.

So what? How does one link these seemingly unrelated insights? Linking Gödel, Heisenberg, and the second law of thermodynamics, Boyd reminded us that "one cannot determine the character or nature of a system within itself; moreover, attempts to do so lead to confusion and disorder." Jumping radically, he asked, "What do the tests of the YF-16 and YF-17 say? . . . The ability to shift or transition from one maneuver to another more rapidly than an adversary enables one to win in air-to-air combat." The implication of the overall message, as Boyd called it, is this:

> The ability to operate at a faster tempo or rhythm than an adversary enables one to fold the adversary back inside himself so that he can neither appreciate nor keep up with what is going on. He will become disoriented and confused; which suggests that
>
> Unless such menacing pressure is relieved, the adversary will experience various combinations of uncertainty, doubt, confusion, self-deception, indecision, fear, panic, discouragement, despair, etc., which will further
>
> Disorient or twist his mental images and impressions of what is happening; thereby
>
> Disrupt his mental and physical maneuvers for dealing with such a menace; thereby
>
> Overload his mental and physical capacity to adapt or endure; thereby
>
> Collapse his ability to carry on.

By combining insights and experiences, by looking at other disciplines and activities and connecting them, one can create new strategies for coping with the world and one's adversaries. Doing so allows one to develop repertoires of competition, ways to contend with multiple adversaries in different contexts. In doing so, one develops a *fingerspitzengefühl* ("finger-tip feel") for folding adversaries back inside themselves, morally, mentally, and physically, so that they can neither appreciate nor cope with what is happening. Thus, the artful manipulation of isolation and interaction is the key to successful strategy.

Boyd paid particular attention to the moral dimension and the effort to attack an adversary morally by showing the disjuncture between professed beliefs and deeds. The name of the game for a moral design for grand strategy is to use moral leverage to amplify one's spirit and strength while exposing the flaws of competing adversary systems. In the process, one should influence the uncommitted, potential adversaries and current adversaries so that they are drawn toward one's philosophy and are empathetic toward one's success.

Boyd then set out to answer the questions he asked at the beginning. He defined strategy as "a mental tapestry of changing intentions for harmonizing and focusing our efforts as a basis for realizing some aim or purpose in an unfolding and often unforeseen world of many bewildering events and many contending interests." Its aim was "to improve our ability to shape and adapt to unfolding circumstances, so that we (as individuals or as groups or as a culture or as a nation-state) can survive on our own terms." Interaction and isolation were the key themes. Analysis and synthesis activate these across a variety of domains and spontaneously generate new mental images that match up with an unfolding world of uncertainty and change. Then, seemingly as an afterthought, the last slide presents two definitions: "Evil occurs when individuals or groups embrace codes of conduct or standards of behavior for their own personal well-being and social approval, yet violate those very same codes or standards to undermine the personal well-being and social approval of others" and "Corruption occurs when individuals or groups, for their own benefit, violate codes of conduct or standards of behavior that they profess, or are expected, to uphold." The briefing ends abruptly on this note.

It should be noted that this was written just after his protégé Col. Jim Burton had fought his battles with the Department of Defense over the testing and evaluation of the Bradley Fighting Vehicle, when the momentum of the military reform movement started to flag. It is symptomatic of Boyd's assessment of those with whom he was contending. Boyd, like Spinney, came to believe that many in the government were evil and corrupt, and Boyd and his closest associates were mired in that corruption.

This combination was new: alternating cycles of interaction and isolation as the essence of strategy with the concept of moral leverage as an essential part of military strategy and the nature of war as a moral and mental as well as physical struggle. Others had spoken of the moral and mental aspects of war, even hinted at the moral leverage necessary to win, but few had spoken of the strategic process as alternating cycles of isolation and interaction. None had combined all three. For Boyd, they were implicit in his notions of strategy and war. One went to war for moral purpose. Using moral leverage was of tremendous advantage, and the pattern of isolation and interaction was critical to success.

This was just as true of personal contests or bureaucratic struggles in the Pentagon over defense policy issues as it was on the battlefield against conventionally arrayed forces or guerrillas in the jungles of Vietnam. Understanding the essence of conflict across the human spectrum gave one a better understanding of how to survive and prosper.

## An Organic Design for Command and Control

The world is full of what Kevin Kelly has called "the rise of the neobiological civilization." That's the subtitle of his book *Out of Control*. His main point is a simple one of immense ramifications: "The realm of the born—all that is nature—and the realm of the made—all that is humanly constructed—are becoming one. Machines are becoming biological and the biological is becoming engineered."[5] They are not quite fused, but they become closer all the time. Both are becoming distorted in the process, as is the role of humans in an increasingly technologically complex and interdependent world. That world is moving at faster tempos of cost and consequence, some of which are known but most of which remain mysterious until after the fact. Is the Internet alive or engineered? Could we have predicted its consequences?

Boyd was particularly concerned with command and control issues, which he called C&C in his briefings and the military refers to generally as $C^2$. Command and control issues are concerned with communication and the implementation of tactics and strategy so that military operations can be carried out as they are supposed to unfold. The problem, of course, is that they rarely do. Denied perfect foreknowledge, one always has to make adjustments. Hence, the flow of information from commander to subordinate units and back is critical to the success of any military engagement. $C^2$ for most military officers suggests hardware and wiring diagrams, the array of communications systems, the radio frequencies to be used, and so forth. Boyd used organic metaphors to emphasize an organic, biological approach to understanding what we are about as counterpoint to the tremendous reliance on technology that we have developed.

Among the basic C&C imperatives for Boyd are the need to understand how well people trust each other, the need to understand the commander's intent, and the purpose for which one needs authority, responsibility, and communication in the first place. He approached the problem not as one of electronic communication from superior to subordinate but of observation relayed from subordinate to superior. This created an outside-in, bottom-up approach dependent first on gathering information about the environment before beginning the OODA loop. First and foremost, one needs to apprehend and comprehend the strategic environment. The critical information flows are thus not down the chain of command but up, for it is only by processing this information that we can adapt successfully as events unfold.

Boyd began his "Organic Design for Command and Control" by asking, "Why the focus on C&C? What do we mean by an organic design?" He then enumerated some failed C$^2$ exercises and the debacles of the evacuation of Saigon and the Desert One incident.

The institutional response for overcoming these fiascoes is: more and better sensors, more communications, more and better computers, more and better display devices, more satellites, more and better fusion centers, etc.—all tied into one giant fully informed, fully capable C&C system. This way of thinking emphasizes hardware as the solution. . . . I think there is a different way—a way that emphasizes the implicit nature of human beings. In this sense, the following discussion will uncover what we mean by both implicit nature and organic design.[6]

What is important for Boyd here is the insight and vision to unveil adversary plans and actions as well as to foresee our own goals and appropriate plans and actions. Without insight and vision there can be no orientation to deal with both present and future. Second, one needs focus and direction to achieve some goal or aim. Without focus and direction, implied or explicit, there can be neither harmony of effort nor initiative for vigorous effort. Third, one must be adaptable to cope with uncertain and ever-changing circumstances. Adaptability implies variety and rapidity. Without variety and rapidity one can neither be unpredictable nor cope with the changing and unforeseen circumstances. Last, we need security, to remain unpredictable. Without security one becomes predictable, hence one loses the benefits of the other elements.

Boyd then reviewed some military history beginning with Sun Tzu and progressing through Bourcet, Napoleon, Clausewitz, Jomini, Forrest, Blumentritt, and Balck, ending with his own take on war. The key points he took from this review are that war involved friction, as Clausewitz showed. Friction is amplified by such factors as menace, ambiguity, deception, rapidity, uncertainty, and mistrust, among others. Implicit understanding, trust, cooperation, and simplicity can diminish friction. For Boyd, the key point was that variety and rapidity tend to magnify friction, while harmony and initiative tend to diminish friction. More particularly, variety and rapidity without harmony and initiative lead to confusion, disorder, and finally chaos. On the other hand, harmony and initiative without variety and rapidity lead to rigid uniformity, predictability, and finally nonadaptability. What fosters harmony and initiative and destroys variety and rapidity? Activities that promote correlation, commonality, and accurate information flows are beneficial. Compartmentalization, disconnected data flows, and plans laid out as recipes to be followed are not. For Boyd, the interactions represented a many-sided implicit cross-referenced process of projection, empathy, correlation, and rejection. In short, one's orientation to the world is one's understanding of reality.

Orientation is a complex amalgam of images, views, or impressions of the world shaped by an interactive process. This process consists of these interactions and shapes and is shaped by the interplay of genetic heritage, cultural traditions, previous experiences, and unfolding circumstances. Orientation, the big O in the OODA loop, is the schwerpunkt. It shapes the way we observe, decide, and act. To be successful one needs to create mental images, views, or impressions (patterns) that match with the activity of the world. Moreover, one needs to deny the adversary the possibility of uncovering or discerning patterns that match one's activity. The essential idea, as Boyd called it, is that patterns (hence, orientation), right or wrong, suggest ability or inability to conduct many-sided implicit cross-references. "How do we set up and take advantage of the many-sided implicit cross-referencing process of projection, empathy, correlation, rejection that makes appropriate orientation possible?" The message for Boyd is to "expose individuals, with different skills and abilities, against a variety of situations—whereby each individual can observe and orient himself simultaneously to the others and to the variety of changing situations."

In such an environment, the bonds of implicit communication and trust that evolve as a consequence of the similar mental images create a harmony, focus, and direction in operations. A strong set of shared impressions is created by each individual. This is committed to memory by repeatedly sharing the same variety of experience in the same ways. What has all this to do with C&C? The secret of a superior command and control system lies in what is unstated or not communicated explicitly to one another. One thereby diminishes friction and compresses time, gaining both quickness and security. Similarly, an inability to operationalize shared impressions may increase friction, reduce adaptability, and make one unable to cope with events. The Marine Corps is working on an extension of this concept called intuitive decision making.

According to Boyd's trinity of Gödel, Heisenberg, and the second law of thermodynamics, "One cannot determine the character or nature of a system within itself. Moreover, attempts to do so lead to confusion and disorder." Applying these ideas, one can see that "He who can generate many noncooperative centers of gravity magnifies friction. Why? Many noncooperative centers of gravity within a system restrict interaction and adaptability of [the] system with its surroundings, thereby leading to a focus inward (i.e., within itself), which in turn generates confusion and disorder, which impedes vigorous or directed activity, hence, by definition, magnifies friction or entropy." Any command and control system that forces adherents to look inward leads to dissolution and disintegration. In other words, as Boyd said, "they become unglued." There is both a positive and a negative aspect to this. If you have these implicit bonds and understandings, you have harmony and initiative within the group. Without them, they are impossible. There is no way that such an organic whole can stay together and cope with a many-sided, uncertain, and ever-changing environment. Without this internal consistency, friction becomes magnified, paralysis sets in, and the system collapses.

One must emphasize the implicit over the explicit to gain a favorable mismatch in friction and time. To do this, one must suppress the tendency to build up explicit internal arrangements that hinder interaction with the external world. Instead, one must arrange a setting among leaders and subordinates alike that gives them the opportunity to interact continuously with the external world and with each other. Doing so allows them to make many-sided implicit cross-referencing projections, empathies, correlations, and rejections more quickly. Simultaneously, they create the similar images or impressions, hence a similar implicit orientation, needed to form an organic whole.

For those that are so organized, the payoff comes as they diminish their friction and reduce time, thereby permitting them

> to exploit variety/rapidity while maintaining harmony/initiative, thereby
>
> to get inside the adversary's OODA loops, thereby
>
> to magnify the adversary's friction and stretch out his time (for a favorable mismatch in friction and time), thereby
>
> to deny the adversary the opportunity to cope with events/efforts as they unfold.

Done correctly, it is a relatively easy and low-cost way to achieve a sizable advantage over a foe, and it does not necessarily involve the use of weaponry. What is at stake is one's orientation to the world and the actions of those in it. Since a first-rate command and control system should possess the above qualities, any design or related operational methods should increase implicit orientation. This really means that the OODA loop can be thought of as the C&C loop. Once again, it is the second O, orientation (the repository of genetic heritage, cultural traditions, and previous experiences) that is the most important part of the OODA loop, since it shapes the way one observes, decides, and acts. Therefore, operating inside an adversary's OODA loop is the same as operating inside the adversary's C&C loop.

Boyd turned next to some "historical snapshots," referring to Napoleon's use of staff officers for personal reconnaissance, Moltke's message directives of few words, British tight control at the Battle of the Somme in 1916, the British GHQ phantom recce regiment in World War II, Patton's household cavalry, and Israeli views on getting accurate assessments of battle. These examples reinforce the notion that command and control must permit one to direct and shape what is to be done as well as permit one to modify that direction and shape by assessing what is being done. "Command must give direction in terms of what is to be done in a clear, unambiguous way. In this sense, command must interact with system to shape the character or nature of that system in order to realize what is to be done. Control," on the other hand, "must provide assessment of what is being done, also in a clear, unambiguous way. In this sense, control must not interact or interfere with system but must ascertain (not shape) the character/nature of what is being done."

Boyd cut to the heart of the matter:

Reflection upon the statements associated with the Epitome of Command and Control leave us unsettled as to the accuracy of these statements. Why? Command, by definition, means to direct, order, or compel, while control means to regulate, restrain, or hold to a certain standard as well as to direct or command. Against these standards it seems that the command and control (C&C) we are speaking of is different than the kind that is being applied. In this sense, the C&C we are speaking of seems more closely aligned to *leadership* (rather than command) and to some kind of *monitoring* ability (rather than control) that permits leadership to be effective. In other words, leadership with monitoring, rather than C&C, seems to be a better way to cope with the multifaceted aspects of uncertainty, change, and stress. On the other hand, monitoring, per se, does not appear to be an adequate substitute for control. Instead, after some sorting and reflection, the idea of *appreciation* seems better. Why? First of all, appreciation includes the recognition of the worth or value and the idea of clear perception as well as the ability to monitor. Moreover, next, it is difficult to believe that leadership can even exist without appreciation.

As Boyd saw it, appreciation and leadership permit one to discern, direct, and shape what is to be done, and they permit one to modify that direction and shape by assessing what is being done or about to be done.

Appreciation, as a part of leadership, must provide assessment of what is being done in a clear and unambiguous way. In this sense, appreciation must not interact or interfere with system but must discern (not shape) the character/nature of what is being done or about to be done; whereas leadership must give direction in terms of what is to be done also in a clear, unambiguous way. In this sense, leadership must interact with system to shape the character or nature of that system in order to realize what is to be done. Assessment and discernment should be invisible and should not interfere with operations, while direction and shaping should be evident to system—otherwise appreciation and leadership do not exist as an effective means to improve our fitness to shape and cope with unfolding circumstances.

To Boyd, C&C represented a top-down and inside-out mentality applied in a rigid, mechanical (or electrical) way that ignores as well as stifles the implicit nature of human beings to deal with uncertainty, change, and stress. He decided, therefore, that the briefing he had just given had been mistitled. "Pulling these threads together suggests that *appreciation and leadership* offer a more appropriate and richer means than C&C for shaping and adapting to circumstances" (emphasis is Boyd's). It should correctly be called "appreciation and leadership."

He left us with a set of definitions to ponder.

*Understanding* means to comprehend or apprehend the import or meaning of something.

*Command* refers to the ability to direct, order, compel, with or without authority or power.

*Control* means to have power or authority to regulate, restrain, verify (usually against some standard), direct, or command. Comes from medieval Latin *contrarotulus*, a counter roll or checklist (*contra*, against, plus *rotulus*, to list).

*Monitoring* refers to the process that permits one to oversee, listen, observe, or keep track of as well as to advise, warn, or admonish.

*Appreciation* refers to the recognition of worth or value, clear perception, understanding, comprehension, discernment.

*Leadership* implies the art of inspiring people to cooperate and enthusiastically take action toward the achievement of uncommon goals.

Trust, appreciation, and leadership are keys to success for any family, church, school, business, political system, or military. They are the real family values, the basic core values, and cultural bedrock that undergird truly successful societies and organizations. The urge to command and control is part of the problem, not part of the solution. It is an impediment to creative adaptation, to true insight, imagination, and innovation. Creating a system that seems to respond intuitively to the challenges and opportunities it encounters is a far more effective way to proceed. Such a system emphasizes the organic, natural aspects of human relationships and interactions rather than the technology, which both connects and separates us from each other.

## The Conceptual Spiral

The result of seven years of additional reading and distillation, "The Conceptual Spiral" sought "to make evident how science, engineering, and technology influence our ability to interact and cope with an unfolding reality that we are a part of, live in, and feed upon."[7] The basic question was: How do we go about adapting successfully in the modern world? Boyd's answer was contained in 30 slides of carefully crafted analysis and synthesis. He began every "Conceptual Spiral" briefing by asking the audience how many had heard of half a dozen important scientists, mathematicians, and inventors or their discoveries. He then asked why they were significant. Though the results varied from audience to audience, they were invariably disappointing. Few were aware of some of the more important contributions to modern science. What follows is a prose version of his thoughts in that briefing and commentary on it. It is written as a discussion similar to one Boyd would have held with his audience. The ideas and most of the words are his. They have been rearranged for clarity.

For openers, Boyd suggested a reexamination of the larger briefing, "A Discourse on Winning and Losing." The theme that weaves its way through "A Discourse" is thinking that consists of pulling ideas apart (analyses) while intuitively looking for connections that form a more general elaboration (synthesis) of what is taking place. The process not only creates the discourse but also represents the key to evolve the tactics, strategies, goals, and unifying themes that permit us to shape and adapt to the world around us.

By examining the practice of science and engineering and the pursuit of technology, one can evolve a conceptual spiral for comprehending, shaping, and adapting to that world. Boyd defined science as a self-correcting process of observation, hypothesis, and test—the essence of the scientific method. Engineering can be viewed as a self-correcting process of observation, design, and test. Technology can be viewed as the wherewithal or state of the art produced by the practice of science and engineering. This in turn raises the question, What has the practice of science and engineering and the pursuit of technology done for us? Boyd then proceeded to list what he considered some of the key advances in scientific knowledge (table 7). His selections were conceptual breakthroughs, leaps in the process of invention and discovery, the macrodiscoveries that enabled others to follow with important inventions that would have been impossible without these mental breakthroughs. The list suggests wide reading and intimate understanding of a wide array of scientific accomplishments.

Boyd's briefings were essentially a dialogue with the audience. A natural teacher, he understood that if he told you something, he robbed you of the opportunity to ever truly know it for yourself. He was skilled at asking a series of leading questions to guide the group's thinking about relationships so that they would figure the lesson out just before he had to tell them. In so doing, he demonstrated the kind of thinking that he sought to demand from others, a set

## Table 7. Examples from Science

| Outstanding Contributors | Outstanding Contributions |
|---|---|
| Isaac Newton (1687) | Exactness-predictability via laws of motion-gravitation |
| Adam Smith (1776) | Foundation for modern capitalism |
| A. M. Ampere, C. F. Gauss (1820s, 1830s) | Exactness-predictability via electronic-magnetic laws |
| Carnot, Kelvin, Clausius, Boltzman (1824, 1852, 1865, 1870s) | Decay-disintegration via second law of thermodynamics |
| Faraday, Maxwell, Hertz (1831, 1865, 1888) | Union of electricity and magnetism via field theory |
| Darwin, Wallace (1838, 1858) | Evolution via theory of natural selection |
| Marx, Engels (1848–1895) | Basis for modern scientific socialism |
| Gregory Mendel (1866) | Inherited traits via laws of genetics |
| Henri Poincare (1890s) | Inexactness-unpredictability via gravitational influence of three bodies |
| Max Planck (1900) | Discreteness-discontinuity via his quantum theory |
| Albert Einstein (1905–1915) | Exactness-predictability via his special and general relativity theories |
| Bohr, de Broglie, Heisenberg, Shrodinger, Dirac et al. (1913, 1920s and beyond) | Uncertainty-indeterminism in quantum physics |
| L. Lowenheim, T. Skolem (1915–1933) | Unconfinement (noncategoricalness) in mathematics and logic |
| Gödel, Tarski, Church, Turing et al. (1930s and beyond) | Incompleteness-undecidability in mathematics and logic |
| Claude Shannon (1948) | Information theory as a basis for communication |
| Crick & Watson (1953) | DNA spiral helix as genetically coded information for life |
| Lorenz, Prigogene, Mandelbrot, Feigenbaum et al. (1963, 1970s and beyond) | Irregular-unpredictability in nonlinear dynamics |
| G. Chaitin, C. Bennett (1965, 1985) | Incompleteness-incomprehensibility in information theory |

*Source:* John R. Boyd, "The Conceptual Spiral," unpublished briefing, August 1992, pp. 9–10.

of implicit and explicit many-sided cross-references to expand people's horizons. He then urged them to continue the process, make their own connections, and continue the spiral of conceptual insights.

Boyd then gave an even more detailed set of examples from engineering that scientific discoveries helped to make possible, mainly during the last 200 years (table 8). He focused on inventions familiar to the audience, easily identified as milestones with connections to technological advancement and social transformations. Boyd commented on his favorites and then pushed on to why they were important and their implications.

Looking at the past via the contributions these people had provided the world, what can one say about our efforts for now and in the future? In a mathematical-

## Table 8. Examples from Engineering

| Outstanding Contributors | Outstanding Contributions |
| --- | --- |
| Savery, Newcomen, Watt (1698, 1705, 1769) | Steam engine |
| George Stephenson (1825) | Steam railway |
| H. Pixil, M. H. von Jacobi (1823, 1838) | AC generator, AC motor |
| Samuel F. B. Morse (1837) | Telegraph |
| J. Nieqce, J. Daguerre, Fox Talbot (1839) | Photography |
| Gaston Plante (1859) | Rechargeable battery |
| Z. Gramme, H. Fontaine (1869, 1873) | DC generator, DC motor |
| Nicholas Otto (1876) | 4-cycle gasoline engine |
| Alexander G. Bell (1876) | Telephone |
| Thomas A. Edison (1877) | Phonograph |
| Thomas A. Edison (1879) | Electric lightbulb |
| Werner von Siemans (1879) | Electric locomotive |
| Germany (1881) | Electric metropolitan railway |
| Charles Parsons (1884) | Steam turbine |
| Benz, Daimler (1885, 1886) | Gasoline automobile |
| T. A. Edison, J. LeRoy, T. Armat et al. (1890–1896) | Motion picture camera, projector |
| Rudolf Diesel (1897) | Diesel locomotive |
| Italy (1902) | Electric railway |
| Wright Brothers (1903) | Airplane |
| Christian Hulmeyer (1904) | Radar |
| V. Paulsen, R. A. Fessenden (1904, 1906) | Wireless telephone |
| John A. Fleming, Lee De Forest (1904, 1907) | Vacuum tube |
| Tri Ergon, Lee De Forest (1919, 1923) | Sound motion picture |
| USA, Pittsburgh (1920) | Public radio broadcasting |
| American Car Locomotive (1925) | Diesel-electric locomotive |
| J. L. Baird (1926) | Television |
| Warner Brothers (1927) | *Jazz Singer,* sound motion picture |
| Germany, USA (1932, 1934) | Diesel-electric railway |
| Britain, USA, Germany (1935–1939) | Operational radar |
| Germany, Britain, USA (1935, 1936, 1939) | Television broadcasting |
| Hans von Ohain, Germany (1939) | Jet engine, jet airplane |
| Eckert & Mauchly (1946) | Electronic computer |
| Bardeen, Brattain, Shockley (1947) | Transistor |
| Ampex (1955) | Video recorder |
| J. Kilby, R. Noyce (1958, 1959) | Integrated electric circuit |
| T. H. Maiman (1960) | Laser |
| Philips (1970) | Videocassette recorder |
| Sony (1980) | Video camcorder |

*Source:* John R. Boyd, "The Conceptual Spiral," unpublished briefing, August 1992, pp. 11–12.

logical sense one can say that taken together, the theorems associated with Gödel, Lowenheim and Skolem, Tarski, Church, Turing, Chaitin, and others reveal a consistent theme and reinforce each other. Not only do the statements representing a theoretical system for explaining some aspect of reality explain that reality inadequately or incompletely, but they also spill out beyond any one system and do so in unpredictable ways. Conversely, these theorems reveal that one cannot predict the future migration and evolution of these statements or just confine them to any one system or suggest that they fully embrace any such system.

Boyd continued by stating that any coherent intellectual or physical system one evolves to represent or deal with large portions of reality will at best represent or deal with that reality incompletely or imperfectly. Moreover, it is impossible to have or create beforehand a supersystem that can forecast or predict the kind of systems that will evolve in the future to represent or deal with that reality more completely or more accurately. Furthermore, such a supersystem can neither forecast nor predict the consequences that flow from those systems that are created later on. Going even farther, one cannot determine or discern the character or nature of such systems (super or otherwise) within themselves.

What Boyd called "the Grand Message" is this: People using theories or subsystems evolved from a variety of information will find it increasingly difficult and ultimately impossible to interact with and comprehend phenomena or systems that move beyond and away from that variety. That is, they will become more and more isolated from that which they are trying to observe or deal with, unless they exploit the new variety to modify their theories and systems or create new ones.

The record reveals that science, engineering, and technology produce change via novelty. To comprehend this process of novelty, one reduces it to patterns and features that make up the pattern. In studying the patterns and features, one can combine and cluster them according to different types of similarities (different advances related to chemistry or electricity, for example). Finding some common features that are shared and connected across disciplines or fields of scientific endeavor helps create a new pattern, new insights. This process of connections is called synthesis. Testing these relationships creates an analytical-synthetic feedback loop for comprehending, shaping, and adapting to the world. Novelty is created through a combination of analysis and synthesis of our environment and our interactions with it.

Now, if our ideas and thoughts matched perfectly with what goes on in the world, and if the systems or processes as designed performed perfectly and matched with whatever one wanted them to do, there would be no basis for evolving or creating new ideas, systems, processes, or materials. There would be no novelty. In other words, it is the presence and production of mismatches that sustain and nourish the enterprise of science, engineering, and technology. Without the intuitive interplay of analyses and syntheses, one has no basic process for generating novelty. There is no basic process for addressing mismatches between one's mental image or impressions and the reality it is supposed to represent and no basic process for reshaping one's orientation toward that reality as it undergoes change. Novelty, mismatches, and reorientation are the stuff of life itself.

This leads to amended definitions of science and engineering. Science can be viewed as a self-correcting process of observations, analyses-syntheses, hypothesis and test. Engineering can be viewed as a self-correcting process of observations, analyses-syntheses, design and test. Why? Without the interplay of analyses and syntheses, one cannot develop the hypothesis, design, or follow-on test. This is all very nice, but, asks Boyd, what does it have to do with winning and losing? The very practice of science and engineering and the pursuit of technology produce novelty. Novelty occurs in nature as well. If there are mismatches, there is a chance for adaptation, and this begets more novelty. The entire course of evolution is a confirmation of this reality. One's own thinking and doing also produces novelty. Indeed, the identification of mismatches (or explanations that are not born out by observations) is responsible for much of the world's progress. It is how we learn. When a mismatch occurs, one must struggle to square the explanation with the facts. Furthermore, novelty is produced continuously, if somewhat erratically and haphazardly. It is the randomness of it all that makes the process so fascinating.

Now, to thrive and grow in such a world, one must match one's thinking and one's actions, hence one's orientation, with that emerging novelty. Yet any orientation constrained by experiences before that novelty emerges will introduce mismatches that confuse and disorient. However, the analytical-synthetic process permits one to address mismatches so that one can reorient one's thinking and action with that novelty. Over and over the continuing whirl of reorientation, mismatches, analyses, syntheses, enables one to comprehend, cope with, and shape as well as be shaped by novelty that flows around and over one continuously.

Why does the world continue to unfold in an irregular, disorderly, unpredictable manner, even though some of the best minds try to represent it as being more regular, orderly, and predictable? More pointedly, with so much effort over so long a period by so many people trying to comprehend, shape, and adapt to a world that one depends on for vitality and growth, why does such a world, although richer and more robust, continue to remain uncertain, ever-changing, and unpredictable? The answer is that the various theories, systems, and processes that one employs to make sense of that world contain features that generate mismatches. These keep the world uncertain, ever-changing, and unpredictable. These features include, but are not limited to:

*Uncertainty* associated with the nonconfinement, undecidability, incompleteness theorems of mathematics and logic

*Numerical imprecision* associated with using rational and irrational numbers in the calculation and measurement processes

*Quantum uncertainty* associated with Planck's constant and Heisenberg's uncertainty principle

*Entropy increase* associated with the second law of thermodynamics

*Irregular or erratic behavior* associated with far-from-equilibrium, open, nonlinear processes or systems with feedback

*Incomprehensibility* associated with inability to screen, filter, or otherwise consider spaghettilike influences from a plethora of ever-changing, erratic, or unknown outside events

*Mutations* associated with environmental pressure, replication errors, or unknown influences in molecular and evolutionary biology

*Ambiguity* associated with natural languages as they are used and interact with one another

*Novelty* generated by the thinking and actions of unique individuals and their many-sided interactions with each other.

The bottom line, given all of this, is simple. If one cannot eliminate these, one must continue the whirl of reorientation, mismatches, analyses, and syntheses to comprehend, shape, and adapt to an unfolding, evolving reality that remains uncertain, ever-changing, and unpredictable. Uncertainty is a basic human condition. It is what we do with it that counts.

Where does this lead us? We have the basis for a conceptual spiral (see page 174). In short, we have a conceptual spiral for generating insight, imagination, initiative. One simply cannot survive without these abilities, says Boyd. The conceptual spiral really is a paradigm for survival and growth. Survival and growth are directly connected with the uncertain, ever-changing, unpredictable world of winning and losing. Therefore, one must exploit this whirling conceptual spiral of orientation, mismatches, analyses-syntheses, so that we can comprehend, cope with, shape, and be shaped by the world and the novelty that arises out of it.

In such a universe and with such a worldview, change is not something to be feared but the very essence of life itself. Life becomes defined as a process of adaptation. Some adaptation is successful. Some is not. The key is the capacity for the combination of analyses and syntheses that enables us to exploit mismatches. This in turn leads to successful adaptation and the repetition of the

| | | | | |
|---|---|---|---|---|
| Exploration | — | Discovery | — | Innovation |
| Thinking | — | Doing | — | Achieving |
| Learning | — | Unlearning | — | Relearning |
| Comprehending | — | Shaping | — | Adapting |

hence a
Conceptual Spiral
for generating

| | | | | |
|---|---|---|---|---|
| Insight | — | Imagination | — | Initiative |

The Conceptual Spiral

cycle all over again as more mismatches are encountered that necessitate creative adaptation and change. The explanation can be seen as a scientific and theoretical explication of the OODA loop. In an astonishing progression, Boyd's inductive method flowed from air-to-air combat to a general theory of change and life itself. The conceptual spiral is the central insight around which "A Discourse on Winning and Losing" itself revolves.

The test of success and the real advantage in the method comes not in reading about it but rather in employing it. Like both muscles and neural networks, Boyd's Way must be exercised, or it will shrivel and atrophy. Hence, you have a responsibility to play with it, to work out with it, to examine it, to reflect on it, to improve it, to amend it, to grow with it, if you will make full use of the opportunity presented. But a discourse, a conversation, is a two-way street. You are invited to continue this important dialogue with yourself and others about Boyd's Way and its meaning for you. Remember, the conceptual spiral is insight, imagination, and initiative. Good luck, and happy idea hunting.

# 11.                    A Retired Fighter Pilot
                              Who Reads a Lot

The world must actually be such as to generate ignorance and inquiry; doubt and hypothesis, trial and temporal conclusions. . . . The ultimate evidence of genuine hazard, contin-
gency, irregularity and interdeterminateness in nature is thus found in the occurrence of
thinking.

                                        **John Dewey,** *Experience and Nature*

**B**oyd had always had misgivings about getting involved with politicians.
Even though his contacts on the Hill were extensive and valuable in or-
chestrating the development of the F-16, Burton and the Bradley Fighting Vehicle, hearings on readiness and spare parts and such, he still didn't like dealing with politicians. He felt they were not honorable men and women. A defense
contractor could always buy them with jobs in their district, or a colleague, a
wealthy donor, or vocal constituency group could call in an IOU. In short, because they were elected, they had chosen to be rather than to do. They thought
they couldn't do anything if they were not in office, so getting elected, and then
reelected, overrode every other consideration. This imperative committed them
to nearly perpetual election campaigns and money raising. Money was the
lifeblood of politics and the means by which they got elected. As far as Boyd
was concerned, all politicians were corrupt because they needed to be elected
to be in office, they needed money to be elected, and they had chosen to be
rather than to do what they should. While some were better than others, it was
a matter of degree, not kind. Politicians couldn't and hence shouldn't be trusted.

Regardless, the military reform movement was over. It had ended with the publication of a piece by Fred Reed in the *Washington Post* on 11 October 1987. Entitled simply "The Reformers," the essay was a scurrilous attack consisting mainly of name-calling. It belittled the purpose, people, and policy of the reformers. The great majority of what was written was simply wrong and filled with innuendo, yet it elicited no response from the Military Reform Caucus. At various places throughout Reed's text, the reformers (identified by name as Dina Rasor, Pierre Sprey, Bill Lind, and, through some strange association in Reed's mind, Norman Cousins) are excoriated. Various other unnamed reformers, most notably Boyd, are included in the blanket charges and referred to with the following phrases:

> They "corrupt thoughtful debate—chiefly by reducing it to clowning."
>
> They are "intellectually not much beyond childhood."
>
> They possess "ignorance of . . . monumental proportions."
>
> They "mix a robust disregard for the truth with a well deserved taste for parody."
>
> They engage in "not analysis but a sort of literary cartooning."
>
> They seek "to lampoon rather than to describe."
>
> They have "an invertebrate's grasp of chemistry."
>
> Their "lack of adherence even to high school standards of research is astonishing."
>
> They are "intellectually dishonest."
>
> They indulge in "relentlessly sloppy research and cultivated ignorance."[1]

The sheer bigotry of these charges is astonishing, and the character assassination without evidence mind-boggling. Indeed, at least one charge leveled by Reed at the reformers is certainly more accurately applied to Reed himself, at best a dilettante on the subject. As he said, "You don't help our boys by making essentially random charges about a highly complex subject whose fundamentals you have made no attempt to master."

Reed attacked the reformers on a variety of issues and weapons systems, making largely unsubstantiated countercharges and, in the process, displaying his ignorance of some of the finer points being argued. The reformers never made many of the charges Reed attributed to them. Dina Rasor did complain about the lack of an optical range finder on an M-1 tank, but she never asserted, as Reed said she did, that it worked as well as a laser range finder. It couldn't be better, for the M-1 didn't have an optical range finder. The differences in data cited by different reformers (4 miles to a gallon fuel consumption for the M-1 cited by Dina Rasor versus 9.3 gallons per mile cited by Bill Lind) that Reed complains about came from separate U.S. Army reports, not from the reformers. If Reed was upset about that, he might have questioned why the performance, measured by fuel consumption rates, was getting worse, increasing over two-fold in five years, rather than averaging out anywhere near the original estimate.

Reed dismissed as nonsense the reformers' charge that the aluminum armor on the Bradley Fighting Vehicle burned. In support of his assessment, he offered the following reasoning. "Does aluminum burn? Of course not. My wife cooks in an aluminum wok on a gas stove, and that wok has yet to go up in a fireball." Applying Reed's own high school standards, Mike Burns and Jim Morrison discovered the following in *Chemistry Made Simple*, a book to prepare people for the high school equivalency exam: "All of these metals burn with a brilliant white light in air or oxygen. . . . One such reducing reaction involving particularly aluminum is known as the thermite reaction. . . . this reaction is highly exothermic and the heat generated is sufficiently great to melt iron." A basic knowledge of high school chemistry might have been useful to Reed.

That Reed was not publicly humiliated instantly for such obviously shoddy work was inexcusable. That so few took umbrage to the character assassination leveled at any who considered themselves reformers was worse yet. After Reed's vitriol reached a crescendo of righteous indignation that would rival a TV evangelist, he declared, "The Reformers are zealots of the classic variety, with the usual self-righteousness and the usual hermetically sealed minds. . . . My objections to the Reformers over the years have not been so much to their ideas but to their slipshod research, chicanery, hermetic pompousness, deceptiveness, emotionalism and general ignorance." It sounds as if Reed made yet another error, substituting an assessment of himself for those with whom he disagrees.

Significantly, the members of the Military Reform Caucus were silent. It took months to get the politicians to reply. Eventually an insert appeared in the Congressional Record, a reprint of a statement by Col. John Boyd, Col. Jim Burton, and Lt. Col. Tom Carter and a strong vote of confidence in the people Reed attacked (save for Norman Cousins). It was hardly from an objective source, though; inserted in the "Extensions" section of the record, it was not delivered on the floor.

The straw that broke the camel's back for Boyd was an encounter with Charlie Bennett (Democrat, Florida) and Tom Ridge (Republican, Pennsylvania), who were then cochairs of the Military Reform Caucus. Boyd was personally and professionally disgusted with both men. Here were two influential members of Congress, both combat veterans themselves, who had supposedly com-

mitted themselves to the reform movement (indeed, they were its political leaders), and they were deserting their own troops when they were under fire. After
a shouting match in Charlie Bennett's office and a tremendous effort from Boyd,
Bennett agreed to sign a rather anemic letter dated 1 April 1988 and to dissemi-
nate the pieces from *Defense News* and the Congressional Record to the
Caucus membership. The caucus eventually published a piece countering
Reed's charges in *Defense News,* on 28 March 1988, five months after Reed's
initial salvo. The response was so belated that the damage had been done.
Bennett eventually retired from Congress in 1992 in his late seventies. Ridge
became governor of Pennsylvania and head of the Department of Homeland
Security. Both Boyd and the military reform movement are dead.

## Retirement, Phase Two

By 1988 Boyd had almost burned out in Washington. He was physically and
mentally exhausted. He had a ringing in his ears, felt sluggish, and grew
irritable. The next-to-last part of "A Discourse on Winning and Losing" was
completed as of August 1987 (the most often cited and distributed version), and
it dealt with what might be called the physics of morality. He was fixated on
moral issues and the need to know why and how people do the right thing. As
Jim Morrison says, Boyd "hit the wall. He got to questions without answers."[2]
Morrison and others think Boyd had a nervous breakdown or came close to one
as a result of his own inability to orchestrate the appropriate behavior. There
was no question that he was physically run down. His friends were worried
about his health and could see the strain on him. He started talking about leaving the Washington area. Despite the loss, his friends thought it best that he go
and urged him to do so. Had he stayed, many figured he would die shortly. He
was not himself, physically, mentally, or emotionally.

Boyd decided to move the family to Florida and leave the area that had been
his home for 22 years. It was a big step, but a necessary one. He would cut himself off from all those friends, issues, contacts, and fights that had been his sustenance for the last decade. Besides, Mary had wanted to leave and go to Florida
for some time. She wanted a warmer climate and a simpler life without the
hassles of D.C. traffic, crime, and urban sprawl. Mary had liked their time in
Florida at Eglin, and the idea of moving back to Florida appealed to her. Once
Boyd decided to leave, Florida was the destination. The family moved to Delray Beach, Florida, in the summer of 1988. There, they rented a three-bedroom
apartment in a new apartment building. It had a pool, a balcony from which
Mary could watch the sunsets, and was close to things they both enjoyed, bookstores for him and the beach and parks for her. His older brother lived nearby,

too, and several old friends from Erie spent the winters in the area. It would be the last move for him and a good one, despite the distance from D.C.

Boyd had several medical problems. Whether from stress and strain, exhaustion, or something more sinister, the ringing in his ears bothered him. He would also find out that he had prostate cancer. As in the past, Boyd's first move was to study the problem. He read medical texts and journal articles. He talked with several doctors. He ended up curing his own ear problem, but he had to make a decision about the cancer, and soon. The options were surgery, with a host of unpleasant side effects; external beam radiation, which was less successful but noninvasive compared to the surgery; or a radioactive isotope seed implant using iodine-125 to kill the cancerous cells. After much study and interviewing several doctors about their preferred methods and experience with each technique, Boyd made his decision. He would go with the radioactive implant.

He jokingly recalled, "Hell, for years people have been telling me that I was an asshole. Well, now I'm even better. I'm a radioactive asshole!"[3]

To exercise his mind and keep up with scientific and mathematical data that he loved, Boyd would calculate the remaining half-life of the isotope on a daily basis. He calculated the rate of radioactive decay out to several decimal places. He also monitored his progress carefully, watched his diet, worked out daily, and took charge of his health. Aside from one night a week when he and Mary would go out to dinner (usually to an Italian restaurant) and have a glass of wine with the meal, he rarely drank. He took nutritional supplements and vitamins, read articles about health and diet, and fell into a routine that was designed to keep him healthy and fit. He became something of a dietary fanatic, taking his cereals, juice, and such with him or buying it along the way as he traveled. The regimen agreed with him. His six-foot-one frame was as lean and as hard as it had been decades ago, and he could wear clothes he'd had for years. That was fortunate, for he didn't buy many, and he traded what might have been spent on a wardrobe for books and telephone bills.

Most important, Boyd exercised his brain. He read. He thought. He talked with his expanded circle of friends on the phone regularly. He revised "The Green Book," as his collection of briefings was now called, after the color of the cover on the first edition of "A Discourse on Winning and Losing." He continued to give the briefing and "take people through it" with regularity, introducing a wider array of people, military and civilian, academic and business, to his ideas. He kept his daughter Mary in Virginia busy retyping his list of ever-expanding sources and text revisions. Since Boyd didn't type, she made all the corrections over the years.

The briefing was always expanding, at least in the oral presentation and often in the text and slides, incorporating new insights, sources, and changes in the presentation. He would agonize for days over changing a single word. I have seen and gone through nineteen separate versions of "Patterns of Conflict" as it became "A Discourse on Winning and Losing." The original version took an hour or two. The last time he gave the whole briefing, it took over thirteen hours over two days. He added to it after that, and my guess is that it would have taken nearly fifteen hours to present. He constantly updated the sources as he read new works or discovered other older ones that were insightful and stimulating.[4]

## Creative Thinking and Telephone Testing

Boyd would find interesting connections and then see what could be done with them. He saw connections everywhere, in much the same way the celebrated author and television host James Burke does. They ranged from the simple to the amazingly detailed and complex, from sports analogies to quantum physics, from air-to-air combat to psychology, from military history to evolution. He used many visual analogies and illustrations to show people how to get outside the box and think about things differently from the way they had in the past. Boyd's approach was to look for interesting connections and then pursue the questions that fit the answers he had collected. According to Chuck Spinney, this drove Pierre Sprey nuts. Pierre would become exasperated that Boyd could arrive at the right answers through analogies, not logic. It may seem backward to most, but it worked for Boyd. An example is shown on page 181.

Boyd argued that all three diagrams in the illustration are the same. How can he say that a square, a triangle, and a box with an X in it are the same thing? All three are a pyramid. Depending on your view of it, the pyramid changes shape. The first is a pyramid viewed from the bottom, the second a side view, and the third a view from the top. It is a graphic insight into Boyd's preference for letting others see what they want to see. It also shows the imperative for making connections and thinking about them differently. Allowing an opponent to jump to conclusions and become a victim of self-deception, while avoiding those pitfalls oneself, was to Boyd the height of strategy.

Anyone who has watched episodes of James Burke's *Connections* and *Connections 2* or his *Day the Universe Changed* or read the books of the same titles has glimpsed the way Boyd's mind worked. How an insight in mathematics in seventeenth-century England can be related to a philosophical discovery made in eighteenth-century France, which in turn can be combined with the experiences of World War I and the development of the nineteenth-century German textile dye industry—well, you get the idea. Boyd, like Burke, was always making connections, from past to present, near to far, art to science, athletics to poli-

What is the following picture?

What is this one?

What is this?

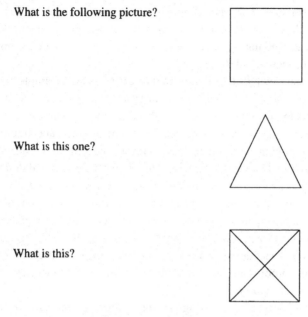

A Boyd Quiz

tics, thinking to acting, flying to life. *Mission Impossible* and *MacGyver* were television's fictional variations on the same concept, making novel connections to solve problems to win against an adversary under severe time constraints. Usually, some deception or other stratagem is required, and the more elaborate the creation of a substitute reality for the adversary, the better the contrived hoax and the more complete the creation of false perceptions. Often, the real success is based on the opponent's willingness to deceive himself, with just a little help in the right direction. Perception is everything, and manipulating that is the essence of strategy.

At times Boyd proceeded at such a dizzy pace that others could not keep up or make the intellectual leaps required to construct the metaphorical equivalent of snowmobiles. For Boyd, it was not even second nature; it was simply how he thought. The randomly firing neurons in his brain touched off a veritable fireworks show of connections that in turn created a dazzling display of synthesis. A conversation with Boyd was a mental travelogue, a cartoon history of the world, a minilecture in theoretical physics, a reference to Michael Jordan or Troy Aikman, with a sidebar allusion to evolutionary theory, reinforced with reference to an article in *Scientific American*. It then shifted into a discussion of the ossified bureaucracy of military procurement coupled with an image from an old movie or a new television show sandwiched between references from "A Discourse," all in support of a particular policy prescription, in less than five minutes. It was exhilarating and exhausting. It was pure Boyd. In his shorthand, it was making snowmobiles.

To Boyd, the revelation in this metaphorical message is simple and compelling. "A *loser* is someone (individual or group) who cannot build snowmobiles when facing uncertainty and unpredictable change; whereas a *winner* is someone (individual or group) who can build snowmobiles, and employ them in appropriate fashion, when facing uncertainty and unpredictable change."[5] For Boyd, not to think this way and act accordingly means defeat and destruction. Hence, sharpening our mental capabilities is critically important if we are to adapt and survive in a complex, uncertain, constantly changing environment. Your best weapon is your mind. Learning how to think well and quickly is the first prerequisite of survival; quite simply, innovate or die.[6] The last years of Boyd's life were spent demonstrating why this was true in a variety of ways and marshaling the proof required from a host of examples and theories from virtually all areas of inquiry.

Boyd particularly enjoyed using comments from sports stars to illustrate some aspect of his cosmology. He once called to ask if I'd heard Dallas Cowboy quarterback Troy Aikman's interview after the Super Bowl. He then proceeded to read it to me from his local newspaper (and he sent me the clipping later). "It was like everybody but me was playing at half-speed. When I'm not playing well, it's like everything is happening too fast. But in that game, it was like I had time to see the whole field and what every receiver was doing."[7] For Boyd, that was a real-world validation of his notions about cycle time. A few months later, a similar call and the eventual clipping came about Michael Jordan's comments during the NBA finals between Chicago and Phoenix. Jordan said, "Things came pretty easy early. As they were making adjustments, we were making adjustments to them quicker than they were making adjustments to us."[8] "That's how you do it," said Boyd. "That's using OODA loops to cause confusion and disorder in the adversary."

On other occasions I would be instructed to read an article on Tuesday from the *New York Times* science section or sent to get a particular book, after Boyd had read a good portion of the more important parts of it over the phone the previous evening. What Boyd characterized as "collecting, sifting, fitting, and shaping" were constant activities in which several of us became willing accomplices. If the first words I heard after picking up the phone were "Let me read you something," I knew I was facing at least an hour-long talk with Boyd, perhaps two or more hours. It could come at the office, at eleven o'clock at night, during dinner — it didn't matter to Boyd. He wasn't always gracious if I begged off, but he would let me go. I knew what he was thinking. "These things are important, damn it, and you should take the time to appreciate the insight, milk everything out of it, and make the connections with everything else remotely linked in order to use this new insight, this new weapon in your arsenal of ideas, as soon as possible."

So much of Boyd's retirement and six years of my life were wrapped up in an effort to make connections, to synthesize, to push the limits of personal knowledge, to expand horizons, to think about myriad apparently unrelated topics, in short, to build snowmobiles. It is art as well as science, simultaneously exciting and frustrating because although important, it often was not what had to be done at the moment. I have a whole bookcase at home of books that Boyd has said were must-read books—scores of them—and another at the office as well. Their subjects were not in my previous orbit of concern, ranging from John Barrow's *Theories of Everything: The Quest for Ultimate Explanation* to Ilya Prigogene and Isabelle Stenger's *Order Out of Chaos,* from Jeremy Campbell's *Grammatical Man* to John Horgan's *End of Science,* from Gary Zukav's *Dancing Wu Li Masters* to Richard Dawkins's *Selfish Gene,* from Stephen Hawking's *Brief History of Time* to Steven Rose's *Making of Memory: From Molecules to Mind.* And you know what? He was right. They are important. The insights gleaned and connections made have changed my thinking accordingly.

## Two Weeks' Worth of Boyd

Let me illustrate by going through my notes of three telephone calls in the space of a single week in November 1995. The books, subjects, current events, theories, implications, and insights contained in these will give you a taste of Boyd's mind at play and the voluminous number of random connections and intriguing questions that he generated. If what appears below seems somewhat disjointed, it is because that's the way Boyd's mind worked. My notes were an effort to capture the substance rather than the dialogue and its transitions from one subject to the next. Hang on. It is an intellectual roller-coaster ride, full of high-speed twists and turns, highs and lows, low-speed pauses and headlong rushes down the track. After it's over, the physical side effects are much the same as the aftermath of an adrenaline rush. That one mind could consistently create these multifaceted forays of thought with such ease is remarkable. The following are heavily excerpted and compressed overviews.

I called Boyd. I was curious to follow up on an earlier conversation in which he said he didn't think like other people. He has an insight, a connection, an interesting observation, and then ponders it. "That's interesting. I wonder what question that is an answer to." He went through the differences in his work, the portion that dealt with static or fixed data (energy maneuverability) and that dealt with potential (aerial attack and aircraft design). He prefers potentialities. He then proceeded to review his latest reading. In rather short order I was instructed to read Konrad Lorenz's *Behind the Mirror*, Ernst Mayer's *Growth of Biological Thought*, Gerard Radnitzky and W. W. Bartley's edited collection entitled *Evolutionary Epistemology* (focus particularly on Karl Popper's essay and that of Donald T. Campbell), and Stuart A. Kauffmann's *Origins of Order*.

In the essay "Blind Variation and Selective Retention," Campbell wrestles with the problem that these are necessary elements of all knowledge. Knowledge is extended inductively, but the real advances are the breakouts of creative thinking beyond the limits of the then known. That is why he calls them blind. Boyd finds fault with his separation of inductive and deductive approaches; one needs both and must mix and match analysis and synthesis. It is not a matter of choosing between deductive and inductive processes; rather, their combination enriches the cumulative inductive and deductive achievements and provides Boyd's "many-sided, implicit cross-references."

Kauffmann's book deals with mutations and systems at the boundaries of chaos. He states that organisms sense, classify, and act on sensory data from their worlds, OODA loops, if you will. They compress data to utilize it quickly so they can respond in time to changing conditions and threats. He laments, on page 232, that no adequate theory exists to explain how this is done. "I guess he doesn't know about mine, does he?" replies Boyd. As gently as possible, I point out that since Boyd has never published these thoughts, poor Mr. Kauffmann can't be expected to know of them. "Yeah, but the point is, you see, that our whole educational system is screwed up because there is a lack of balance in our thinking. We need both synthesis and analysis, not just an overemphasis on analysis." A relatively brief call, we hang up after only about 40 minutes.

The next night, Boyd calls. He wants to discuss some things he has tripped over that I should know about. We begin with his injunction to check out the new book by Coveney and Highfield (they wrote *The Arrow of Time*), *Frontiers of Complexity: The Search for Order in a Chaotic World*. It has some problems, but it is still worth looking at, says Boyd. "Oh, have you ever read Cleary's *Japanese Art of War*? You should. It's important." We then move to John Hall's notion of genetic algorithms, the notion that discovery takes place by combining ideas, and the query "Where do the ideas come from?" Boyd's answer is that you use changing metaphors, thought association, and forced analogies to make connections and explore for them. He cautions that every time you do an analysis of something, you should conduct a synthesis that uses it in a novel way. Nuances, analogies, and metaphors produce new concepts. "They're there," says Boyd, "it's just that they are prisoners of other concepts, and you need to liberate them. It's a sort of guerrilla warfare of the mind." We then discuss how to go about playing with ideas to see new facets and connections with other ideas: turn them upside down and inside out, reverse order insights, be deductive and inductive. All these will produce new insights and generate novelty that may be valuable.

The conversation turns to how to go about protecting an airbase in the twenty-first century. How will the Air Force's Security Police (SPs) have to change to protect Air Force installations? Boyd says the SPs should be indistinct from others, quicker to respond, irregular, not in uniform, outside the perimeter as well as inside. The locus of threat may well be internal rather than external, domestic not foreign. They should be ready to cope with different types of attacks. What about information warfare attacks, I ask. Boyd muses, "You could put autodialers on generators and shut down the telephone and computer systems of a base pretty easily, thus destroying much of the communications." Warming to the possibility, Boyd expounds on the notion of how to confound the United States using terror tactics. "Attackers should maximize ambiguity and leave no calling cards, the wrong calling cards, or multiple calling cards. How would you respond to such attacks?" Under current conditions, we agree, with great difficulty. We need to emphasize what Boyd calls the amorphous, what Sun Tzu and Musashi called formlessness.

To combat opponents successfully, says Boyd, there are multiple strategies to employ. We could maximize our appearance of ambiguity and uncertainty. Or we could create false images through deception. We could be a chameleon and change appearance, behavior, or reality with frequency. Or be our real self, just not for long. Ideally we should adopt a strategy that does all of the above combined, to mix and match randomly. Or we could bedevil an adversary by mirror-imaging him. Anyone who has taught a younger sibling to play chess can appreciate how frustrating such a tactic is. Or we could shut down entirely and have no image, electronic signatures, or traffic whatsoever. Or we could indulge in an interplay of any two courses of action for uneven amounts of time and switch back and forth at will. We could play with any or all of the building blocks of reality (time, space, energy, matter, or information) and hide, emphasize, alter, or sustain any one for strategic effect.

Pogo, the cartoon character, had it right, allows Boyd. "We have met the enemy and he is us." We are hampered by our own inability to generate novelty and our propensity to be predictable. We have become easy prey for others if they are clever enough. "Look at the Ames case," says Boyd. He then reads part of CIA director John Deutsch's testimony from the 1 November 1995 *New York Times*. Ames "gave the agency information and misinformation so craftily mixed that it has yet to sort fact from fiction."[9] I offer Goethe's admonition, "We are never deceived. We only deceive ourselves." How do you decide what portion of your perceptions are accurate? How do you prove it? How much time and effort will it take to confirm or deny what has been tainted? The real impact of such a strategy is the dissipation of resources, the creation of both self-fulfilling and suicidal prophecies, and the destruction of truth and trust. It maximizes confusion and disorder and destroys the organization's resilience, adaptability, core values, and ability to respond.

The key to such a strategy, says Boyd, is less deception (the creation of a false order) and more ambiguity (confusion about reality itself). You want to combine fact and fiction to create ambiguity for an adversary, for the combination creates more problems, requires longer to sort out, and calls more into question than merely inserting false information. As an example, he recalled the story of a group of Germans after the Normandy invasion who had stolen some American uniforms and jeeps. They went around the French countryside changing all the road signs to confuse the allies as they advanced through the area. Soon, the Americans figured out that the directions had been reversed and simply did the opposite of whatever the signs indicated. How much more effective it would have been if the Germans had changed only a portion of the signs, a third to a half, and created even more problems for the Americans. Creating ambiguity about the signs' accuracy and prolonging the time it would take to discover the problem would have been far more effective than changing all the signs in a consistent fashion.

From biology to chaos, future defense scenarios to information war, Sun Tzu and Musashi to the Ames spy case, genetic algorithms to how one thinks and learns, airbase security and police to the Japanese art of war, evolutionary epistemology and the growth of biological thought—to Boyd, they are all clearly interrelated. The next week's calls bring discussions of the DNA double helix and spiral galaxies, sensory deprivation experiments and animal behavior in zoos, neurobiological activity and the differences between subjective experience and sensory intake regarding color and music and the importance of harmony. Then follows a discussion of the relation of variety, rapidity, harmony, and innovation to the OODA loop cycle, how Boyd reads a book, and the importance of tempo and rhythm. In addition, I get Boyd's views on improving education, an article by David Chalmers in *Scientific American* entitled "The Puzzle of Conscious Experience," and Brian Goodwin's *How the Leopard Changed Its Spots*. Now, imagine the education one gets from six years of such tutelage. It left me breathless but greatly enriched. Imagine what an education based on connections and synthesis instead of mere analysis could provide to children at an early age. What formidable adversaries they would be.

## Rehabilitation

Despite Boyd's recognized brilliance on projects for the Air Force, his work on maneuver warfare and effect on the Army and the Marines, and his importance in the military reform movement, his obvious talents were not showcased, at least not within the U.S. Air Force. He was not invited to share his views with rising officers, and in fact he lectured at the Army War College and to the Marines at Quantico far more often than to his own service. He was invited just once to lecture to the Air War College. It happened on a Friday afternoon at 1400 in 1981. He was asked to present "Patterns of Conflict" and was allotted two hours to do what he knew would take four. It was a disaster. The students, used to leaving around noon, were not pleased about being in class on a Friday afternoon. Boyd, anxious to cram the briefing into the time given, was not at his best. Neither thought much of the experience. It was the only time Boyd made a presentation to an entire Air War College class.

Boyd was not invited back for over a decade. Col. Ray Bishop, who as a young officer on the Air Staff had heard Boyd more than a dozen years earlier, invited him back to address a small elective class he taught called "Strategy beyond Clausewitz" in the fall of 1991. Boyd's "Discourse on Winning and Losing" was a principal text for the course. Boyd spent two days taking the class through it. It was an exhausting and exhilarating experience. Some of the dozen or so students in the class were intrigued; others were just overwhelmed. Invited to sit in on these sessions, I experienced my first encounter with Boyd, and I was fascinated.

Ray Bishop and I gave out copies of "A Discourse" to others on the faculty, to students who seemed interested, and quietly pushed Boyd's ideas and discussed them with people in academic circles at Air University. As the concepts percolated through the community, some of Boyd's ideas and techniques became better known to a small coterie of faculty who saw value in his approach. The elective using Boyd's materials was continued, and more copies of "A Discourse" were distributed. I decided to begin the long process of writing a book about him and his ideas and began to invite Boyd to Maxwell with some frequency, after an initial week of interviews in January 1992. Other members of the faculty (Dr. George Stein, Col. Richard Szafranski, and Col. Jae Engelbrecht in particular) became Boyd aficionados.

In 1993 Boyd was asked to participate in a study sponsored by the Chief of Staff of the Air Force called Spacecast 2020. It was to investigate where the Air Force should be with respect to the control and exploitation of space nearly 30 years later. It required creative, synthetic thinking and an ability to speculate on future security environments, asking tough questions and pursuing complex scientific and technological concepts and possibilities. Boyd was a natural to help the more than 200 students and faculty involved in the project come to grips with the process. Among the captains of industry, scientists, and serving and retired general officers on the board of advisors, he was listed simply as "maverick thinker." He concurred with the designation and was proud of it. It was 18 years after he retired. His first visit in this role was only the fourth time he had been to Maxwell since leaving Squadron Officer School in the 1950s. Thereafter, until cancer began to take its toll, Boyd was a regular visitor to various schools at Air University. To some degree, he was rehabilitated within the Air Force and compensated for the vilification he had endured in the late 1980s at the hands of critics of the military reform movement.

It was the Gulf War that really increased his fame, or notoriety, depending on one's point of view. Suddenly, it seemed as if Boyd were everywhere in a variety of publications covering the war. There were articles in *Aerospace America*, *Forbes*, and *U.S. News and World Report*. A book was dedicated to Boyd and based on his synthetic thinking, chronicles of the Gulf War recounted Boyd's impact, articles in the *Wall Street Journal* and the *Boston Globe* mentioned him, books highlighted Boyd's role in the military reform movement and fighter design, and eventually a master's thesis considered his strategic thought.[10] More important, the concepts that he had been preaching gained widespread currency; phrases Boyd had pushed for years ("get inside the opponent's decision-making cycle," "have a faster OODA loop," "shape the battle space and conflict arena") were becoming routine and were enshrined in doctrine in all the services. At last there was some acknowledgment of Boyd and his ideas.

## The Big Squeeze

On 28 June 1995, Boyd made the last major revision to "A Discourse." Returning to his love of compressibility, he tried to boil down the essence of "A Discourse" into four slides, its thirteen hours into maybe thirteen minutes, and he titled it "The Essence of Winning and Losing." The process took him about three months, with frequent phone calls to his inner circle at the time: Chuck Spinney, Pierre Sprey, Barry Watts, Chet Richards (an Air Force Reserve colonel who was a business strategist for Lockheed Martin), and me. Boyd affectionately referred to the results as "the big squeeze," the ultimate compression of all he had learned and thought about winning and losing and what was really important about the process. It is a synthesis too of all of Boyd's work, from "Aerial Attack Study" and OODA loops to his most recent interests in coevolution, sociobiology, genetic engineering, chaos theory, complexity, and nonlinearity. It is an impressive effort but one that can be easily overlooked. It is somewhat akin to saying, "Life is a double helix of DNA." It is, but the richness contained in that statement and the variety and possibilities of life that a double helix may contain are so vast as to be incomprehensible. It is pregnant with potential, and the possibilities, though finite, are great in number for the organism that emerges. For Boyd, it all boils down to OODA loops and what they in turn contain, represent, and illuminate. He had come full circle and validated his intuitive hunch of more than 40 years ago.

Properly understood, the world is not as complex in its processes as we might think. The process of observation-orientation-decision-action is rich with possibilities and nearly infinite in its variety; yet it is profoundly simple in the way in which all organisms utilize the same processing of stimulus and response to make their way in the world, to spend their lives, winning and losing in the struggles of life. For Boyd, the model of the OODA loop (page 190) illustrates the keys to life itself and the way in which one wins and loses in its many competitions. It is not difficult, but it is disarming. As Colin Gray remarked at the beginning of this book, it is simple yet comprehensive and elegant.

The key statements for Boyd's "Essence of Winning and Losing" are as follows:

> Without our genetic heritage, cultural traditions, and previous experiences, we do not possess an implicit repertoire of psychophysical skills shaped by environments and changes that have been previously experienced.

> Without analysis and synthesis, across a variety of domains or across a variety of competing independent channels of information, we cannot evolve new repertoires to deal with unfamiliar phenomena or unforeseen change.

> Without a many-sided implicit cross-referencing process of projection, empathy, correlation, and rejection (across many different domains or channels of information), we cannot even do analysis and synthesis.

> Without OODA loops, we can neither sense, hence observe, thereby collect a variety of information for the above processes, nor decide as well as implement actions in accord with those processes.

> Or put another way, without OODA loops embracing all the above and without the ability to get inside other OODA loops (or other environments), we will find it impossible to comprehend, shape, adapt to, and in turn be shaped by an unfolding, evolving reality that is uncertain, ever-changing, and unpredictable.

The key to everything then, is the OODA loop. Just what is it again? There are some related insights. Note how orientation, what Boyd has always called the

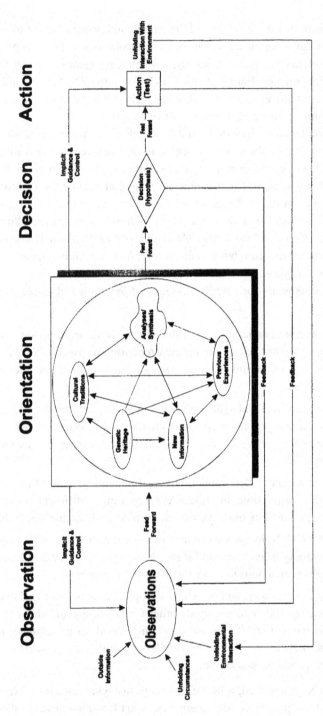

The OODA Loop. Boyd's final sketch of the OODA loop, as presented in his summation of "A Discourse on Winning and Losing," which he referred to as "the big squeeze," 28 June 1995.

big O, shapes observation, shapes decision, shapes action, and in turn is shaped by the feedback and other phenomena coming into our sensing or observation window on the world. Also note how the entire loop, not just orientation, is an ongoing, many-sided, implicit, cross-referencing process of projection, empathy, correlation, and rejection.

Putting it all together for Boyd brings one to the realization that the key statements, the OODA loop, and the related insights represent an evolving, open-ended, far-from-equilibrium process of self-organization, emergence, and natural selection. Each of these modifiers is critically important. Collectively, they mean we are faced with a dynamic, novel, unstable world that we must constantly adapt to even as we try and shape it for our own ends.

## The Importance of Mismatches and Discontinuity

Some people become so comfortable in their routines and habits that they seek to impose them on the reality around them. In one sense, there is nothing wrong with that. Man has tamed a wild environment and bent it to his needs over the millennia. In another sense, a failure to recognize change or, more correctly, the need for change, and a continuance of routine out of habit when it no longer suffices to accomplish what we must, is foolhardy. Before one can do something about change, one has to recognize it. Then the OODA loop must cope with it effectively if we are to survive. The whole process depends in the first instance on recognizing that something no longer fits as it should, on seeing a mismatch, on recognizing a discontinuity. Once that has been observed, we can proceed to answer Lenin's famous question, "What is to be done?"

From these mismatches, discontinuities, things that don't fit reality or our perceptions of it, progress comes. Without the difference to contend with, we would have no reason to address it and its consequences. It is the mismatch, the lack of fit, the incongruity, that is the spur to creativity. It is our recognition of it and ability to contend with it and make something of the opportunity that determines our success or failure, our prosperity, the quantity and quality of life itself. Not being able to read the environment and take advantage of opportunities that it presents is the essence of original sin, in Boyd's catechism. OODA loops are the answer. From that process come the possibilities for success, failure, life, and death. Coming to grips with these opportunities or threats faster than others gives us greater advantage still. A failure to recognize these truths will mean we fail to survive and prosper.

This gave Boyd a rather perverse glee in finding that all was not right with the world, for in that reality, he saw the possibility of continuing to improve it. He did not fall victim to the ultimate heresy of the Enlightenment, in believing in earthly perfection. He did not shrink from what he saw as the continuing need for improvement and adaptation, either. For Boyd, discontinuities were the norm and harmony the exception. That doesn't mean we should seek to abolish discontinuities in pursuit of a widening gyre of harmony. It means rather that there is a sort of yin and yang balance between the two in the long run and that we are the agents of transformation among them. Humankind is responsible for much of the change that has been wrought on the planet, though by no means the bulk of it, thus it is incumbent on us to muddle through as best we can.

Life that was perfect, where everything fit, with no loose ends, late arrivals, imperfect understandings, poor connections, blown fuses, failures, or mismatches, would not be worth living for Boyd. In such a life, man would become an automaton, incapable of adaptation. Without the need to adapt, without the excuse to become creative, without the puzzles that need to be solved, we would become a mere part of the environment and not a thinking agent of change within it. Such would not be a life for Boyd or, one suspects, for most of the rest of us either. One needs to work, to be responsible, to have chores, to be needed to do something, have others to assist, problems to solve, things that need fixing, to justify our sense of self-worth and some reason for being beyond even ultimate salvation.

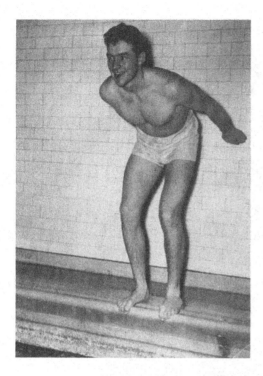

John Boyd as a swimmer, Erie
Strong Vincent High School.
Family photograph.

Private John R. Boyd, U.S.
Army Air Forces, 1945–1947.
Family photograph.

John and Mary Boyd on their wedding day, December 23, 1951. Family photograph.

John Boyd as a lifeguard at Presque Isle State Park near Erie, Pennsylvania. Family photograph.

First Lt. John Boyd and his F-86 in Korea. USAF photograph.

The A-10 Thunderbolt II (Warthog). USAF photograph.

The F-15 Eagle, after being refueled by a tanker. USAF photograph.

The F-16 Fighting Falcon (Viper). USAF photograph.

Col. John R. Boyd's official Air Force photograph, 1974.

Colonel Boyd's retirement ceremony. A handwritten inscription on the family's print of this photograph reads: "To Colonel John R. Boyd with my sincere gratitude for your great contributions to the Air Force. You will be sorely missed. John McLucas, Secretary of the Air Force."

Boyd explaining a fine point to a listener, January 1995. Family photograph.

Boyd before his descent into poor health, spring 1996. Family photograph.

# 12.     That Marvelous Pitch of Vision

What this task requires in the way of higher intellectual gifts is a sense of unity and a power of judgment raised to a marvelous pitch of vision, which easily grasps and dismisses a thousand remote possibilities which an ordinary mind would labor to identify and wear itself out in so doing.

Carl von Clausewitz, *On War,* Book 1, Chapter 3

**B**oyd was a multidimensional man of remarkable talent, skill, and compassion. He was ruthless when he needed to be, gentle when he wanted to be, demanding always, controversial and provocative routinely. He tilted at various windmills in the establishment, relished it, and drew sustenance from it. A natural leader of great moral suasion, Boyd aroused in those who joined him an adulation and willingness for sacrifice. They were his disciples and followers, and he had many. The inner circle of Spinney, Burton, Sprey, and Christie and the far more numerous outer circle of converts to the cause remain acolytes to his vision, pilgrims on a journey. Many others, mostly the politicians, have forgotten his teachings or avoided the sacrifices Boyd's beliefs required.

Many officers in the military, people in business and the academy, are rediscovering his message. They are joining a movement to teach others about the moral dimension of human conduct, the need for creative adaptation, the evils of business as usual, the rigors of successful competition, and the Boydian trinity of people first, ideas second, things third. His legacy endures through Internet exchanges, Web sites, symposia, courses at public and private schools throughout the world, and articles and books that continue to spread the word. Internationally, there have been articles in South Korean newspapers, Internet discussions of Boyd in Chinese, and graduate business courses in Denmark.

Over the years, Boyd's ideas have penetrated not only other military services but also the business community and academia here and abroad. Scores of books and articles chronicle his ideas and exploits and mention Boyd in a variety of roles. Thousands of copies of the 327-slide magnum opus, "A Discourse on Winning and Losing," are out there, copies from ones he gave away. Many of the ideas, words, and phrases in Boyd's briefings have found their way into numerous doctrinal statements and joint publications throughout the U.S. military. All the services use the OODA loop as a standard description of decision-making cycles. John Fialka of the *Wall Street Journal* summarizes Boyd's influence: "Like the rain coming in through a leaky roof, Boyd's ideas thoroughly penetrated the winning strategy of the U.S. forces during the Gulf War, which was based on speed, maneuver and stealth. Later, generals and admirals borrowed liberally from Boyd's unpublished "Discourse on Winning and Losing" to explain their theories on information warfare. Some of them even passed off Boyd's ideas as their own."[1] That didn't bother Boyd. He gave away good ideas and didn't care who took credit for them. It was the bad ones he wanted to root out.

The concepts of shaping the strategic environment, adaptation to the fluidity of the modern battlefield, coping with uncertainty, using time as an ally, using more rapid OODA loop cycles to degrade an adversary's ability to cope, are now routine. His emphasis on innovation and empathy (not normally seen as skills of warfighters), leveraging asymmetries, the importance of trust and teamwork, the necessity for considering moral factors, is no longer seen as strange. Nor are the need for nonlinear thinking and the emphasis on such elements as awareness, the commander's intent, information, and the quality of leadership. All are enshrined in the *Concept for Future Joint Operations* (May 1997) and numerous other DOD and service publications.[2] Though not unique to him, Boyd made consideration of them routine in an important period in the evolution of the American military. He was a great synthesizer as well as an original thinker and a singular individual.

John Boyd committed his greatest sin—challenging orthodoxy—routinely, and with glee. He relished doing so, and others either believed in him or hated him for it. He is regarded simultaneously as one of the greatest military minds of the twentieth century and a crackpot, as a great pilot and a one-trick pony, as a threat to the nation and one of its greatest unsung heroes. The reality lies somewhere between those extremes but tends toward greatness.

## Boyd on Warfighting

What Boyd is all about is a way of thinking and the creation of organizations and organisms that are adaptive and capable of rapidity, variety, harmony, and initiative. Only in this way can they hope to survive and prosper in the face of complex change and uncertainty. The most comprehensive application of Boyd to date is found in FMFM-1, the U.S. Marine Corps manual entitled "Warfighting."[3] Conceived by the commandant of the Marine Corps Gen. Albert M. Gray, the manual was largely written by Capt. John F. Schmitt. Gray minces no words in his accompanying foreword. "I expect every officer to read—and reread—this book, understand it and take its message to heart. The thoughts contained here represent not just the guidance for actions in combat, but a way of thinking in general. This manual thus describes a philosophy for action which, in war and peace, in the field and in the rear, dictates our approach to duty." A synthesis of Clausewitz, Sun Tzu, Liddell Hart, Napoleon, Patton, and, most especially, John Boyd tailored to the Marine Corps, "Warfighting" is the essay Boyd should have written instead of only giving briefings.

The synthesis that FMFM-1 represents rests largely on the one that Boyd created. Boyd is cited in the manual for his ideas, and parts of it are taken verbatim from Boyd's presentations.

> On uncertainty, "The very nature of war makes absolute certainty impossible; all actions in war will be based on incomplete, inaccurate, or even contradictory information."

> On maneuver warfare, "The goal is the application of strength against selected enemy weakness. By definition, maneuver relies on speed and surprise, for without either, we cannot concentrate strength against enemy weakness. Tempo itself is a weapon—often the most important. The need for speed in turn requires decentralized control. While attrition operates principally in the physical realm of war, the results of maneuver are both physical and moral. The object of maneuver is not so much to destroy physically as it is to shatter the enemy's cohesion, organization, command, and psychological balance."

> On trust, "Consequently, trust is an essential trait among leaders—trust by seniors in the abilities of their subordinates and by juniors in the competence and support of their seniors."

Certain terms used throughout the pamphlet are thoroughly Boydian: fluidity, shaping the battle, intuition, harmony, decision-making cycles, the moral aspects of war, dispersion and concentration, the importance of trust, increasing the adversary's friction, promoting uncertainty and disorder, decentralizing decision making. Chapter 4, "The Conduct of War," is a tightly woven synthesis of Boyd's more rambling briefings, particularly the sections on maneuver warfare and decision making. Indeed, its definition of maneuver warfare is Boyd's preferred vision of how wars should be fought: "Maneuver warfare is a warfighting philosophy that seeks to shatter the enemy's cohesion through a series of rapid, violent, and unexpected actions which create a turbulent and rapidly deteriorating situation with which he cannot cope."

Other portions of the manual are beautifully written syntheses of Boyd's Way. The introduction to the chapter "The Conduct of War" is entitled "The Challenge." It is useful to cite it in full.

The challenge is to identify and adopt a concept of warfighting consistent with our understanding of the nature and theory of war and the realities of the modern battlefield. What exactly does this require? It requires a concept of warfighting that will function effectively in an uncertain, chaotic, and fluid environment—in fact one that will exploit these conditions to advantage. It requires a concept that, recognizing the time-competitive rhythm of war, generates and exploits superior tempo and velocity. It requires a concept that is consistently effective across the full spectrum of conflict, because we cannot attempt to change our basic doctrine from situation to situation and expect to be proficient. It requires a concept which recognizes and exploits the fleeting opportunities which naturally occur in war. It requires a concept, which takes into account the moral as well as physical forces of war, because we have already concluded that the moral forces form the greater part of war. It requires a concept with which we can succeed against a numerically superior foe, because we can no longer presume a numerical advantage. And, especially in expeditionary situations in which public support for military action may be tepid and short-lived, it requires a concept with which we can win quickly against a larger foe on his home soil, with minimal casualties and limited external support.

That is in effect a summary of what Boyd was able to do in "A Discourse on Winning and Losing."

## Military Genius

In Carl von Clausewitz's famous treatise *On War,* chapter 3 of book 1 is devoted to the subject called "Military Genius." Clausewitz defines genius as outstanding "gifts of intellect and temperament," "a very highly developed mental aptitude for a particular occupation," and "a harmonious combination of elements."[4] What constitutes this "harmonious combination of elements"? Although Clausewitz was obviously thinking of Napoleon and other "great captains," could those of lesser rank exhibit military genius? Boyd was not an aerial ace, never made general officer, and was to many more trouble than he was worth. How does he measure up? Did he meet Clausewitz's standard of military genius?

First among the elements Clausewitz requires for military genius is courage. This is of two kinds: courage in the face of personal danger and courage to accept responsibility. Courage in the face of personal danger is divided further into two kinds. Courage is indifference to danger, and it is also that which flows from positive motives of "ambition, patriotism or enthusiasm of any kind." Summarizing his views on courage, Clausewitz says, "These two kinds of courage act in different ways. The first is the more dependable; having become second nature, it will never fail. The other often will achieve more. There is more reliability in the first kind, more boldness in the second. The first leaves the mind calmer; the second tends to stimulate, but it can also blind. *The highest kind of courage is a compound of both*" (p. 101). Boyd obviously displayed both kinds of courage. There wasn't anything he wouldn't try in an airplane. He also displayed high levels of patriotism and enthusiasm, if not ambition for wealth or rank. His ambition was for the success of good ideas. Boyd was courageous in both senses, often risking all to do what he thought was right, at the expense of a career, promotion, assignments, and income.

Clausewitz continues with his catalog, noting, "war is the realm of physical exertion and suffering. These will destroy us unless we can make ourselves indifferent to them." Boyd didn't much care about his living circumstances, the length of his days (or nights) on the job, the lousy offices or tasks he was given, as long as he was learning, contributing, pushing ahead with the ideas that counted. He had what Clausewitz called "a certain strength of body and soul," and it was the latter that was more important. Boyd was passionately committed to truth, and all else paled in comparison. What Clausewitz characterized as "the powers of intellect," Boyd possessed in abundance. "War is the realm of uncertainty; three quarters of the factors on which action in war is based are wrapped in a fog of greater or lesser uncertainty. A sensitive and discriminating judgment is called for; a skilled intelligence to scent out the truth." The ability "to scent out the truth" is a wonderful metaphor and near-perfect description of the way Boyd searched a thicket of ideas and unraveled the tangle to capture his prey, the truth. He certainly possessed "sensitive and discriminating judgment," much to the chagrin of many of his superiors. He had high standards, and he held himself and others to them with equal conviction.

Clausewitz next reminds us that "war is the realm of chance" and that "chance makes everything more uncertain and interferes with the whole course of events." War is an environment where "all information and assumptions are open to doubt," where "the commander continually finds that things are not as he expected," where new information calls into question the commander's intentions, where we become "more, not less uncertain." It is the world as Boyd understood it, where perfection and exact measurement always elude us, where Gödel, Heisenberg, and the second law are the norm, not the exception. Boyd not only understood but also reveled in the realization that war is, as Clausewitz put it, the realm of uncertainty. Fog and friction come with the territory, to Boyd and to Clausewitz. War was art, not science, and highly dependent on morale, perception, and attitude as well as aptitude.

Clausewitz explains further, "If the mind is to emerge unscathed from this relentless struggle with the unforeseen, two qualities are indispensable: first an intellect that, even in the darkest hour, retains some glimmering of the inner light which leads to truth; and second, the courage to follow this faint light wherever it may lead. The first of these qualities is described by the French term *coup d'oeil*, the second as *determination*." *Coup d'oeil* is French for an insightful glance, for knowing in an instant what is going on, for a flash of insight derived from a quick look at the situation. Clausewitz defines it simply as "the quick recognition of a truth that the mind would ordinarily miss or would perceive only after long study and reflection" (p. 102). His explanation of its derivation and importance flows from decision making in combat. As he explains it,

The aspect of war that has always attracted the greatest attention is the engagement. Because time and space are important elements of the engagement, and were particularly significant in the days when the cavalry attack was the decisive factor, *the idea of rapid and accurate decision* was first based on the evaluation of time and space, and consequently received a name which refers to visual estimates only. Many theorists of war have employed the term in that limited sense. But soon it was also used of any sound decision taken in the midst of action—such as recognizing the right point to attack, etc. *Coup d'oeil* therefore refers not alone to the physical but, more commonly, to the inward eye. The expression, like the quality itself, has certainly always been more applicable to tactics, but it must also have its place in strategy, since here as well quick decisions are often needed. (p. 102)

Boyd certainly met this test, given his concern for time and space, for quick decision and OODA loop cycles, for rapid assessment of an always changing circumstance. Clausewitz would have no trouble recognizing the capacity for coup d'oeil in Boyd. The whole notion of rapid OODA loops is coup d'oeil in action.

What of determination, the other element that Clausewitz says characterizes the mind of the military genius? It proves to be far more important to Clausewitz. He makes several significant distinctions in defining it.

Determination in a single instance is an expression of courage; if it becomes characteristic, a mental habit. But here we are referring not to physical courage but to courage to accept responsibility, courage in the face of moral danger. . . . the role of determination is to limit the agonies of doubt and the perils of hesitation. . . . Determination, which dispels doubt, is a quality that can be aroused only by the intellect, and by a specific cast of mind at that. . . . It is engendered only by a *mental act;* the mind tells the man that boldness is required, and thus gives direction to his will. (pp. 102–103)

The Air Force's adoption of the F-16 is proof enough of Boyd's determination. Boyd battled over a long period of time, against long odds, in spite of numerous obstacles, and at the risk of his career. Few have exhibited such commitment to bucking the system. Courage and determination are for most of us episodic characteristics, if attributes at all. We will ask once, challenge perhaps twice, but rarely push consistently for what we know others think unpopular, unwise, difficult, or wrong. Boyd was different; he wouldn't take no for a final answer.

Clausewitz's next requirement for military genius is "presence of mind." This Clausewitz generally defines as "an increased capacity for dealing with the unexpected." It requires quick thinking in the face of danger, demonstrated by apt repartee and the "speed and immediacy of the help provided by the intellect." Boyd, whose core concept of the OODA loop deals with quick assessment, response, and adaptation to a constantly changing environment, seems to fit the bill exactly. He reveled in the unexpected, cherished opportunities to grapple with it, and always sought to outthink his adversary in time before outmaneuvering him in space. Boyd was a walking example of presence of mind.

The four elements that make up the climate of war, says Clausewitz, are danger, exertion, uncertainty, and chance. These require, in turn, if one is to be successful in war, energy, firmness, staunchness, endurance, emotional balance, and strength of character. If one could possess these six traits, then he could cope successfully with the four dangers. Boyd possessed extraordinary energy and focus. "Firmness" is hardly strong enough to describe a man who would argue against all comers late into the night for what he thought right. Few have exhibited the endurance in support of unpopular causes and positions on multiple occasions that Boyd displayed routinely. Boyd was noted for his anger and temper at times, but overall, he possessed a great degree of emotional balance.

Clausewitz spends a great deal of time discussing strength of mind and strength of character.[5] They depend on a capacity for self-control, "the gift of keeping calm even under the greatest stress" (a factor of temperament), and the urge "to act rationally at all times" (a matter of intellect). Clausewitz wanted men as warriors and commanders who were not easily roused or excited. Second, he wanted those who were "sensitive but calm." Third, he wanted men with some spirit, whose passions could be inflamed and be motivated to make sacrifices in pursuit of the desired end. It was not just powerful feelings that were important but also "maintaining one's balance in spite of them." He sought men of character, "whose views are *stable and constant*." This is a tall order, to be passionate but balanced, sensitive but calm, and controlled and rational at all times. Boyd may fail here, but his outrageous antics were all purposeful and calculated and, hence, controlled, however wild they may have seemed at the time. His emotional outbursts were designed more to destabilize an opponent than to vent true anger, to give himself an edge by causing others to underestimate him.

For Clausewitz, military genius required a man of conviction, character, and constancy. He used many different phrases to describe the necessary qualities he had in mind. Among them were:

> instinct, a sensing of the truth
>
> clear and deep understanding
>
> a strong faith in the overriding truth of tested principles
>
> a balanced temperament
>
> a sense of locality . . . the faculty of quickly and accurately grasping the topography of any area
>
> the mental gift we call imagination
>
> a good memory
>
> outstanding effort, the kind that gives men a distinguished name
>
> the commander-in-chief is simultaneously a statesman. (pp. 109–111)

Military genius is a rare blend of all those qualities.

In the end, it is that capacity to see things—as they are, as they were, as they should be—and to make that vision a reality that lies at the heart of military genius. It is, as Boyd would state it, a capacity for insight, imagination, intuition, and innovation. Clausewitz concludes this section by asking and answering the question this way: "If we then ask what sort of mind is likely to display the qualities of military genius, experience and observation will both tell us that it is an inquiring rather than the creative mind, the comprehensive, rather than the specialized approach, the calm rather than the excitable head to which in war we would choose to entrust the fate of our brothers and children, the safety and honor of our country" (p. 112). John Boyd was both an inquiring and creative mind, but as "Destruction and Creation" reveals, his focus was first and foremost on inquiring about the mismatches. He was a synthesizer of rare breadth and depth who combined observations to achieve new insights and understanding. He never was solely entrusted with the safety and honor of the country, but his ideas have done much to shape those who are. By any reasonable test of Clausewitz's criteria, John Boyd was a military genius. Compared with most of his contemporaries and products of the American military in this century, the same verdict would be rendered. Few, if any, have achieved that "unity and power of judgment raised to a marvelous pitch of vision."

## Prophet without Honor

Boyd was hurt that for many years he was virtually ostracized by the service to which he had devoted his life. His boss and fellow conspirator in promoting the F-16, Rich Riccioni, went so far as to say, "Fighter aviation can never be the same for the advent of Lt. Col. Boyd. Aircraft and battle analysis will never be the same. The entire spectrum of aircraft contractors has modified their analysis and presentations. Air combat tactics can never revert to the pre-Boyd era."[6] He was so gifted in so many ways, one would expect the Air Force to be eager to use him and his ideas in its educational programs. Such was not the case. Meanwhile, the Army had Boyd speak at Leavenworth (the Command and General Staff College) and Carlisle (the Army War College) on multiple occasions over the years. West Point held a conference on military reform in 1982 and invited Boyd as a principal speaker. The Marine Corps had him speak at Quantico several times a year at the Basic School, and he briefed the officers of the Second Marine Division, which prompted one of the higher accolades Boyd was to receive. Brig. Gen. Joe Hopkins, an assistant division commander, had been reluctant to participate in Boyd's briefing but was ordered to attend by Commander Al Gray. When he was asked afterward what he thought of the briefing, his reply was effusive. "Well, General, I got nine months at Newport [Naval War College] in one day with John Boyd."[7] The Marines made use of his "Green Book" briefing on "Patterns of Conflict" and eventually "A Discourse on Winning and Losing." Even the Navy made use of Boyd through his visits to Cecil Field in Florida to talk with pilots in naval aviation. The Air Force did none of that. The Air Force rediscovered Boyd and OODA loops only after the Gulf War, when getting inside the adversary's decision-making cycle became a given for military strategy and tactics and was much discussed in the press and among the defense intellectual community.

Here was one of the finest military minds this country has produced. He was a model of integrity. He had made major contributions to the design and development of the fighter aircraft the Air Force flies today, and the Air Force had little or no use for him. It would give time to nearly any retired three- and four-star general officer, regardless of intellect, character, or accomplishments, but not to Boyd. Rank has its privileges, you know, even in retirement. Retired colonels generally don't count for a lot, and maverick thinking is not to be promoted. It is difficult for those in a military hierarchy to remember that rank × IQ is a constant.

Admittedly, Boyd was not an easy person to deal with, in uniform or out, for the Air Force. He broke nearly every rule on how to be successful in the Air Force. He went outside the chain of command, and he made end runs around his boss or his boss's boss routinely. He challenged cherished corporate values and traditions in service culture. He was abrasive, irritating, pushy, at times arrogant. He had little respect for rank, only high-quality thinking and behavior. He made many enemies by pushing his unpopular ideas. Boyd was a shining example of what the service could not tolerate. When various high-ranking officers in the Air Force learned of my interest in Boyd and my decision to write about him, I was told a number of times that my talents could be better utilized on other people or other subjects. To their credit, however, no one told me not to do it. They simply regretted the emphasis on Boyd and his ideas. They thought they were done with him.

Perhaps more egregious is the Air Force's failure to provide an occasion for Boyd to experience what he helped to create. Though nearly any reporter or local television anchorman can get a public relations ride in an Air Force fighter, Boyd never flew in an F-15 or in his beloved F-16. In fairness to the Air Force, Boyd never asked—he wouldn't, as a point of honor—and they never offered.

Boyd's ideas have had a greater influence on other services, certainly the Marines and to some degree the Army. Partially rehabilitated in the early 1990s, Boyd spoke at Air University to students at the Air War College, Air Command and Staff College, and the Squadron Officers School. He also served as an advisor to Spacecast 2020, the Air Force study to forecast the service's needs related to space. He appreciated his designation as "maverick thinker" on the list of project advisors. It took a while, but the Air Force finally appreciated that there is a need and a role for mavericks.

A listing of Boyd's accomplishments, arranged as a military citation for an award, might well read:

His prescient insights into strategy and tactics, his brilliant analytical and synthetic thinking skills, his superb understanding and practice of aerial combat, his seminal contributions to energy maneuverability theory, his outstanding concept of the OODA loop and the importance of cycle time, his skillful training of hundreds of pilots and sharing of aerial combat skills with thousands of others, his superior design genius and contributions to development of the F-15 and the F-16, his unflagging efforts to promote understanding of and adoption of the principles of maneuver warfare by the American military, his unstinting initiatives to improve the planning and budgeting process for national defense, and his continuous efforts to improve the procurement processes of the Air Force reflect great credit on Colonel Boyd and the United States Air Force.

His protégé Jim Burton would go even farther. "My personal belief is that history will also show that, during the past two decades, John Boyd has had more influence on the military than any other single individual."[8] Regrettably, no such citation was ever presented.

To contribute to the defense of the nation by defying others is a hard kind of patriotism. To challenge orthodoxy as a part of a military hierarchy meant challenging one's superiors. Challenging one's superiors risked assignments, promotions, and ultimately one's career and very livelihood. To do so routinely for an entire career and continue to challenge the system in retirement exacts an even heavier toll. To do so as a matter of principle and not for private gain marks one as dangerous. Such conviction requires self-sacrifice and loyalty to an authority higher than one's superiors. Unfortunately, there are few rewards, virtually no ribbons and medals, and few thank-yous, even for jobs well done. The satisfaction gained from success, whatever the victories won, is relatively short-lived. The system will return to its accustomed inefficiency until nudged temporarily out of its lethargy by the next crusader, always coming back to rest essentially where it was before. Boyd and company nudged harder and longer than most. Though Forty-Second Boyd's service to his country is over, a grateful nation may continue to profit from his insights.

## Taps

Among the mourners at Boyd's funeral at Arlington National Cemetery, with full military honors, more were from the other services than from the Air Force. That wasn't hard to arrange. With the exception of the Air Force Band and Honor Guard, there was only one three-star general, the token representative from Boyd's service, and a major who had heard of Boyd and wished to pay his respects. The general had no clue who Boyd was or what he had done. He was merely attending a ceremony as ordered. Large numbers of civilians and a few officers from the Navy and Army were present. So too were the Marines, in large numbers, one of whom laid his eagle, globe, and anchor at the grave as a mark of the respect the Marine Corps had for Boyd.

Friends worked hard to arrange a flyover for the graveside service. Had it not been for the efforts of retired general officers, particularly Howard Leaf, who had flown with Boyd in Korea, it would not have been possible. A flyover was dutifully arranged with F-15s, not his beloved F-16 (that would have been too much for the Air Force to take), but even that didn't occur. As we stood there at Arlington Cemetery, watching civilian airliners landing at National Airport every few minutes, we were informed that the flyover had to be cancelled because of inclement weather.

Shortly after Boyd's death, I received a phone call from a major on the Air Staff at the Pentagon, who wanted to know if anything had been done at Air University to memorialize John Boyd. "Not to my knowledge," I replied; though several initiatives had been made, none had been implemented. He then inquired if the book I was writing could be considered an Air Force recognition of Boyd. I said no, it was my book, not an Air Force project. When I asked why he was asking these questions, he explained that he was answering a congressional inquiry regarding Boyd.

A little detective work solved the puzzle. Boyd's disciples had learned well and were still pushing. Ron Catton, Boyd's former student at Nellis, had written to his congressman, Rep. George Nethercutt (the Republican who had defeated Speaker of the House Tom Foley). He in turn had written to the Air Force to inquire "what the USAF was doing to honor the memory of Col. John R. Boyd, USAF (ret.)" for his valuable contributions to the Air Force and the American victory in the Gulf War. The Air Force was scrambling to find out what could count as recognition for Boyd. I sent the major some materials on Boyd and volunteered my help in any way. I never heard from him again.

Over two years later, I got a call from Nellis asking for materials on Boyd and informing me that the old photo lab at Nellis was to be converted into the USAF Weapons School Adversary Support Building and would be named for Boyd. The congressional inquiry had raised a mild effort to do something, and this was deemed both appropriate and low profile enough to fill the bill and not embarrass the Air Force. Several requests (none from me) to do more, for instance at Air University, a more appropriate venue to acknowledge his ideas rather than his tactics or hardware contributions, had been rebuffed.[9] So the Air Force memorialized Boyd with a small plaque on a building at the Fighter Weapons School at Nellis. The building was named for Boyd in a short ceremony at 0930 on 17 September 1999. Boyd's widow, Mary, his older brother, and one of his sons were in attendance, as were friends from his hometown of Erie, Pennsylvania, and some colleagues from over the years. Even then, however, the Air Force got in its digs. The commander of the Fighter Weapons School was instructed by a retired general officer to shorten his remarks from eleven minutes to no more than five. The Air Force does not intend to tolerate mavericks, as evidenced by the absence of any mention of Boyd in the public materials distributed about the Fighter Weapons School or its history.

Though belated and belittled, Boyd would applaud even that token recognition. Linking him with the aggressors in the annual Red Flag air-to-air exercises at Nellis is at least in keeping with his approach. Within Air Force culture, being a good stick and showing others how to be good at air-to-air combat 40 years ago has a greater value than learning about better thinking for the future. Several senior Air Force officers—serving and retired—have explained to me that although Boyd was an important figure in the evolution of the Air Force, public recognition would be difficult because he dared to buck the system on so many occasions. Challenging the orthodoxy of the senior leadership is not something that can be easily forgiven.

Within 48 hours of Boyd's death, the commandant of the Marine Corps contacted the family about preserving his papers. Today, all of John Boyd's books and papers are housed in the archives of the Marine Corps Research Center at Quantico. There is a large display case honoring Boyd, an Air Force officer, at the center of the Marine Corps university. It is odd to see the flight suit, flight logs, decorations, and papers of an Air Force colonel displayed in the halls of the Marine Corps Library, along with famous battles and accomplishments of the Marine Corps. That's not what Congress had in mind with the Goldwater-Nichols Act of 1986 encouraging "jointness" among the services, but it is one of the better testimonials to it that can be found. If any one person exuded a commitment to jointness, in the sense of pushing ideas about how to organize, train, and equip for war without regard to service parochialism, it was Boyd.

All this would seem to suggest that many of the principles of Boyd's beliefs—trust, initiative, innovation, adaptation—are still in short supply in the military in general and the Air Force in particular. To date, his challenge to both has been greater than the change that has resulted. John Boyd's ideas live on, but they have had far more impact on the Marine Corps and the Army than on the Air Force. After two military triumphs without victory in the Gulf War and Kosovo, perhaps his thoughts on winning and losing are being revisited. The investment in the minds of people is far overshadowed by the investment in the technologies of war. Greater attention to the thought behind the deployment and employment of military force and its ultimate purpose rather than on the tools of winning and losing would serve us well.

## Protect the Mavericks

What are we to learn from a life such as Boyd's? What are we to take from the chronicle of his experiences? What do we do with "A Discourse on Winning and Losing?" These are important questions, and the answers are not easy. There are several lessons to be learned. The first views Boyd's story as a cautionary tale. National security is important, but it should not be so all consuming that the invocation of the term causes unthinking compliance with whatever remedies are proposed first. A healthy debate about not only "How much is enough?" but also the corollary and more important question "To do what?" has to be sustained. We need devil's advocates, nay-sayers, doubting Thomases, those who question our assumptions, ends, means, and costs of the course of action the nation adopts. Doing so places great strain on rank-conscious hierarchical systems, which are top down, not bottom up, in orientation and worried more about command and control than appreciation and leadership or the nurturing of good ideas.

Gen. Matthew B. Ridgway, one of our ablest military leaders, was a tough, capable, intelligent airborne soldier of World War II and later a United Nations commander in Korea. He went on to become Army Chief of Staff. At his retirement ceremony, he was asked what his most significant role had been in the mid-1950s as Army Chief of Staff. His answer shocked many with its promptness and simplicity. He said simply, "to protect the mavericks." As Arthur Hadley relates it,

Ridgway went on to explain that, like wars in the past, any future war was apt to be completely different from what the planners had forecast. Yet when such crises came, there would have to be plans and methods ready to meet the unforeseen challenge. All he could hope to do was to have some mavericks around who were looking at the future from points of view different from the orthodox beliefs and school solutions. Since the Army, Navy and Air Force were such powerful and rigid institutions, such maverick officers were not always popular and their careers usually at risk. He felt his chief contribution had been in protecting such men.[10]

In that sense, perhaps the real heroes of this saga about Boyd, the Fighter Mafia, and the military reform movement are people like Air Force Chief of Staff John P. McConnell, Gen. James Ferguson in Air Force Systems Command, and Brig. Gen. Allman T. Culberson at Eglin Air Force Base, who put up with, supported, protected, and promoted Boyd when he needed it. Without them, Boyd and his work would not have had the impact they did. They are to be commended, as are many others who acted in a similar fashion throughout his career.

The Air Force is not much different from most large enterprises. The sheer size, scope, and scale of the operations, bureaucracy, regulations, and standard operating procedures are so large that a certain amount of stultifying routine and a lack of imagination are to be expected. In saying this, one should realize that most of corporate America, academia, and many other institutions of some size and complexity (be they churches or the American Medical Association, unions or political parties) share the same characteristics most of the time. The trick is to allow the mavericks to exist and to be heard, to select those who have real contributions to make from those who merely complain, to keep a certain amount of in-house criticism and nay-saying as a counterpoise to the routine.

Somebody has to keep the system honest by asking the novel and tough questions and pushing radical ideas.

Taking care of the mavericks is not something the American military does well. Few make it to general officer, and most don't make colonel, deciding to leave rather than continue to get hammered in the effort to create change. Making a place for diversity of thought on the team rather than requiring sycophantic cheerleading for the boss is hard but necessary for successful competition. The worst climate is one where no one speaks up for fear of retribution and the organization obtains nonconcurrence by silence. At that point the diversity, ferment, uncertainty, and mismatches that are required for creative problem solving, true insight, and real progress are all stifled and suppressed. The organization's ability to adapt is impaired, perhaps destroyed.

Permitting diversity of thought and opinion is a prerequisite for "thriving on chaos," as Tom Peters described it. The interaction with one's environment and the constant monitoring of it and one's opportunities and reactions is a requirement for continued existence and prosperity. Boyd's Way is, on one level, little more than the extrapolation of that rather simple, commonsense observation to the specific choices of our lives. OODA loops are merely an explanation for our existence, the general process by which we cope and interact with others and our environment. As an insight, it is hardly earth-shattering. As a thought process, it is rich in consequence and an empowerment tool of limitless possibilities. The habit of mind of synthesizing as well as analyzing makes one routinely and expansively creative, not merely analytically critical. Connections enrich us. Conflict challenges us. Competition motivates us. Our responses (insight, imagination, innovation, and initiative) give us hope and inspiration.

## Boyd and the American Way of War

Boyd's sin was no less than a complete challenge to the way the American people and military were used to doing business. Schooled to prefer formulaic answers, checklists, and school solutions, the American military is decidedly Jominian, not Clauswitzian. It shuns openness, nonlinearity, and *auftragstaktik* in favor of technology, attrition, and mass. It dislikes the political aspects of war and would prefer merely to apply military force to the targets selected. The syllogism runs something like this: Strategy equals targeting. The number and nature of targets destroyed best measure success. When all the targets are destroyed, the war is over. It is playing checkers, not chess. It is an attrition approach to war. It ignores the reality that it is the adversary who may determine if he will surrender, when, and on what terms. The American military in general and the Air Force in particular see war as science, not art, and are disposed to treat it as such. Despite using terminology stressing strategic effects, the military still tends to focus on outputs (keeping score on targets) instead of on outcomes (the effects they seek to achieve).

In a brilliant essay, Colin Gray lists eight attributes of the American approach to strategy.[11] In effect, Boyd took them all on in his assault on the way the American military does its business. The attributes and Boyd's views are:

1. "An indifference to history." Americans tend to eschew the past and historical insights. Boyd's "Patterns of Conflict" is based on a review of war and warfare for the past 2,500 years and seeks to glean from the past the clues to how war and warfare have developed over time.

2. "The engineering style and the technical fix." Americans believe there is a technological solution for every problem. Boyd shunned the latest high-tech solution as neither necessary nor sufficient to gain victory in the next war. There was more to it than that.

3. "Impatience." Americans tend to want quick results to a given problem. Boyd's formula for success is a strategy of long-term adaptation to a constantly changing world environment, a never-ending OODA loop of adaptive security. It demands patience and understanding.

4. "Blindness to cultural differences." Americans want others to "be reasonable and do it our way" and have little experience with or use for other cultures and their values and procedures. Boyd kept trying to get the U.S. military to analyze the perceptions of the adversary and the importance of his orientation—historical experience, cultural values, and moral vision. It didn't take. The military preferred massive doses of firepower as the key to victory.

5. "Continental *weltanschauung*, maritime situation." We incorrectly equate war with "war in Europe," says Gray. Boyd looked not at war but at winning and losing, not a particular kind of war or war in a particular place but the essence of violent conflict of all kinds. Most of the U.S. military didn't understand.

6. "Indifference to strategy." We have a proclivity toward reducing war to narrowly military undertakings with little appreciation of the social and economic as well as the political circumstances that gave rise to them or the end states that should follow. We have produced "triumphs without victory" in both the Gulf War and Kosovo. Boyd sought to elucidate the linkages inherent in conflict to improve his understanding of the process of winning and losing.

7. "The resort to force, belated but massive." We may not realize

what's happening or take action until late in the game, but when America flexes its military might, it tends to do so massively. This hardly corresponds with Boyd's preaching of strategic agility, the ability to adapt constantly to a complex and ever-changing world environment, and his emphasis on the other dimensions of power that come into play in the affairs of state.

8. "The evasion of politics." Here Gray contends that "The United States has a strategic culture more comfortable with administration than with politics, and centered upon the quaint belief that the country can purchase the right weapons in the right numbers to serve both as deterrent in peacetime and as an adequate arsenal in crisis or war. The American literature on force planning quite resolutely declines to recognize that its subject is an art and not a science." Boyd took politics and perceptions, moral as well as physical dimensions, nonmilitary means as well as weaponry, as essential aspects of war and warfare. It is small wonder his ideas were viewed with skepticism by the system.

In retrospect it is amazing that John Boyd succeeded as well as he did in nudging military and political consideration of an utterly different approach to strategy, winning and losing.

## The Continuing Legacy

John Boyd is dead, but he has left a legacy of how to think about war and conflict that is useful, if abstract. An amalgam of the ideas of many others selected from throughout history, it attempts a creative synthesis of insights from both science and technology on the one hand, philosophy and social science on the other. It is imperfect and incomplete. It was done over many years and never written in prose format. It did, however, infect a generation of senior military and political leaders with the virus of novelty and led them to think in different ways about the conduct of war. Much of what he attempted to do still exists, enshrined in service doctrine and certain joint publications. Much of this doctrine Boyd would find dangerously self-delusional. He never accepted the concept of synchronization as enshrined in Army doctrine. He railed against the hubris of attaining perfect knowledge and information dominance amid the fog, friction, chance, and luck of war.

If alive and on active duty today, Boyd would be developing the low-cost alternative to the F-22, arguing against it as he had the F-15, not on the basis of performance but on the basis of cost. Most important, Boyd would be looking for other maverick thinkers, people with unquestioned integrity and moral purpose, willing to challenge orthodoxy and committed to making the system more honest and capable than it is. Boyd led the charge to challenge much of our strategic thinking, doctrinal rigidity, and lack of understanding about the art of war and the profession of arms. He was, oxymoron though it may be, a loyal heretic, and proud of it.

Concern for purpose, not merely process, ends over means, and the ethical dimension and moral consequences of our conduct is important. We need people who are more concerned about the mental and moral aspects of challenge, success, and failure (both on the battlefield and in the boardroom, in Congress and in the classroom) rather than merely the material aspects and technological prowess of our capabilities. Technology springs from the mind of humankind and should be a servant, not our master. It is in our minds that we conjure up both good and evil. It is in our minds that we must seek to have an impact if we wish to change behavior. The perception of the opponent is always the target. Time is a free good, which if used to our advantage can be a force multiplier of immense proportions. Acting at the right time is as important or more important than acting at the right place. Wars are planned and fought first in the minds of human beings in peacetime. What we do between the conflicts during ostensible periods of peace is critical to what we will do and how well we will fare in the next conflict.

Boyd and his ideas remind us of these simple truths. He synthesized the work of others. He created superbly and adapted well to the circumstances around him by thinking through things, using analogies from what he knew and applying them to situations that were novel. He kept pushing the envelope of his own mental performance by encountering new ideas, pondering the mismatches, solving the problems he encountered, and telling us how to do the same. His attempt to define and refine our understanding of war and warfare continues. His legacy is our commitment to continue the effort.

That Boyd's ideas have infected those concerned with American security is undeniable. This was amply demonstrated at a conference hosted by the Potomac Institute for Policy Studies on 26–27 June 2000 in Washington, D.C., entitled "Out of the Box and into the Future: A Dialogue between Warfighters and Scientists on Far-Future Warfare (2025)." The old warhorse Al Gray was there and paid homage to Boyd and OODA loops. He emphasized both spatial and temporal aspects of war, the need to pit strength against weakness, the importance of maneuver warfare, the need for fluidity, speed, empowerment, and decentralization. Boydian concepts all, these were to be expected from him, but others continued the themes that Boyd had labored to instill.

Frank Fernandez, director of the Defense Advanced Research Projects

Agency, emphasized Boydian themes, declaring, "Change is the norm, not the exception. . . . one has to stay ahead with speed, flexibility, and adaptability." He declared that what was needed was "innovation more than invention" and that this "requires leadership, dedication, and protection." Ralph Peters, a retired Army lieutenant colonel and prolific author, reminded the group that "the military's problems are at base human, not technological." He stated that "control of human behavior is the key problem for weapons of the twenty-first century" and that the competition would be between "self-correcting societies versus those who believe lies that deny empirical reality." Most pointedly, he maintained, "the unifying factor that ties Timothy McVeigh to the Taliban is that there are winners and losers, and losers don't like it." Even Maj. Gen. Robert Scales, retiring commandant of the Army War College, maintained that speed is essential and declared that what was required for this century was "smaller, cheaper, precision weapons." Adm. Arthur Cebrowski, president of the Naval War College, sounded like John Boyd incarnate: "Battles are won and lost in the minds of commanders." Commenting on information technology, he summarized its effects: "The value of time versus the cost of speed; demassification; flattened hierarchies; higher shared awareness." He commented on the need for tacit knowledge over explicit knowledge and stated flatly, "Until we solve the command and control problems and time delay, money spent on weapons accuracy is wasted." It seems that at least some of Boyd's notions have taken root.

Whether John Boyd was a military genius or not is less important in the long run than the use to which his ideas are put and the degree to which they help us shape an international security environment in which the United States can survive and prosper. His contributions are a set of important insights of transforming power. What we make of them is up to us. Whether we can learn Boyd's Way and profit from the insights contained within it is up to us. "On Winning and Losing" is a salute to maverick thinking, to synthesis, to understanding the moral aspects of our behavior, and learning how to adapt. About this there can be no doubt: Boyd's Way provides "a marvelous pitch of vision" for how to go about doing just that. We would do well to heed it.

This too is certain: the integrity of the man and his ideas should be celebrated. We would all do well to emulate Boyd's dictum, "Ask for my loyalty and I'll give you my honesty. Ask for my honesty and you'll have my loyalty." Rest in peace, John. The discourse on winning and losing continues. *Semper Fi.*

## Epilogue

Much has changed since the first publication of this book in 2001, and subsequent editions in 2004 and 2007. It was originally published before 9/11, before the war on terrorism, Operation Enduring Freedom, Operation Iraqi Freedom, the Arab Spring, civil war in Syria, Putin's grab for Crimea, attempted secession in Ukraine, and China's hard line and show of force in the East and South China Seas. What has not changed is the relevance and increasing awareness of the validity of John Boyd's counsel on strategy. If anything, the era of continuous competition and conflict that defines our circumstances today calls for Boyd's insight, imagination, and innovation even more.

Yet many of Boyd's ideas—notably the OODA Loop—have been reduced to mere caricatures of what they really reveal. But the concept that one's target in any kind of competition or conflict is always the same—the opponent's perception—has gained acceptance. His insights on the human dimension of conflict are as important as those on technology and airpower. Both Boyd and his ideas continue to grow in stature here and abroad. How he thought, as well as what he thought, are equally important. His views on command and control and how he conceptualized isolation and interaction provide useful insights on the cyber conflict of today.

Several other books, and a number of articles, have been written about Boyd, most notably Franz Osinga's *Science, Strategy and War: The Strategic Theory of John Boyd*. Indeed, the literature on Boyd now numbers in the hundreds. Boyd's reputation is now worldwide, his ideas and concepts studied by militaries, politicians, and businesses in Europe and Asia as well as in the U.S. If anything, his notions of rapidity, variety, harmony, and initiative as ways to contend successfully in an uncertain, ever-changing strategic environment are more relevant today. His ideas are even studied in his own Air Force, albeit belatedly. He was the subject of the U.S. Air Force Academy's prestigious Harmon Memorial Lecture series in January 2012.

Boyd died wondering if he had really made a difference, if people either knew or cared about his ideas, and if these ideas could be used to improve his beloved air force and the nation he served. They have. The insights contained in his briefings combined in his magnum opus, "A Discourse on Winning and Losing," have become widely known and continue to influence the thinking of those concerned with strategy, competition, and conflict around the globe. Boyd's personal integrity, his courage, and his dedication to improving the performance of his service and his country are role models for us all. The calling to be a maverick who is a "loyal heretic" is not an easy path to follow, especially in the military. But we need such people. Rest in peace, John, the "discourse on winning and losing" continues, and has been forever improved by your example and counsel.

# Notes

## 1: The Man and His Mind

1. I am indebted to Mr. James Morrison for this characterization of Boyd.
2. The obituary in the *New York Times* appeared on 12 March 1997. See also the "One Week" column by James Fallows entitled "A Priceless Original," *U.S. News and World Report*, 24 March 1997, p. 9, and "Col. John Boyd: Requiem for a Warrior," in *Defense Week*, 24 March 1997, p. 20. The best short published overview of Boyd's life, career, and accomplishments is Franklin C. Spinney, "Genghis John," *U.S. Naval Institute Proceedings*, July 1997, pp. 42–47.
3. General Krulak's letter was published in *Inside the Pentagon*, 13 March 1997, p. 5.
4. Colin S. Gray, *Modern Strategy* (Oxford: Oxford University Press, 1999), p. 91.
5. John R. Boyd, Capt., USAF, *Aerial Attack Study*, 50, 10-6e, revised 11 Aug. 1964 (147 pp.). The original version was completed in Feb. 1960 and classified. The revised version was declassified and is available from the Air University Library, Maxwell AFB, Ala. (call number M-U 43947-5).
6. Gen. Wilbur Creech, USAF (ret.), former head of the Tactical Air Command, has maintained that he beat Boyd in an air-to-air encounter but that both promised they would not disclose the fact. There is no way to corroborate this claim.
7. James G. Burton, *The Pentagon Wars: Reformers Challenge the Old Guard* (Annapolis, Md.: Naval Institute Press, 1993), p. 14.
8. Ibid., p. 20. The insight is Burton's. The contention that the record will stand is mine.
9. Bill Minutaglio, "Tales of the Fighter Mafia," *Dallas Life Magazine*, 3 May 1987, p. 12.
10. Burton, *Pentagon Wars*, p. 37.
11. "The Winds of Reform," *Time*, 7 March 1983, and "A Survey of Defense Technology: The Software Revolution," *Economist*, 10 June 1995.

12. See for instance, Joseph J. Romm, "The Gospel According to Sun Tzu," *Forbes*, 9 Dec. 1991, pp. 154–162; J. L. Bower and T. M. Hout, "Fast Cycle Capability for Competitive Power," *Harvard Business Review*, Nov.-Dec. 1988 (6), pp. 110–118; George Stalk, "Time: The Next Source of Competitive Advantage," *Harvard Business Review*, July-Aug. 1988, pp. 15–20; Stephan H. Haeckel and Richard I. Nolan, "Managing by Wire," *Harvard Business Review*, Sept.-Oct. 1993, pp. 122–132, esp. p. 128. Also see Chester W. Richards, "Riding the Tiger: What Do You Really Do with OODA Loops?" *The Handbook of Business Strategy*, 1995, reproduced along with many other Boyd-related pieces on the Web site www.belisarius.com.

13. Burton, *Pentagon Wars*, p. 10.

14. Ray Leopold recounted the story, interview with the author in Phoenix, Ariz., 20 May 1994.

15. Boyd, interview with the author, 9 Dec. 1993.

16. "The Windmills of Your Mind" was Boyd's favorite song. Composed by Michel LeGrand, it was the theme to the 1968 movie *The Thomas Crown Affair*.

17. John R. Boyd, "Destruction and Creation," unpublished essay, 3 Sept. 1976, p. 1. I am grateful to Mr. Barry Watts for the ideas relating to the singularity of implication in these three concepts. Both he and I originally saw a different set of emphases but were repeatedly told by Boyd that they all dealt with the same thing.

18. Boyd, interview with the author, 14 Nov. 1994.

19. General Loh, interview with the author, 1 Nov. 1994. The phone number was 354-7634.

### 2: The Making of a Maverick

1. Unless otherwise noted, Boyd's quotations and dialogue are taken from the U.S. Air Force Oral History Interview, Col. John R. Boyd, Corona Ace, K239.0512-1066. As these references are frequent, specific page numbers are not given, but the material is available from the USAF Historical Research Agency, Maxwell AFB, Alabama.

2. I am indebted to Robert Coram for this information and insight.

3. Murray Gell-Mann, *The Quark and the Jaguar: Adventures in the Simple and Complex* (New York: W. H. Freeman, 1994), p. xiii.

4. *USA Weekend*, 19–21 July 1996, p. 5.

5. Boyd related the incident in a set of discussions with the author in Oct. 1993. It is also discussed in a special profile on Boyd by Jim Booth, "John Boyd: An American Patriot," *Erie Daily Times*, 4 July 1994 (Boyd's comments on this event are cited on p. 7A). Here is an instance in which Boyd's memory failed him. In his oral history interview and elsewhere he refers to the "Eleven General Orders" being in effect, yet the injunction for an officer to tend to the welfare of his men is a part of the "Principles of Leadership." I am indebted to Lt. Gen. Van Riper for pointing this out. Whether the rest of the story is accurate, I do not know.

6. Boyd's college roommate Robert Busch related this story in an interview with the author, 20 March 1997.

7. Booth, "John Boyd: An American Patriot," p. 6A.

8. Col. Everest Riccioni, USAF (ret.), interview with the author in Los Angeles, Oct. 1994.

9. Boyd, interview with the author, 6 Nov. 1994.

### 3: Air-to-Air Combat

1. This information is contained in data supplied by the Tactical Fighter Division, Directorate of Operations, Headquarters, USAF, 19 May 1982, cited in Walter Kross, *Military Reform: The High-Tech Debate in the Tactical Air Forces* (Fort Lesley J. McNair, Washington, D.C.: National Defense University Press, 1985), p. 97.

2. See James P. Stevenson, *The Pentagon Paradox: The Development of the F-18 Hornet* (Annapolis, Md.: Naval Institute Press, 1993), p. 33 ff., citing comments made by Myers, Sprey, and Riccioni.

3. Ibid., p. 45.

4. Ibid., p. 47.

5. James G. Burton, *The Pentagon Wars: Reformers Challenge the Old Guard* (Annapolis, Md.: Naval Institute Press, 1993), p. 11.

6. U.S. Air Force pilot Roland Parks, interview with the author in Montgomery, Ala. Parks confirmed that when he was shot down and became a POW in the Korean War, he was well inside Chinese airspace. Many of his fellow POWs were pilots who had been shot down over China, not North Korea.

7. Charles D. Bright (ed.), *Historical Dictionary of the U.S. Air Force* (New York: Greenwood Press, 1992), pp. 221–222.

8. Ron Catton, "Reflections," Memorial Service for Col. John R. Boyd, USAF (ret.), 20 March 1997, Main Chapel, Arlington National Cemetery.

9. Interviews with Vernon Spradling, Ron Catton, and others who witnessed these exploits and have confirmed them independently of each other.

10. Ron Catton, interview with the author at the Cosmos Club, Washington, D.C., 20 March 1997.

11. Capt. John R. Boyd, "Air Combat Maneuvering," *Fighter Weapons School Newsletter,* June 1957.

12. Vernon Spradling, interview with the author in Las Vegas, Nev., 1 July 1993.

13. Boyd, interview with the author, 12 Sept. 1994.

14. Spradling, interview.

15. Burton, *Pentagon Wars,* p. 12.

16. Maj. Barry Watts, USAF, "Fire, Movement, and Tactics," *Top Gun* (Navy Fighter Weapons School Journal), Winter 1979–1980, p. 9, cited in Burton, *Pentagon Wars,* pp. 12–13. (See note 5 under chapter 1 for bibliographic data on *Aerial Attack Study.*)

17. This version of events comes from the USAF Oral History Interview, Col. John R. Boyd, Corona Ace, K239.0512-1066, pp. 50–53. These are Boyd's recollections, but I have no reason to doubt them, given corroboration from Vern Spradling about the general course of events.

18. Dugan and McPeak's presence in the audience was revealed the day I introduced

John Boyd to General McPeak in the spring of 1993 at the Air War College, where Boyd was visiting and General McPeak was speaking. McPeak said, "John, it is a real privilege to meet you. I have known of your work for years and have seen you before, but we had never formally met until now." Then he related the story, which I later confirmed with General Dugan. McPeak was one of the few senior leaders in the Air Force who valued Boyd's ideas and said so publicly. See Gen. Merrill A. McPeak, "Flexibility and Airpower," *Air Force Update for Senior Air Force Leaders,* June 1993, pp. 1–6 (speech presented at the Air Mobility Command Dining-In, Scott AFB, Ill., 12 June 1993).

### 4: Energy Maneuverability

1. Boyd, interview with the author, 19 Sept. 1994.
2. Chuck Cooper, telephone interview with the author, 6 Oct. 1999. I am indebted to Mr. Cooper for these insights and Georgia Tech yearbook materials from those years as well.
3. Vernon Spradling, interview with the author, 1 July 1993.
4. James Fallows, "A Priceless Original," *U.S. News and World Report,* 24 March 1997, p. 9.
5. Thomas P. Christie, interview with the author, 7 Nov. 1995.
6. James P. Stevenson, *The Pentagon Paradox: The Development of the F-18 Hornet* (Annapolis, Md.: Naval Institute Press, 1993), p. 75. The work on energy maneuverability did not end here. Boyd and Christie kept refining the concepts they had developed and published extensively within the Air Force on their findings and their implications. These works included, among others, "Expanded Maneuverability Theory," *USAF Fighter Weapons Newsletter,* Dec. 1969, pp. 1–33; "Introducing Handling and Agility into Energy Maneuverability," unpublished manuscript, 30 Aug. 1970; and John R. Boyd, Thomas P. Christie, and Robert E. Drabant, "Maximum Maneuver Concept," unpublished manuscript, June 1972 (43 pp.).
7. Thomas P. Christie, USAF Oral History Program interview with Jack Neufeld, 3 Oct. 1973, p. 13.
8. Boyd, interview with the author, 22 April 1995.
9. First Lt. John F. Gulick, "Remember the Name," *Eglin Eagle,* 30 Sept. 1966, p. 8.

### 5: Designing Fighters: The F-15

1. James P. Stevenson, *The Pentagon Paradox: The Development of the F-18 Hornet* (Annapolis, Md.: Naval Institute Press, 1993), p. 29. Stevenson comments further, "If Boyd, Sprey and Riccioni were to get credit for painting the *Lightweight Fighter,* Myers prepared the pigments, stretched the canvas, and was instrumental in creating an audience for a private showing."
2. Winston Churchill, cited in Steven F. Hayward, *Churchill on Leadership: Executive Success in the Face of Adversity* (Rocklin, Calif.: Prima Publishing, 1997), p. 29.
3. For the saga of the TFX, see Robert J. Art, *The TFX Decision: McNamara and the Military* (Boston: Little, Brown, 1968).

4. Robert D. Goartz, "An Analysis of Air-to-Air Missile Capability in Southeast Asia" (Montgomery, Ala.: Maxwell AFB, June 1968), pp. 1–2.
5. Ibid., p. 59.
6. I am indebted to Mr. Barry Watts for these insights regarding the complexities of air-to-air combat.
7. Charles D. Bright (ed.), *Historical Dictionary of the U.S. Air Force* (New York: Greenwood Press, 1992), pp. 211–212.
8. Stevenson, *Pentagon Paradox,* p. 22.
9. Ibid.
10. J. P. McConnell, "Air Superiority," Memorandum to all Major Commands, Department of the Air Force, Office of the Chief of Staff, 3 May 1965. Cited in Stevenson, *Pentagon Paradox,* pp. 26–27.
11. Bright, *Historical Dictionary,* p. 53.
12. See Carl H. Builder, *The Icarus Syndrome: The Role of Air Power Theory in the Evolution and Fate of the U.S. Air Force* (Santa Monica, Calif.: RAND, 1993), for the coevolution of the U.S. Air Force and strategic bombing as its core mission.
13. See Col. Mike Worden, *The Rise of the Fighter Generals: The Problem of Air Force Leadership* (Maxwell AFB, Ala.: Air University Press, 1998).
14. See, among others, Eliot Cohen, "The Mystique of Air Power," *Foreign Affairs* 73, no. 1 (Jan.-Feb. 1994), pp. 109–124, and James A. Winnefeld, Preston Niblack, Dana J. Johnson, *A League of Airmen: U.S. Air Power in the Gulf War* (Santa Monica, Calif.: RAND, Project Air Force), 1994. The cheerleading for airpower and its decisiveness is to be found in USAF historian Richard Hallion's *Storm over Iraq: Air Power and the Gulf War* (Washington, D.C.: Smithsonian Institution Press, 1992), especially pp. 188–200. An antidote to that school of thought is Grant T. Hammond, "Myths of the Gulf War: Some Lessons Not to Learn," *Air Power Journal,* Fall 1998, pp. 6–18.
15. Robert A. Pape, Jr., *Bombing to Win: Air Power and Coercion in War* (Ithaca, N.Y.: Cornell University Press, 1996), p. 318.
16. R. Ernest Dupuy and Trevor N. Dupuy, *The Encyclopedia of Military History from 3500 B.C. to the Present,* 2nd rev. ed. (New York: Harper & Row, 1986), pp. 1233–1234.
17. Jeff Ethell, *F-15 Eagle* (London: Ian Allen, 1981), pp. 13–14.
18. Roy S. Dickey, "The Advocacy of the F-15," Professional Study 4893, Air War College, Maxwell AFB, Ala., 1973, p. 21.
19. E-mail communication with Barry Watts, Northrop-Grumman Analysis Center, 5 May 2000.
20. Col. Everest E. Riccioni, "An Evaluation of Lt. Col. John R. Boyd's Creative, Professional Contributions to the USAF," cited in Stevenson, *Pentagon Paradox,* p. 351 (Appendix A).
21. As explained by Jeff Ethell in *F-15 Eagle,* there was a great deal of infatuation with the turbofan or bypass engine, "which pumps a great deal of cold air out of the first compressor stages without heating it in the combustion chamber. In other words, it

is passed out around the side of the engine. High bypass engines are seen on most airliners today because they are very economical on fuel for long range flying. The problem with high bypass engines for fighters, however, comes from their heavier weight and an afterburner that consumes more than the usual turbojet afterburner. Not mentioned at the time was the still unsolved tendency of afterburning fan engines to suffer severe stall/stagnation and overheating problems, particularly when manoeuvring" (p. 14).

22. Riccioni, "An Evaluation of Lt. Col. John R. Boyd."
23. Michael J. Getting, *F-15 Eagle* (New York: Arco, 1983), pp. 5–6.
24. Capt. David R. King and Capt. Donald S. Massey, "History of the F-15 Program: A Silver Anniversary First Flight Remembrance," *Air Force Journal of Logistics,* Winter 1997, p. 10.
25. Lt. Col. Jerauld R. Gentry, "Evolution of the F-16 Multinational Fighter," Industrial College of the Armed Forces, ICAF Student Research Report 163.
26. Riccioni quoted in James Fallows, *National Defense* (New York: Random House, 1981), p. 43.

## 6: Designing Fighters: The F-16

1. James G. Burton, *The Pentagon Wars: Reformers Challenge the Old Guard* (Annapolis, Md.: Naval Institute Press, 1993), p. 10.
2. James P. Stevenson, *The Pentagon Paradox: The Development of the F-18 Hornet* (Annapolis, Md.: Naval Institute Press, 1993), p. 77.
3. Roger Franklin, *The Defender: The Story of General Dynamics* (New York: Harper & Row, 1986), p. 238.
4. Myers may have been the first person to use the word "stealth" in describing the ideal characteristics of a fighter, in a document entitled "F-X Review" in Oct. 1969. He later promoted the concept under Project Harvey in a plan for an ultralightweight fighter. The first stealth plane, the F-117, was operational in 1982 but not made public until 1989.
5. Harry Hillaker, interview with the author, 17 April 1997. Unless otherwise noted, comments made by Hillaker in this chapter are from this interview.
6. John J. Fialka, interview with the author, 28 Oct. 1996.
7. Bill Minutaglio, "Tales of the Fighter Mafia," *Dallas Life Magazine,* 3 May 1987, p. 10.
8. Ibid. p. 29.
9. Stevenson, *Pentagon Paradox,* pp. 100, 103.
10. Ibid., p. 97.
11. Memorandum, Riccioni to Gen. D. Smith, 29 March 1970, cited in Stevenson, *Pentagon Paradox,* p. 97.
12. James Fallows, *National Defense* (New York: Random House, 1981), p. 102.
13. Ibid., p. 103.
14. Burton, *Pentagon Wars,* p. 17.
15. Lt. Col. Jerauld R. Gentry, USAF, "Evolution of the F-16 Multinational Fighter," Student Research Report 163, Industrial College of the Armed Forces, June 1976, p. 23.

16. Ibid., Riccioni interview cited on p. 28.

17. Ibid., pp. 27–28.

18. Burton, *Pentagon Wars,* p. 19.

19. Gentry, "Evolution of the F-16," p. 46.

20. There are many sources on this aspect of U.S. involvement in Southeast Asia. One of the earlier ones is the concise overview of the development of these programs and operations found in "The Electronic Battlefield: Counterguerrilla Surveillance and Detection," chapter 7 of Michael T. Klare, *War without End: American Planning for the Next Vietnams* (New York: Alfred A. Knopf, 1972), pp. 165–202. More detailed information can be found in U.S. Senate, *Investigation into Electronic Battlefield Program,* Armed Services Committee, Electronic Battlefield Subcommittee, Hearings, 91st Congress, 2nd Session, 1971, and Lt. Col. John N. Dick, Jr., USAF Oral History Program, interview with Gen. John D. Lavelle, 12–24 April 1974.

21. Doug Richardson, *F-16 Fighting Falcon* (New York: Arco, 1983), p. 7.

22. Burton, *Pentagon Wars,* p. 19.

23. Boyd, interview with the author, 17 Nov. 1994.

24. James R. Schlesinger, "Some Ruminations on the Office of Secretary of Defense," address delivered in Louisville, Ky., fall 1983, cited in Richard A. Stubbing with Richard A. Mendel, *The Defense Game: An Insider Explores the Astonishing Realities of America's Defense Establishment* (New York: Harper & Row, 1986), p. 325.

25. Bill Gunston and Mike Spick, *Modern Air Combat: The Aircraft, Tactics, and Weapons Employed in Aerial Warfare Today* (New York: Crescent Books, 1983), p. 190.

26. Fallows, *National Defense,* p. 106.

27. Dennis Smith, "The Roots and Future of Modern-Day Military Reform," *Air University Review,* Sept.-Oct. 1985, p. 38.

28. Harry Hillaker, "Tribute to John Boyd," *Code One* 12, no. 1 (July 1997), p. 15.

29. The most comprehensive assessment of the initial foreign sale to the European Participating Governments, called the sale of the century, is that of Ingemar Dorfer, *Arms Deal: The Selling of the F-16* (New York, Praeger, 1983). For additional information on some of the later sales, see also Grant T. Hammond, *Countertrade, Offsets, and Barter in International Political Economy* (London: Pinter Publishers, 1990).

30. Minutaglio, "Tales of the Fighter Mafia," p. 10.

**7: Military Reform**

1. Among many other sources, see Gordon Adams, *The Politics of Defense Contracting: The Iron Triangle* (New Brunswick, N.J.: Transaction Books, 1982); James A. Blackwell, Jr., and Barry M. Blechman (eds.), *Making Defense Reform Work* (New York: Brassey's, 1990); James Fallows, *National Defense* (New York: Random House, 1981); Gary Hart and William S. Lind, *America Can Win: The Case for Military Reform* (Bethesda, Md.: Adler & Adler, 1986); Franklin C. Spinney, *Defense Facts of Life: The Plans/Reality Mismatch* (Boulder, Colo.: Westview Press, 1985); and Richard Stubbing, *The Defense Game* (New York: Harper & Row, 1986).

2. The President's Blue Ribbon Commission on Defense Management, "An Interim Report to the President," 28 Feb. 1986, p. 5.

3. Hedrick Smith, *The Power Game: How Washington Works* (New York: Ballantine Books, 1988), p. 202.

4. Ibid., p. 175.

5. This statement is by Boyd. The quotation, cited in numerous books and articles critical of defense spending, is usually attributed to an anonymous source or at best associated with "an Air Force colonel" or "a colonel in the Pentagon." It was one of Boyd's most successful public relations gambits.

6. "Military Reform Caucus Oral History Seminar," 27 June 1992, draft transcript, Center for Legislative Archives and Historical Office, U.S. House of Representatives, pp. 4–5.

7. The document is entitled "Development Planning Interim Report," sent from Col. John R. Boyd to AF/RDQ on 9 Aug. 1974. My copy came from Ray Leopold's files. This was not the first effort to change procurement and acquisition. In a paper entitled "System Acquisition Evaluation," dated 22 Feb. 1971, Boyd tried to change the in-house system advocacy to a more objective set of analytical reviews.

8. Michael R. Gordon, "Budget Crunch Gives Shot in the Arm to Growing Military Reform Movement," *National Journal,* 5 Sept. 1981, p. 1573. "Military Reform Caucus Oral History Seminar," pp. 55–57, makes the same point about Boyd's central role.

9. These famous phrases came from a single speech delivered by President Reagan. See "Excerpts from the President's Speech to the National Association of Evangelicals," *New York Times,* 9 March 1983. For more on this entire period and the Reagan approach, see Daniel Wirls, *Buildup: The Politics of Defense in the Reagan Era* (Ithaca, N.Y.: Cornell University Press, 1992).

10. Serge Herzog, *Defense Reform and Technology: Tactical Aircraft* (Westport, Conn.: Praeger, 1994), pp. 3–4.

11. Ibid., pp. 6–7.

12. Walter Kross, *Military Reform: The High-Tech Debate in the Tactical Air Forces* (Washington, D.C.: National Defense University Press, 1985), p. 84.

13. James P. Stevenson, *The Pentagon Paradox: The Development of the F-18 Hornet* (Annapolis, Md.: Naval Institute Press, 1993), p. 6. Despite the subtitle, this detailed study includes a great deal of information on the military reform movement in general and the F-15 and F-16 in general.

14. James Fallows, *National Defense* (New York: Vintage Books, 1982), p. 100.

15. Among the more strident examples, see Fred Reed's article "The Reformers," in the Outlook section of the *Washington Post,* 11 Oct. 1987, and the numerous exchanges between Col. Alan L. Gropman and William S. Lind in the Fire/Counter Fire section of *Air University Review* from 1982 to 1984, with such pointed titles as "Winnowing Fact from Opinion" (Gropman) and "Analysis by Hyperbole: A Response" (Lind).

16. See Jeffrey Record, "The Military Reform Caucus," *Washington Quarterly,* Spring 1983, pp. 125–129.

17. Among a host of books on the subject, see Gordon Adams, *Controlling Weapons Costs: Can the Pentagon Reforms Work?* (New York: Council on Economic Priorities, 1983); Jeffrey C. Barlow (ed.), *Reforming the Military* (Washington, D.C.: Heritage Foundation, 1981); Asa A. Clark (ed.), *The Defense Reform Debate: Issues and Analysis* (Baltimore: Johns Hopkins University Press, 1984); Richard A. Gabriel, *Military Incompetence* (New York: Hill & Wang, 1985); Arthur T. Hadley, *Straw Giant, Triumph and Failure: America's Armed Forces* (New York: Random House, 1984); Jeffrey Record, *Revising U.S. Military Strategy: Tailoring Means to Ends* (New York: Pergamon Brassey's, 1984) and *Beyond Military Reform: American Defense Dilemmas* (New York: Pergamon Brassey's, 1988); Richard Stubbing, *The Defense Game* (New York: Harper & Row, 1986); in addition to the other works by Adams, Burton, Crackel, Fallows, Fitzgerald, Hart and Lind, Herzog, Rasor, Smith, Spinney, and Stevenson cited elsewhere in this chapter. Note that the criticism flows from the Heritage Foundation, defense industry officials, congressional staffers, and former military officers, besides the more liberal critics who would prefer greater expenditures on social programs as well as greater efforts in arms control and disarmament.

18. The opening salvos were articles by Gary Hart, "The Case for Military Reform," *Wall Street Journal*, 23 Jan. 1981, and "What's Wrong with the Military?" *New York Times Magazine*, 14 Feb. 1982. They were largely the work of his principal staff assistant on defense, William S. Lind. Newt Gingrich contributed a later article entitled "Think Now, Buy Later," *Washington Post*, 21 April 1981.

19. See James Fallows, "The Muscle-Bound Super Power: The State of America's Defense," *Atlantic Monthly*, Oct. 1979, pp. 59–78. Fallows also published other pieces, one near the end of the military reform movement entitled "The Spend-Up," *Atlantic Monthly*, July 1986, pp. 27–33.

20. Theodore J. Crackel, "Reforming Military Reform," *Heritage Foundation Backgrounder*, 12 Dec. 1983.

21. Tom Amlie was a radar expert who had worked for the Navy at China Lake and supplied many critics with information about radar performance. He wrote a controversial article, "Radar: Shield or Target?," that appeared in the *IEEE Spectrum* in April 1982. Ernie Fitzgerald, who endeared himself to the DOD and President Nixon as a whistleblower on the C-5A transport plane, lost his job, and was reinstated after a celebrated court case, later wrote about his experiences and the problems in the Pentagon. See A. Ernest Fitzgerald, *The Pentagonists: An Insider's View of Waste, Mismanagement, and Fraud in Defense Spending* (Boston: Houghton Mifflin, 1989). Dina Rasor was a frequent and vociferous critic in numerous pieces, including Dina Rasor, *Pentagon Underground* (New York: Times Books, 1985). More pointed is a collection of articles she edited in a volume entitled *More Bucks, Less Bang: How the Pentagon Buys Ineffective Weapons* (Washington, D.C.: Fund for Constitutional Government, April 1983). Andrew Cockburn, a journalist, wrote many pieces on various aspects of the reform movement. He first drew the wrath of the DOD for his book *The Threat: Inside the Soviet Military Machine* (New York: Random House, 1983) and remains critical of the defense establishment to this day as a writer for *Vanity Fair*.

22. See James G. Burton, "Case Study: The Navy Runs Aground," in *Pentagon Wars*, pp. 213–232. Also see James Stevenson's new book on the A-12, *The Five-Billion-Dollar Misunderstanding* (Annapolis, Md.: Naval Institute Press, 2000).

23. Burton, *Pentagon Wars*, p. 66.

24. Anthony Cave Brown, *Bodyguard of Lies* (New York: Harper & Row, 1975). The Churchill quotation appears on p. 10.

25. Walter Isaacson et al., "The Winds of Reform: Runaway Weapons Costs Prompt a New Look at Military Planning," *Time*, 7 March 1983.

26. Among these assessments see, for example, T. N. Dupuy, "The Pied Pipers of Maneuver-Style Warfare," *Armed Forces Journal International* 119, no. 3 (Nov. 1981), pp. 73–78; James M. Lindsay, "Congress and Defense Policy, 1961–1986," *Armed Forces and Society* 13 (Spring 1987), pp. 371–400; John J. Mearsheimer, "The Military Reform Movement: A Critical Appraisal," *Orbis*, Summer 1983, pp. 285–300; Thomas McNaugher, "Weapons Procurement: The Futility of Reform," *International Security* 12 (Fall 1987), pp. 63–104.

### 8: Patterns of Conflict

1. John R. Boyd, "Destruction and Creation," unpublished essay, 3 Sept. 1976, pp. 12–13.

2. Ibid., p. 9.

3. Pierre Sprey, interview with the author, 30 June 1993.

4. For information on the A-10 and the Army's Apache helicopter, see Ray Bonds, *Modern Weapons* (New York: Crescent Books, 1985).

5. Maj. Gen. Jack N. Merritt, Commandant, Army War College, quoted in *Washington Post*, 4 Jan. 1981, and cited in James G. Burton, *The Pentagon Wars: Reformers Challenge the Old Guard* (Annapolis, Md.: Naval Institute Press, 1993), p. 53.

6. John Boyd, quoted by Henry Eason, "New Theory Shoots Down Old War Ideas," *Atlanta Constitution*, 22 March 1981.

7. There are numerous translations of Sun Tzu. The best is by Ralph D. Sawyer, *Sun Tzu: The Art of War* (Boulder, Colo.: Westview Press, 1994). Others are by Samuel B. Griffith (Oxford, 1963), James Clavell (Delacorte Press, 1983, and Delta, 1988), Yuan Shibing (Sterling Publishing, 1987), and Thomas F. Cleary (Shambhala, 1988). Boyd used the Griffith translation originally but read all the others for the nuances in translation and emphasis.

8. Ch'i suggests "unique," "rare," "surprising," and "novel" as well as "unorthodox." The concepts Sun Tzu had in mind in discussing successful tactics and strategies can be characterized under the term "cheng" as: fixed, form, knowledge, logic and reason, control, space. Under "ch'i" the related concepts are: flexible, formlessness, secrecy, spontaneity and emotion, spirit, time.

9. David G. Chandler, *The Campaigns of Napoleon* (New York: Macmillan, 1966), pp. 67–68. The excerpt is from a commentary by "the noteworthy contemporary soldier General Foy," which Chandler describes as a "rather romanticized picture."

10. Ibid., pp. 363–364.

11. See Carl von Clausewitz, *On War*, originally published in 1832, edited and translated by Michael Howard and Peter Paret (Princeton, N.J.: Princeton University Press, 1984), and Baron Antoine Henri de Jomini, *The Art of War*, originally translated by Capt. G. H. Mendell and Lt. W. P. Craighill (Philadelphia: J. B. Lippincott & Co., 1862; reprinted by Greenwood Press in 1971 and 1975).

12. Clausewitz, *On War*, vol. 8, ch. 4, p. 595.

13. Jomini's theory of lines of operation and flanking maneuvers is found in chapter 7 of his *Treatise on Grand Military Operations: Or a Critical and Military History of the Wars of Frederick the Great as Contrasted with the Modern System*, vol. 1, translated from the French by Col. S. B. Holabird (New York: D. Van Nostrand, 1865). Additional commentary can be found in Crane Brinton, Gordon A. Craig, and Felix Gilbert, "Jomini," pp. 77–92 in: Edward Meade Earle (ed.), *Makers of Modern Strategy: Military Thought from Machiavelli to Hitler* (Princeton, N.J.: Princeton University Press, 1948).

14. Observations on these theorists are summarized in Emil Schalk, *Summary of the Art of War* (Philadelphia: J. B. Lippincott & Co., 1862).

15. See Capt. Andre Laffargue, "The Attack in Trench Warfare: Impressions and Reflections of a Company Commander," translated for *Infantry Journal* by an officer of the Infantry (Washington, D.C.: U.S. Infantry Association, 1916). For a description of tactics associated with Gen. Oskar von Hutier, see Paddy Griffith, *Forward into Battle: Fighting Tactics from Waterloo to the Near Future* (Novato, Calif.: Presidio Press, 1992), p. 100. See also Bruce I. Gudmundsson, *Storm Troop Tactics: Innovation in the German Army, 1914–1918* (New York: Praeger, 1989). John English, in *A Perspective on Infantry* (New York: Praeger, 1981), maintains that "Hutier tactics" should be credited to Ludendorff.

16. Gen. Paul Emil von Lettow-Vorbeck and T. E. Lawrence are the two most famous early proponents and practitioners of guerrilla warfare in their century, eclipsed more recently by Mao Tse Tung and Nguyen Vo Giap. On Lettow-Vorbeck, see Brian Gardner, *On to Kilimanjaro: The Bizarre Story of the First World War in East Africa* (Philadelphia: Macrae Smith Co., 1963). Lawrence's exploits are chronicled in his *Seven Pillars of Wisdom* (New York: Doubleday & Co., 1935) and *Revolt in the Desert* (New York: George H. Doran Co., 1927).

17. Quotations are from Lawrence, *Seven Pillars of Wisdom*, pp. 195, 192, 337, 338.

### 9: From Patterns of Conflict to Maneuver Warfare

1. See J. F. C. Fuller, *The Reformation of War* (New York: E. P. Dutton & Co., 1923), and his *Lectures on F.S.R. II* (London: Sifton Praed & Co., 1931), which are commentaries on volume 2 of the British Field Service Regulations and Fuller's views on how mechanized war will change infantry tactics. Heinz Guderian, *Achtung-Panzer: The Development of Armoured Forces, Their Tactics, and Operational Potential*, translated by Christopher Duffy (London: Arms and Armour, 1992), was first published in 1937. Guderian later wrote his memoirs, *Panzer Leader* (Washington, D.C.: Zenger, 1979; reprint of the original 1952 edition, translated by Constantine

Fitzgibbon). See also Kenneth Macksey, *Guderian: Creator of the Blitzkrieg* (New York: Stein & Day, 1976), and Charles DeGaulle, *The Army of the Future* (New York: J. B. Lippincott, 1941; originally published in French in 1934).

2. Technically, there was no doctrine called blitzkrieg. It was merely the name for the style of warfare the Germans perfected and demonstrated in 1939–1940. For a cautionary note about reading more into blitzkrieg than may have been in German doctrine, see Daniel J. Hughes, "The Abuses of German Military History," *Military Review* 66, no. 12 (Dec. 1986), pp. 66–75, and his entry under "Blitzkrieg" in *Brassey's Encyclopedia of Land Forces and Warfare,* edited by Franklin D. Margiotta (Washington, D.C.: Brassey's, 1996), pp. 155–162.

3. The quotations in this section are from John R. Boyd, "Patterns of Conflict," pp. 67–68, which is part of the Aug. 1987 version of the larger unpublished briefing "A Discourse on Winning and Losing." Not being academically trained, Boyd did not properly cite selections he referred to from others. Where possible, I have tried to do so; however, the number of citations from Marx and Lenin and the voluminous writings of each have made this difficult, if not impossible. Therefore, the quotations used in this chapter are all from "Patterns of Conflict" rather than the original sources.

4. "Nebenpunkt" is a word Boyd coined after conferring with others who were German. It was to emphasize the opposite of "schwerpunkt," the focus of main effort, to create a concept to use in tandem with it.

5. The two Blumentritt works Boyd relied on are available as copies of the originals in the Pentagon library: Gunther Blumentritt, "Experience Gained from the History of War on the Subject of Command Technique," 27 Jan. 1947, 13 pages, no translator listed, prepared by the Historical Division, Headquarters, U.S. Army, Europe, Foreign Military Studies Branch, and "Operations in Darkness and Smoke," 1952, 26 pages, translated by A. Schroeder and identified as a draft translation from the German done by the Historical Division, European Command, Foreign Military Studies Branch. All the Blumentritt quotations are from those works.

6. Boyd, "Patterns of Conflict," p. 87. Emphasis is Boyd's.

7. There is a large literature on maneuver warfare. The relevant articles are too numerous to cite. Among some of the more prominent books are William S. Lind, *Maneuver Warfare Handbook* (Boulder, Colo.: Westview Press, 1985); Robert R. Leonhard, *The Art of Maneuver: Maneuver Warfare Theory and AirLand Battle* (Novato, Calif.: Presidio Press, 1991); and Richard D. Hooker, Jr. (ed.), *Maneuver Warfare: An Anthology* (Novato, Calif.: Presidio Press, 1993).

8. Alvin and Heidi Toffler, *War and Anti-War: Survival at the Dawn of the Twenty-First Century* (Boston: Little, Brown, 1993), pp. 9–12.

9. James G. Burton, *The Pentagon Wars: Reformers Challenge the Old Guard* (Annapolis, Md.: Naval Institute Press, 1993), pp. 51–55.

### 10: A Discourse on Winning and Losing

1. John R. Boyd, "The Strategic Game of ? and ?," part of the June 1987 version of the larger unpublished briefing, "A Discourse on Winning and Losing." All the "Strategic Game" excerpts in this chapter are from this version of the briefing.

2. Unless otherwise noted, Boyd's papers do not contain and I did not find complete citations for the sources of these quotations.

3. Ilya Prigogene and Isabelle Stenger, *Order Out of Chaos: Man's New Dialogue with Nature* (New York: Bantam Books, 1984), p. 127.

4. Alexander Atkinson, *Social Order and the General Theory of Strategy* (London: Routledge & Keegan Paul, 1981), ch. 4.

5. Kevin Kelly, *Out of Control: The Rise of Neobiological Civilization* (Reading, Mass.: Addison Wesley Publishing, 1994), p. 1.

6. John R. Boyd, "An Organic Design for Command and Control," part of the May 1987 version of the larger unpublished briefing, "A Discourse on Winning and Losing." All the "Organic Design" excerpts in this chapter are from this version of the briefing.

7. John R. Boyd, "The Conceptual Spiral," part of the Aug. 1992 version of the larger unpublished briefing, "A Discourse on Winning and Losing." All the "Conceptual Spiral" excerpts in this chapter are from this version of the briefing. ("The Conceptual Spiral" was not part of the most widely disseminated version of "A Discourse," dated Aug. 1987.)

## 11: A Retired Fighter Pilot Who Reads a Lot

1. Fred Reed, "The Reformers," *Washington Post,* 11 Oct. 1987.

2. Jim Morrison, phone interview with the author.

3. Boyd, conversation with the author, n.d.

4. Boyd's list of sources is reprinted in Appendix A of James G. Burton, *The Pentagon Wars: Reformers Challenge the Old Guard* (Annapolis, Md.: Naval Institute Press, 1993), pp. 257–265.

5. John R. Boyd, "Revelation," part of the Aug. 1987 version of the larger unpublished briefing, "A Discourse on Winning and Losing."

6. Jack Matson, a professor in the engineering school at Penn State University, passes out buttons with a picture of *Tyrannosaurus rex* in a red circle with a slash across it. The motto is "Innovate—or Die!" That's Boyd's kind of guy.

7. *Boca Raton News,* Sunday, 7 Feb. 1993.

8. *Fort Lauderdale Sun-Sentinel,* Thursday, 10 June 1993.

9. Tim Weiner, "CIA Admits Failing to Sift Tainted Data," *New York Times,* 1 Nov. 1995.

10. Jeff Ethell, "Lessons from Desert Storm's Air War," *Aerospace America,* May 1991, pp. 16–18; Joseph J. Romm, "The Gospel According to Sun Tzu," *Forbes,* 9 Dec. 1991, pp. 154–162; Peter Cary, "The Fight to Change How America Fights," *U.S. News and World Report,* 6 May 1991, pp. 30–31. Joseph J. Romm, *The Once and Future Superpower: How to Restore America's Economic, Energy, and Environmental Security* (New York: William Morrow & Co., 1992). U.S. News and World Report, *Triumph without Victory: The History of the Persian Gulf War* (New York: Random House, Times Books, 1993). John Fialka, "A Very Old General May Hit the Beaches with the Marines," *Wall Street Journal,* 9 Jan. 1991; Fred Kaplan, "The American Military: The Force Was with Them," *Boston Globe,* 17 March 1991. James P. Stevenson, *The Pentagon Paradox: The Development of the F-18 Hornet*

(Annapolis, Md.: Naval Institute Press, 1993); James G. Burton, *The Pentagon Wars: Reformers Challenge the Old Guard* (Annapolis, Md.: Naval Institute Press, 1993). Maj. David S. Fadok, "John Boyd and John Warden: Air Power's Quest for Strategic Paralysis," master's thesis, School of Advanced Aerospace Studies (Maxwell AFB, Ala.: Air University Press, Feb. 1995).

## 12: That Marvelous Pitch of Vision

1. John Fialka, *War by Other Means: Economic Espionage in America* (New York: W. W. Norton, 1997), p. 197.
2. See *Concept for Future Joint Operations: Expanding Joint Vision 2010* (Fort Monroe, Va.: Commander, Joint Warfighting Center, May 1997).
3. U.S. Marine Corps, "FMFM-1: Warfighting," Quantico, Va., 6 March 1989.
4. Carl von Clausewitz, *On War,* edited and translated by Michael Howard and Peter Paret (Princeton, N.J.: Princeton University Press, 1984), p. 112.
5. Ibid., pp. 106–107.
6. Col. Everest E. Riccioni, "An Evaluation of Lt. Col. John R. Boyd's Creative, Professional Contributions to the USAF," memo cited in James P. Stevenson, *The Pentagon Paradox: The Development of the F-18 Hornet* (Annapolis, Md.: Naval Institute Press, 1993), p. 351 (Appendix A).
7. Gen. Al Gray, USMC (ret.), interview with the author, at Gray's home in Alexandria, Va., n.d.
8. James G. Burton, *The Pentagon Wars: Reformers Challenge the Old Guard* (Annapolis, Md.: Naval Institute Press, 1993), p. 4.
9. There is a silly but probably lasting monument to Boyd at Air University. In front of the Air Force Doctrine Center and the JAG School buildings, a U-shaped road connects with another road to form a circle around a static display of a B-52 bomber. Though Boyd had little use for USAF doctrine and nothing to do with bombers, someone at the Doctrine Center persuaded the Civil Engineers to make a sign and designate the road the OODA Loop. It is the only permanent recognition of Boyd or any of his accomplishments at Maxwell AFB.
10. Arthur T. Hadley, *The Straw Giant: Triumph and Failure, America's Armed Forces* (New York: Random House, 1986), pp. 165–166.
11. Colin S. Gray, "Strategy in the Nuclear Age: The United States, 1945–1991," in Williamson Murray, MacGregor Knox, and Alvin Bernstein, *The Making of Modern Strategy: Rulers, States, and Wars* (Cambridge: Cambridge University Press, 1996), pp. 592–598.

# Index

A7D Corsair, 69
A-10 Thunderbolt, 98, 115, 116, 121
A-12, 113
active defense, 154
adaptation, 15, 163, 167
*Aerial Attack Study,* 7, 39, 44–48, 50, 60, 73
*Aerospace America,* 188
Air Combat Maneuver (ACM), 7, 60
Agan, Maj. Gen. Arthur, USAF, 72
aggressor squadron, 204
Aikman, Troy, 181–82
AIM-9L, 69
Air Command and Staff College, 202
Air Combat Command, 16
Air Force, U.S., 1, 4, 6, 8, 9, 32–34, 112, 187, 199, 201, 203–4, 206–7
*Air Force 2025,* 116
Air Force Academy, 10
Air Force Institute of Technology (AFIT), 51–52
Air Force Manual, 31, 47
air superiority, 69–74
Air Superiority Society, 71
air-to-air combat, 4, 7, 37–38, 41, 160
Air Training Command, 45
*Air University Review,* 112

Air War College, 187
AirLand Battle, 9, 154
Alexander the Great, 125
ambiguity, 123, 147, 149, 186
American Institute for Aeronautics and Astronautics (AIAA), 84
Ames, Rich, 185–86
Amlie, Tom, 112
ancient warfare, 125–26
Apache helicopter, 116
appreciation, 166–67
Arbuthnott, Cdr. James, RN, 114
Armstrong, Neil, 42
Army Air Forces, 4, 24, 71
Army War College, 122, 201
Army, U.S., 1, 139, 187, 203
*Art of Maneuver: Maneuver Warfare and AirLand Battle,* 35
Atkinson, Alexander, 157–58
*Atlantic Monthly,* 5, 111
attrition warfare, comparison with guerrilla, 155
*Auftragstaktik,* 152, 207

B-1 Lancer, 70, 92, 115–16
B-2, 116
B-25 Mitchell, 19, 71

Balck, Gen. Herman, 163

Baldwin, Stanley, 73

Barrow, John, 183

Bartley, W. W., 184

Battle of Arbela, 125; Britain, 19; Cannae, 122, 142; Leuctra, 125, 142; Leuthen, 130; Marathon, 125; Midway, 19; Somme, 165

Beard, Amanda, 22

Belasarius, 125

Berlin, 4

Bennett, Charles, 177–78

"Big Squeeze," 188–91

Bishop, Col. Ray, USAF, 187

blitz-guerrilla themes, 147–49

blitzkrieg, 123, 137, 139–44; WW II to 1973, 144; essential aspects of, 140–41

Blumentritt, Gen. Gunther, 141–42, 163

*Bodyguard of Lies*, 114

Boeing, 75

*Boston Globe*, 188

Bourcet, 126, 163

Boyd, Elsie, 19, 34

Boyd, family and children, 19, 28–29, 52, 59, 114, 179

Boyd, Hubert, 19

Boyd, John R.: and American way of war, 207–9; anomaly, 16–18; awards, 65; "Boyd it," 49; burning hangar, 24–25; childhood, 18–20; college, 25–28; confrontational style, 56; creative thinking, 180–83; dedication of building for, 204; first flight, 20; flying, 29–34; honorary Marine, 3–4; hypothetical citation for, 202–3; integrity, 13–15; intensity, 13–15; legacy, 48–50, 209–11; making of a maverick, 6–8; man and his mind, 11–13; military genius, 196–201; pilot training, 29–31; poor health, 178–79; quiz, 181; rehabilitation of, 187–88; retirement, 104–5; simple truths of, 210; sports, 20–24; strategist, 4–6, 195–96; suggested reading, 183–86; swimming, 27–28; taking on system, 8–10; water polo, 23–24; why he did not write, 17

Boyd, Mary, 28–29, 34, 52, 59, 178–79, 204

"Boyd cycle." *See* OODA loop

Boyd's way, 15–16, 174, 211

Boyne, Walter J., 67

Braddock, Maj. Gen. Edward, 127

Bradley fighting vehicle, 10, 113, 115, 161, 175

Brown, Anthony Cave, 114

Brown, Gen. George, USAF, 96

Burke, James, 196

Burns, Mike, 112

Burton, Col. James. G., USAF (ret.), 10–11, 37, 84, 92, 105, 113–14, 161, 175, 177, 193, 203

Busch, Bob, 26

BVR–beyond visual range, 69, 79

C-5, 90

C-130 Hercules, 94

*Call of the Wild*, 21

Campbell, Donald T., 184

Campbell, Jeremy, 183

Carter Lt. Col. Tom, USAF, 177

Catholic bishops, 106

Catton, Ron, 41–43, 204

Cebrowski, Adm. Arthur, USN, 211

Cecil Field, Florida, 6, 201

center of gravity, 130

Chalmers, David, 188

Chandler, David, 127–28

character, 199–200

Cheatham, Tom, 68

Cheng and Ch'i, 125, 145

Cheney, Richard, 6, 111, 113

Christie, Tom, 8, 51, 55–63, 65, 105

Churchill, Winston, 18, 68, 114

Clausewitz, Carl von, 106, 109, 122, 129–31, 152, 163, 187, 195, 196–201, 207

Cleary, Thomas, 184

Clifton, Maj. Leroy, USAF, 43, 48

Cockburn, Andrew, 112

Cohen, Eliot, 74

Cohen, William S., 111, 115

Columbus Air Force Base, Mississippi, 30

commander's intent, 152–53

Committee on the Present Danger, 106

Concept for Future Joint Operations, 194

Concept Formulation Package (CFP), 75

"conceptual spiral," 13, 155–56, 167–74
*Connections, Connections 2,* 180
context of 1920s and 1930s, 18–19; of
   1975–1985, 105–7
Cooper, Chuck, 53
corruption, 161
courage, 197
Coveney, Peter, 184
Council for a Livable World, 106
Councilman, "Doc," 26, 53
Crackel, Theodore J., 111
Culbertson, Brig. Gen. Allman, USAF,
   62–63, 206
"Curve of Unilateral Disarmament," 109

DDR&E (Director, Defense Research and
   Engineering), 68, 75, 91–92, 116
Darwin, Charles, 12
Dawkins, Richard, 183
*Dawn Patrol,* 19
*Day the Universe Changed, The,* 180
deception, 147, 149, 163
Defense Advanced Research Projects
   Agency, 210
Defense Communications Planning Group
   (later, Defense Special Projects Group),
   93
*Defense News,* 178
*Defense Week,* 2
DeGaulle, Gen. Charles, 137
Dempsey, Jack, 49
Dempster, Gen. K. C. "Casey," USAF, 8, 77
Desert One, 163
Desert Storm, 3, 81
"Destruction and Creation," 118–21, 156,
   158, 159, 200
determination, 198–99
Deutsch, John, 185
Dewey, John, 175
Dicks, Norman, 111
Dilger, Bob, 115
DIVAD, 103
"Discourse on Winning and Losing," 2, 6,
   13, 119–21, 154, 155–74, 180, 187, 194,
   196, 205
DNA, 186, 188
Domodedovo Air Show, 75

Donohue, J. Ray, 72
Douhet, Giulio, 73
Drabant, Bob, 80
Dugan, Gen. Mike, CSAF, 50

Easterbrook, Gregg, 1
Eckerd, Jack, 20, 27
*Economist,* 11
Edwards Air Force Base, California, 52, 63
Edwards, Jack, 41, 112
Eglin Air Force Base, Florida, 8, 55–57, 66
Energy maneuverability theory (EM), 8,
   55–64, 76, 80, 91, 202; importance of,
   59–61
Engelbrecht, Col. "Jae," USAF, 187
Engels, Friedrich, 132, 135
engineering, outstanding contributors and
   contributions, 170
environment, importance of, 157–59
Erie Strong Vincent High School, 22
*Essence of Winning and Losing, The,*
   188–89
Ethell, Jeff, 76
Evans, David, 103, 112
evil, 161
Ewalt, Professor, 52
Ewbank, Brig. Gen. John N., Jr., USAF,
   49–50
*Experience and Nature,* 175

F-4 Phantom, 58, 61, 69–70, 75–76, 78
F-5 Freedom Fighter, 90
F8U Crusader, 45
F9F Panther, 71
F-15 Eagle, 1, 8, 68, 73, 76–82, 83, 86,
   89–90, 96, 98, 102–3, 209; characteris-
   tics, 80–182; development of, 76–79
F-15E Strike Eagle, 81–82
F-16 Fighting Falcon, 1, 9, 17, 68, 73,
   88–100, 105, 175, 199, 201, 202, 203;
   decision to procure, 95–98; foreign
   purchasers and coproducers of, 99;
   implications of, 98–100; process to
   develop, 94–95
F-18 Hornet, 108, 115
F-20 Tigershark, 99, 116
F-22 Raptor, 209

F-80 Shooting Star, 31, 33
F-86 Sabre, 7, 33, 36, 41, 78, 91, 123
F-100 Super Sabre, 41, 49, 69, 85
F-104 Starfighter, 61
F-105 Thunderchief, 61, 69, 72
F-106 Delta Dart, 61
F-111 Aardvark, 8, 69–71, 73, 76, 90
F-117 Nighthawk, 98
F-X, 8, 67–68, 75–81, 84
F-XX, 84, 94
Fairchild-Hiller, 80
Fallows, James, 5, 56, 89, 98, 111
fast transients, 7, 123
Ferguson, Gen. James, USAF, 206
Fernandez, Frank, 210
Fialka, Howard, 5, 87, 111, 194
Field Manual, 100–5; operations, 154
fighter mafia, 9, 87, 91, 95, 97, 99–100,
    104, 105, 106, 111
fighter production, U.S., 98
Fighter Weapons School, 7, 10, 39–50,
    51, 204
*Fighter Weapons School Newsletter,* 43, 50
*Fingerspitzengefeuhl* ("fingertip feel"), 6, 160
Fitzgerald, Ernest, 112
FMFM-1, warfighting (Fleet Marine Forces
    Manual-1), 154, 195–96
fluid separation, 43–44
fluidity, 151
"fly before you buy procurement," 84, 94–95
Foley, Thomas, 204
*Forbes,* 11, 188
Foreign Technology Center, 58, 61, 63
Forrest, Nathan Bedford, 163
Foster, John, 91–92
Fort Myers, Viginia, 154
"40-Second Boyd," 7, 45, 203
Frederick the Great, 130
friction, 129, 141, 143, 163–65, 195
Fuller, J. F. C., 137, 142, 148

GAU-8, 115, 121
Gell-Mann, Murray, 14, 21
General Dynamics, 9, 71, 84, 87–89, 94
Georgia Institute of Technology, 30, 52,
    66, 68
German operational philosophy, 141–43
Getler, Michael, 111

Ghenghis Khan, 125–26
Gingrich, Newt, 105, 111
Giraudo, Col. John, USAF, 40
Glasser, Lt. Gen. Otto, USAF, 81, 88–89
Goethe, Johann Wolfgang von, 186
Godel, Kurt, 16, 119, 120, 159, 164, 198
Gordon, Michael, 105, 111
Goodwin, Brian, 186
Graff, George, 77
Grassley, Charles, 111
Grau, Mister, 114
Gray, Gen. Al, USMC, 151, 195, 210
Gray, Colin S., 5, 208–9
"Green Book," 13, 179, 201
Grumble, Col. "Red," USAF, 64
Guderian, Heinz, 137
guerrilla war, 127, 135, 139, 143–51;
    counter-guerrilla campaign, 150–51;
    keys to success, 146; results over last
    200 years, 147
Gulf War, 116, 123, 194, 201, 204, 205, 208
Guibert, Count Jacques Antoine Hippolyte
    de, 126

Hadley, Arthur, 206
Hagerstrom, Col. Jim, 36
Hall, John, 184
Hannibal, 125
harmony, 124, 126, 143, 163–65, 192, 195
Hart, Gary, 6, 110, 111, 113, 115, 151
*Harvard Business Review,* 11
Hawking, Stephen, 183
Heisenberg, Werner, 6, 119, 120, 159, 164,
    198
Herzog, Serge, 107
Highfield, Roger, 184
Hillaker, Harry, 9, 86–88, 100
hi/lo mix, 98
*Hindenburg,* German dirigible, 18
*Historical Dictionary of the U.S. Air
    Force,* 74
Ho Chi Minh Trail, 93
Hopkins, Brig. Gen. Joe, USMC, 201
Horgan, John, 183
Hutier, Gen. Oscar von, 133

IFF (identification, friend or foe), 37
Igloo White, 93

incompleteness theorem, 119
infiltration tactics, 133–35, 149
information warfare, 185
initiative, 124, 163–65
*Inside the Pentagon,* 3
interaction, 159–61
Iowa, University of, 30
Iraq, 3
Isaacson, Walter, 111
isolation, 159–61

JSTARS (Joint Surveillance Target Attack Radar System), 116
*Joint Vision 2010,* 116
Jomini, Baron Antoine Henri de, 122, 129–31, 152, 158, 207
Jones, Gen. David C., CSAF, 96
Jordan, Michael, 181–82

*Kampfgruppen,* 133
Kassebaum, Nancy, 111
Kaufmann, Stuart A., 184
Kelly, Kevin, 162
Kennelly, Janet, 13
Kent, Gen. Glenn, USAF, 104
Korea, 5, 34, 35, 203, 206
Korean War, 29, 68, 71
Kosovo, 74, 205, 208
Kross, Col. Walter, USAF, 107
Krulak, Gen. C. C., USMC, 4
Kuwait, 3

Laffargue, Capt. Andre, 133
Laird, Melvin, 90, 92
Lambeth, Benjamin, 83
Langley Air Force Base, Virginia, 17, 62
Laos, 93–94
*Last of the Mohicans,* 21
Lawrence, T. E., 135–36
Lawson, Col., USAF, 64
leadership, 126, 158
Leaf, Gen. Howard, USAF, 203
Lenin, Vladimir Ilyich, 135, 136–38
Leonhard, Robert, 35
Leopold, Ray, 11, 86, 103, 105
Lettow-Vorbeck, Gen. Paul Emil von, 127, 135
Liddell Hart, B. H., 195

lightweight fighter (LWF), 68, 83, 88–92, 94
Lind, William, 9, 112, 136, 151, 154, 177
Lockheed, 71, 75, 188
Loh, Gen. John "Mike," USAF, 11, 16–17, 86
Lorenz, Konrad, 184
loser, 159, 182
Ludendorff, Field Marsh. Erich von, 133–34, 136, 142, 148
Luke Air Force Base, Arizona, 32

*MacGyver,* 181
McConnell, Gen. John P., USAF, 68, 72–73, 206
McDonnell Aircraft (McAir), 75
McDonnell, Douglas, 80, 94
McLucas, John, 96
McNamara, Robert S., 70–71, 92, 99
McPeak. Gen. Merrill "Tony," CSAF, 50
McVeigh, Timothy, 211
Maitland, Jock, 37–38
Major Command Manual (MCM) 31, 47
Mao Tse Tung, 137
Mandelker, Jacob, 52–53
maneuver warfare, 136–54, 195–96;
    comparison with attrition warfare, 153;
    instilling in U.S. military, 153–54;
    theory of, 151–53
"many-sided implicit cross references,"
    165, 169, 184, 189
Marine Corps, 1, 3, 4, 9, 112, 129, 195, 201, 203, 205
*Marine Corps Gazette,* 112
Marx, Karl, 132, 135, 136, 138
mavericks, 6–8, 202, 206; need to protect, 205–7
Maxwell Air Force Base, Alabama, 17, 44–45, 187
Mayer, Ernst, 184
ME-109, 42
Merritt, Maj. Gen. Jack N., USA, 122
Meyer, Gen. Edward, USA, 13
MiG 15 "Fagot," 35–38, 123; 19 "Farmer," 61; 21 "Fishbed," 11, 70; 23 "Flogger," 75; 25 "Foxbat", 17, 75; 27 "Flogger D," 75; 17 "Fresco," 61, 70, 72
Mikheyev, Dimitri, 158
Military Reform Caucus, 6, 103, 109, 110–13, 177–78

military reform movement, 101–17: assessment of, 116–17; critique by Fred Reed, 176–77; end of, 177–78
military genius, 196–201, 211
mind-time-space, 148
Miramar Naval Air Station, California, 7, 45
mismatches and discontinuity, 171–72, 191–92
"Miss Dolphin," 27
*Mission Impossible*, 181
mission-type orders, 152
Moltke, Count Helmuth von, 165
moral dimension of conflict, 157, 158, 159–61
Morelli, Brig. Gen. Don, USA, 154
Munich crisis, 18
Murphy, Charles, 112
Musashi, 27, 186
mutations, 172
Myer, Gen. John C., USAF, 88
Myers, C. E. "Chuck," Jr., 8, 36, 68, 71–72, 86, 94, 105,

Napoleon, 126, 130, 131, 163, 195, 196
Napoleonic warfare, 122, 126–29
NASA (National Aeronautics and Space Administration), 41
*National Defense*, 111, 118
Navy, U.S., 76, 80–81, 88–89, 112, 203
Nebenpunkt, 140
Nellis Air Force Base, Nevada, 7, 32–33, 39, 42, 66, 73
Nethercutt, George, 204
Newport, 201
*New World Vistas*, 116
*New York Times*, 2, 188
Newman, Col. Ralph F., 42
Nietzsche, Friedrich, 21
Nineteenth-century warfare, 131–32
Nitze, Paul, 106
NKP (Nakom Phanom Air Base, Thailand), 93–94
Nixon doctrine, 90
Noncooperative centers of gravity, 130, 134, 141, 143, 145, 164
North American Rockwell, 75, 81
Northrop, 84, 89, 94–95, 99

novelty, 171–73, 185
Nuclear Freeze Campaign, 111
Nunn, Sam, 6, 111, 115
NVA (North Vietnamese Army), 93

officers' clubs, 86
Okinawa, 4, 69
*Once and Future Superpower: How to Restore America's Economic, Energy, and Environmental Security*, 155
OODA (Observation, Orientation, Decision, Action) Loop, 2, 3, 15, 35, 88, 123, 126, 141–42, 152–54, 156, 164–65, 174, 182, 184, 188–91, 194, 198, 201, 202, 207; diagram, 190; explained, 4–5; orientation emphasized, 164–65
*Order Out of Chaos*, 157
"Organic Design for Command and Control," 13, 162–67
*Out of Control: The Rise of Neobiological Civilization*, 163

P-530 Cobra, 95
Packard Commission, 102
Packard, David, 92, 99, 102
Pape, Robert, 74
"Patterns of Conflict," 13, 105, 112, 120, 122–54, 155, 156, 159, 180, 201; ancient world, 124–26; blitz-guerrilla themes, 147–49; blitzkrieg and guerrilla strategies, 139–41; German operational philosophy, 141–43; guerrilla and counterguerrilla campaigns, 149–51; modern Guerrilla campaigns, 143–47; Napoleonic synthesis, 126–29; overview, 122–24; technology, ideology, society, and war, 131–33; theories of war (Clausewitz and Jomini), 129–31, WWI and emergence of infiltration and guerrilla tactics, 133–35
Patton, George S., 166, 195
*The Pentagon Paradox: The Development of the F-18 Hornet*, 71, 95
*The Pentagon Wars: Reformers Challenge the Old Guard*, 10
perceptions, 147–48, 181, 210
Perry, William, 116
Petain, Marshal Henri Philippe, 135

Peters, Ralph, 211
Peters, Tom, 6, 207
Pettinato, Frank, 23–24
pk (probability of kill) ratio, 69
planning process, 103–4
politicians, Boyd's view of, 175
Popper, Karl, 184
Potomac Institute for Policy Studies, 210
*The Power Game: How Washington Works,* 102
Pratt and Whitney, 94–95
predictability, 185
presence of mind, 199
President's Blue Ribbon Commission on Defense Management. *See* Packard Commission
President's Scientific Advisory Board, 6
Presque Isle State Park, 23–24, 25
Prigogene, Ilya, 157, 183
Princeton, 6
procurement process, 1, 93, 103–4

Quantico, 6, 187, 201

Radnitzky, Gerard, 184
rapidity, 124, 126,143, 163–65
Rasor, Dina, 112, 176–77
Red Flag, 37, 204
Reed, Fred, 176–77
Rensberger, Boyce, 156–57
request for proposals (RFP), 75–76, 80
Restak, Richard M., 157
Ricci, Col., USAF, 8
Riccioni, Col. Everst E. "Rich," USAF, 8, 29, 79, 85–86, 88–99, 91, 94, 104, 105, 201
Richards, Chet, 188
Ridge, Thomas, 177–78
Ridgway, Gen. Matthew B., USA, 206
*Right Stuff, The,* 32
Roberts, Gen. John W., USAF, 62–63, 64
Romm, Joseph J., 155
Rose, Steven, 183
ROTC (Reserve Officer Training Corps), 4, 27–28

Saddam Hussein, 123
Saigon, 4, 105,163

Salter, Betty Jo, 64
SAM (surface-to-air missile), 69–70
Saxe, Count Maurice de, 126
Scales, Maj. Gen. Robert, USA, 211
Schmitt, John, 195
Schlesinger, James S., 92, 96–97, 99
School of Advanced Military Studies (SAMS), 6
Schriever, Gen. Bernard, USAF, 62
Schwerpunkt, 140, 142, 149
science, 168; outstanding contributors and contributions, 169
*Scientific American,* 181, 186
sidewinder missile, *69*
Simon Study, 92
Six-Day War, 74
*Sixty Minutes,* 11
Slay, Gen. Alton, USAF, 97
Smith, Dennis, 111
Smith, Maj. Gen. Donovan, USAF, 88
Smith, Hedrick, 102
snowmobiles, 156, 182
*Social Order and the General Theory of Strategy,* 157
*Spacecast 2020,* 116, 187, 202
Sparrow missile, 69–70, 115
Spinney, Franklin C. "Chuck," 11, 86, 103, 105, 107, 114–15, 161, 180, 188, 193
Sprey, Pierre, 8, 83–85, 91–92, 105, 108, 114, 121, 180, 188, 193
Squadron Officers School, 30, 44–45, 188, 202
Stalin, Marshall Joseph, 136–38
Starry, Maj. Gen. Don, USA, 154
Stein, George, 187
Stevenson, James, 71, 95, 108
Stimson biplane, 20
*Stosstruppen,* 133
Strategic Air Command (SAC), 74
Strategic bombing, 74
Strategy, 159, 161, 181, 186, 207; American approach to, 208–9
"Strategic Game of ? and ?," 155, 156–62
Stuka, 121
Sullivan, Gen. Gordon, Army Chief of Staff, 187

Sun Tzu, 27, 105, 107, 122, 124–25, 135, 147–48, 158, 195
Sweeney, Gen. Walter C., USAF, 62
synchronization, 154
synthesis, 171–73, 184, 186
systems command, 8, 55, 61–63, 65

T-6 Texan, 30
T-33 "T-bird," 58
TACAIR shop, 105
Tactical Air Command (TAC), 8, 45, 55, 58, 61–63, 81
Taft, Robert Jr., 112
Taliban, 211
Tamerlane, 125
Task Force Alpha, 93
technology, 107–9, 131–32, 168, 210
TFX (Tactical Fighter Experimental), 69–71, 76
Than Hoa Bridge, 72
thermodynamics, second law of, 16, 119–120, 159, 164, 198
Thunderbirds, 41–42
Tice, Clay, 33
Ticonderoga class frigates, 113
time and timing, 123, 141–43, 151, 160, 210
*Time*, 11, 114–15, 210
"To Be or To Do?," 10–11
Toffler, Alvin and Heidi, 154
Topgun, 7, 37, 47
TRADOC (U.S. Army Training and Doctrine Command), 112, 154
trade-off analyses, 77–81, 91
trade-off thinking, 110, 120
trust, 141, 163, 167, 195

uncertainty, 173, 195
uncertainty principle, 119, 159
*U.S. News and World Report*, 2
unpredictability, 123, 173

Vanguards, 132, 137–139, 146
*Variety*, 124, 126, 143, 163–65
VFAX Fleet Defense fighter, 76, 80–81
Vietcong, 93
Vietnam, 1, 68–69, 72, 93, 101, 105, 127
Vincent, Capt. Hal, USMC, 45–46

*Wall Street Journal*, 5, 86, 111, 188, 194
"Warthog," 121
*Washington Post*, 11, 111, 156–57
Wass de Cega, Gen. Huba, USA, 151
Watts, Barry, 11, 47, 78, 105, 188
Weed, Bob, 112
Welch, Lt. Col. Larry (later Gen. and CSAF), USAF, 77
West Point, 153, 201
Wheeler, Winslow, 112
White, Lt. Col. Floyd W., USAF, 45
Whitehurst, William G., 103, 110, 112
Wieble, Art, 22, 53
Williams Air Force Base, Arizona, 31, 33, 66
Wilson, Gwen L. L., USAF, 80
winner, 182
Wolfe, Tom, 32
Woods, Sidney, 33
Woolsey, James R., 101
World War I, 133–34, 142
World War II, 142, 166
Wright Patterson Air Force Base, Ohio, 58, 61, 63
Wyly, Col. Mike, USMC, 151

YF-16, 94–95, 97, 160
YF-17, 94–95
YF 101 engine, 94–95
Yom Kippur War, 95

Zukav, Gary, 183